JOURNEYS TO RENEWED CONSECRATION

RELIGIOUS LIFE AFTER FIFTY YEARS OF VATICAN II

EMEKA XRIS OBIEZU, OSA

& JOHN PAUL SZURA, OSA

Editors

PACEM IN TERRIS PRESS

*Devoted to the global vision of Saint John XXIII,
prophetic founder of Postmodern Catholic Social Teaching,
and in support of the search for a Postmodern Ecological Civilization,
which will seek to learn from the spiritual wisdom-traditions
of Christianity and of our entire global human family.
(www.paceminterrispress.com)*

Copyright © 2017 Emeka Xris Obiezu, OSA & John Paul Szura, OSA
All Rights Reserved

Cover Photograph
St. Peter's Basilica in Rome seen from the roof of Castel Sant'Angelo.
Wolfgang Stuck (Own work), September 2004
Reprinted with Permission

ISBN-13: 978-0999608814
ISBN-10: 0999608819

Pacem in Terris Press publishes scholarly books directly or indirectly related to
Catholic Social Teaching with its commitment to justice, peace, ecology,
and spirituality, and on behalf of the search for a Postmodern Ecological Civilization.

In addition, in order to support ecumenical and interfaith dialogue as well as dialogue
with other spiritual seekers, Pacem in Terris Press publishes scholarly books from other
Christian perspectives, from other religious perspectives, and from perspectives
of other spiritual seekers, that promote justice, peace, ecology,
and spirituality for our global human family.

Opinions or claims expressed in publications from Pacem in Terris Press
represent the opinions and claims of the authors and do not necessarily represent
the official position of Pacem in Terris Press, the Pacem in Terris Ecological Initiative,
Pax Romana / Catholic Movement for Intellectual & Cultural Affairs USA,
or its officers, directors, members, and staff.

PACEM IN TERRIS PRESS
is the publishing service of

PAX ROMANA
Catholic Movement for Intellectual & Cultural Affairs
USA
1025 Connecticut Avenue NW, Suite 1000,
Washington DC 20036
www.paceminterris.net

TABLE OF CONTENTS

Introduction
EMEKA XRIS OBIEZU, OSA & JOHN PAUL SZURA, OSA   1

PART I
PRINCIPLES & EXPERIENCES OF THE RENEWAL

1. Vatican II & My Religious Life Journey
   JOHN PAUL SZURA, OSA   13

2. With All Devotedness: Women Religious &
   the Reception of the Second Vatican Council
   DIANNE BERGANT, CSA   31

PART II
EVANGELICAL COUNSELS VATICAN II: UNDERSTANDING AND LIVING

3. "We Have Left Everything and Followed You":
   Challenges of Being a Religious in Today's World
   in Light of the Second Vatican Council
   FRANCIS CHIDI EZENEZI   49

4. Until All Have Enough: Vow of Poverty &
   the Continued Impact of Vatican II
   JOAN F. BURKE, SND DE NAMUR   69

PART III
RELIGIOUS LIFESTYLE

5. Religious Community Life: Then & Now
   THERESA EKE, DC   89

6. Living & Thriving in Religious Community in
   Light of Contemporary Social Changes
   CHRISTIANA CALICE MATRIS (NGOZI) IDIKA, DMMM   113

PART IV
THE WAY FORWARD: QUESTIONS & PROPHECY

7. Religious Life in The Post-Vatican II Era   145
   ROBERT DUEWEKE, OSA

8. Wake Up the World:
   Religious Life as a Prophetic Witnessing
   EMEKA XRIS OBIEZU, OSA   171

PART V
LONG RANGE VIEWS &
VARIED PERSPECTIVES FROM EXPERIENCE

9. New Consecrated Life: Still in the Making
   GUILLERMO CAMPUZANO, CM   207

10. Consecrated Life: Global Concerns and
    the Demand for Renewal
    IKECHUKWU ANTHONY KANU, OSA   233

References & Sources   251

Contributors   267

Other Books from Pacem in Terris Press   270

INTRODUCTION

Emeka Xris Obiezu, OSA
John Paul Szura, OSA

In his November 21, 2014 Apostolic Letter *To All Consecrated People,* Pope Francis inaugurated for members of consecrated life institutes a year of celebration to commemorate the fiftieth anniversaries of two Second Vatican Council documents dealing with religious life: *Perfectae Caritatis,* the Decree on the Adaptation and Renewal of Religious Life, dated October 28, 1965; and *Lumen Gentium,* the Dogmatic Constitution on the Church, dated November 21, 1964.

Using the words of Pope John Paul II's March 25, 1996 Apostolic Exhortation *Vita Consecrata,* Francis reiterates: "You have not only a glorious history to remember and to recount, but also a great history still to be accomplished! Look to the future, where the Spirit is sending you in order to do even greater things" (Pope Francis, 2014).

The invitation of Pope Francis to celebrate the fiftieth anniversary of Vatican II religious life renewal was received by men and women religious, and indeed by the whole Church, with great enthusiasm and hope. A series of special events was organized throughout the world, locally and internationally, within and among various religious congregations of men and women to realize the richness of this celebration —"to offer an opportunity for renewal for men and women in consecrated life; to offer thanksgiving among the faithful for the service of brothers, priests and sisters; and to extend an invitation to young Catholics to consider a religious vocation" (Pope Francis, 2014).

The United States Conference of Catholic Bishops (USCCB) referred to this celebration in its "Days with Religious" as providing the Church with the "initiatives and resources to help families learn about the consecrated life of religious men and women" (USCCB Committee on Clergy, *Consecrated Life and Vocations*, 2014). This learning was the focus of the various activities that marked this year-long celebration called for by Pope Francis, such as sharing experiences of prayer, service and community life with those living a consecrated life. This same learning is the intention of our present volume focused on how "to look to the past with gratitude, to live the present with passion and to embrace the future with hope" (Pope Francis, 2014).

In 2015 at the fiftieth anniversary of *Perfectae Caritatis*, several male and female religious working at the United Nations with their institutes' Non-Governmental Organizations (NGOs) began a process of reflection upon the impact of the Council on their lives. After several months of reflection, and with the addition of other religious collaborating with them, this book has developed as the fruit of that process.

Indeed, immediately upon the December 1965 close of the Second Vatican Council, institutes of consecrated life plunged into the long and sometimes contentious processes of renewal by updating their rules, constitutions, lives, and apostolates. The Council invited them to return to their roots, namely the Gospel and their founding charisms. This radical call to renewal challenged them to rethink their responses to the "signs of the times." Similar to the experience of the Council members themselves, religious felt impelled by the Spirit to work day and night at discerning how and where in the contemporary world they were being called.

Postconciliar religious life renewal experienced a mix of both positive and negative consequences. That time was felt as exciting and also dangerous, as spiritually uplifting and a cause of great tension and deep struggle, as enthusiastic with new beginnings of phenomenal growth as well as decline and extinction. In some regions, postconciliar religious life suffered a membership exodus of massive numbers. In other regions, religious life enjoyed a vocation boom of a mass influx of new members, along with an emergence of new enthusiastic groups. Despite all the risks involved, religious institutions kept up their reform process with courage, bearing the fruit of the personal and spiritual development of members and their communities. This sustained courage also revealed new meanings of religious life for the People of God today.

Change is a process, not an event. Thus, fifty years later, Vatican II's clarion call for religious-life renewal still echoes. Its challenges are as new as they were at their outset. The celebration of the fiftieth anniversary of the Council presented an opportunity to assess the progress made so far by the institutions of religious life in achieving the Council's call to renewal in a changed and changing world. As in those early days following Vatican II, religious are once more confronted with fundamental questions: Who are we to ourselves? Who are we today to the Church and to the world? What does it mean to be a religious? What are the essential and indispensable elements of our particular group identities?

This volume attempts to articulate what these questions mean to various selected individual religious and their institutes, and how they were and are today being responded to. We attempt this by way of reflections on aspects of the renewal project written by individual religious from several institutes of consecrated life. These reflections highlight the successes, lessons learned, challenges and prospects of this renewal.

Contributors enhance the quality of this volume by their personal experiences. The contributions are of high scholarly quality yet communicated in a manner easily readable by a wide audience. Though our contributors were gathered from religious with some connection to United Nations ministry, part of this volume's strength nevertheless is diversity among the authors. They are diverse in terms of their generational and socio-cultural roots. Some were formed by pre-Vatican II experience and others entered religious life after the Council. Some come from the global North and others from the global South. Their theological and spirituality outlooks are varied.

While this volume highlights the seeming changes between the eras, the challenges of realizing the intended renewal, and how various religious communities responded and are responding to it, it pays close attention to the elements that would ensure a future for this way of life. It discusses how these elements are impacting religious life especially in the context of the signs of the time.

What is clear from the voices presented here is that the renewal project placed upon religious life represents the spirit of Vatican II both in its continuity (*ressourcement*) and in its updating (*aggiornamento*). In the following chapters, each contributor captures this spirit of the Council as lived out by different religious communities' attempts at the renewal called for by the Council itself. Some contributors take up a rather evaluative approach that assesses the reception of the invitation to renewal in the light of the place of religious life today and tomorrow. These chapters are a testament to the fundamental nature of conciliar renewal—to "make a grateful remembrance of the recent past," while embracing "the future with hope."

With the title "Vatican II & My Religious Life Journey," **John Paul Szura,** OSA opens his contribution with a graphic presentation of a very inspiring narrative of one with an all-round experience of Vatican II's impact on religious life. He identifies these influences in the issues and the documents of the Council in general, and more so in the call for religious life renewal. Without attempting a full theological analysis of Vatican II document perspectives, teachings, or directives, he rather offers an anamnesis of the living impact of Vatican II upon the multi-year journey of religious candidates in formation and beyond. He opens up with Vatican II's liturgy renewal, which he sees as a fundamental breakthrough and then moves to the Council's religious life renewal in the light of identity.

Dianne Bergant, CSA in her chapter "With All Devotedness: Women Religious & the Reception of the Second Vatican Council," provides the readers with the varying opinions describing the dynamics of the religious reception of the Second Vatican Council and its call for renewal. Focusing on the typical experiences of women religious, she claims that the religious women received the Second Vatican Council with utter devotedness. She underscores the radical changes women's religious life was thrown into following the Council.

In general it may be agreed that new forms of religious life emerged for women religious mirroring more of the "Church in the modern world." "Their lives and ministries were interwoven like a tapestry, so that even the slightest change reverberated throughout." Some opinions maintained that the reception went too far and led to the secularization of many women religious, upon which was blamed the crisis in vocations to religious life today. Indeed, we can say, "Congregations and individuals went through this period of change in very different ways."

In his chapter "'We have Left Everything and Followed You' (Cf. Mark 10:28): Challenges of Being a Religious in Today's World in the Light of the Second Vatican Council," **Francis Chidi Ezenezi** (the only contributor to this volume not of a religious institute) provides an outsider's view that complements those of the insiders, thus enhancing the richness of this entire work. He examines the contemporary living of the religious vow of poverty drawing on his personal experience of living with members of religious institutes and his academic background as a pastoral theologian with expertise in the reception of the Second Vatican Council.

Maximizing his privilege of living and working in North America and being an African, he structures his chapter as a comparative study of the North American and Sub-Saharan African regions in order to appreciate their unique values and consequences in today's changing and challenging world. His proposals to deal with some of the issues he identifies prove seminal to the type of renewal envisaged by the Council and echoed by Pope Francis as he inaugurated the year of consecrated life.

In her chapter "Until All Have Enough: Vow of Poverty and the Later Impact of Vatican II," **Joan Burke, SND de Namur**, provides an insider's and diverse perspective on the vow of poverty that complements Ezenezi's approach. She presents the vow of poverty as typically illustrative of how Vatican II made its impact, changing and expanding the scope of understanding and living religious life. Quite unlike the limited explanation of the vow of poverty in an earlier time "as a personal question, a matter of permissions, and also the obligation of common life," she sees this vow today calling us "to try both to model an alternative way of living and to restructure our world —so that all may indeed have enough."

Theresa Eke, DC, in her chapter "Religious Community Life: Then & Now," traces the historical shifts that had occurred in the understanding and living of religious community life. She discusses religious community life in the preconciliar era, highlighting its particular form with some characteristic features and implications. She also examines religious community life in the postconciliar period with its problems and prospects, seeing how individual personality styles, group dynamics, and styles of leadership impact the quality of the common life in religious institutes. It is hoped that this chapter informs the readers of the value of community life within the legacy of the Second Vatican Council and poses challenges for further reflection.

In her chapter "Living and Thriving in Religious Community in the Light of Contemporary Social Changes," **Christiana Calice Matris**

(Ngozi) Idika, DMMM studies how contemporary social changes and challenges are impacting and redefining religious community life. She discusses under this topic the enduring adverse effects of the many and diverse dynamics of this age upon the healthy living of religious life in this era. She identifies two examples of major challenges: namely, the individual versus the community and the value of personal freedom versus an authority strengthened by vows of obedience. Her claim is that the tensions in these areas are at the root cause of some of the visible conflicts among the religious institutes and within individual religious today.

She proposes using insights from behavioral philosophers, Church authorities, and other sources to overcome this conundrum that requires a sincere and humble exploration of the issues at stake. Structured within the contemporary issues of individuality, freedom, and responsibility, her chapter explores an understanding of religious obedience and communal living that neither sacrifices the evangelical way of life at the altar of anarchy nor slips into the absolutist elevation of authority to the level of the divine so as to compromises the realization of personal fulfillment.

In his chapter "Religious Life in the Post-Vatican II Era," **Robert Dueweke, OSA** begins his study with a rather heart-searching question: "Is religious life obsolete and coming to an end?" Several indices point to a gloomy future for religious life, sometimes suggesting its demise. Though Dueweke refuses to accept this prognosis as inevitable, he nevertheless warns that if religious institutes and individual religious fail to undertake the task of questioning themselves, an inevitable demise may follow.

His methodology is built on a Lonergarian approach setting the steps of renewal as a chain of questions. Dueweke challenges, "How we approach the question and what other questions are asked are important. What we do with the answers to those questions will depend on the courage of the one who becomes aware of new possibilities. Such possibilities emerge as an invitation to go deeper into the inquiry." He then sets his meta-question: "Are we able to face the situation and dig below the surface to see what underlies it?" What he offers in this chapter is an examination of the crises and trends of religious life from a phenomenological perspective that sees the religious bearing witness to the life they live, by which alone they can ward off the inevitable "demise of religious life."

Emeka Xris Obiezu, OSA's chapter "Wake up the World: Religious Life as a Prophetic Witnessing" makes the bold claim that religious life is first and foremost prophetic and by that stance essentially "other-focused." Religious as prophets are called to be risk takers, bold enough to take up the challenge of ungodliness everywhere it lurks – both in society and in the Church. His chapter is structured around two questions. In what does prophetic witnessing consist for consecrated life institutes particularly in our time? What examples can we derive from our founding charisms and from the Scriptures to which we must always return?

He considers the evolution of the understanding, the meaning and the demands of prophetic witnessing in the context of today's challenges in Church and society. Drawing on the lived-experience of the prophets and his own experience as an Augustinian from the Nigerian-African socio-economic, political and religious milieu, he grapples with the challenges of living in Church and society today as religious. He concludes that the only way for religious to be faithful to their calling is by embracing this prophetic dimension of their way of life in openness to suggestions and to the risks arising from today's reality.

In his chapter "New Consecrated Life: Still in the Making," **Guillermo Campuzano,** CM points to the direction which religious life is to go if it is to be worthy of its beginnings. He sees a new consecrated life that is still yet to come and will emerge only when religious become incarnate in their time and circumstances. He draws examples for the authenticity of this way of being from the prophets, from Jesus and from the early founders and foundresses of this way of life. He recognizes these figures as those who entered into their time with the deep faith and genuineness that offered a light of new hope to their contemporaries. He warns religious to beware of seeking comfort in the security of the past and of avoiding the risks and bruises of the present.

Finally, **Ikechukwu Anthony Kanu, OSA**, in his chapter "The Consecrated Life: Global Concerns & the Demand for Renewal," brings this volume to its conclusion by re-echoing why renewal is not only necessary but urgent by exploring what he considers as some major worrisome features of concern in consecrated life today. His contribution witnesses to his wide experience in education and formation as well as his work with the Conference of Major Superiors of Religious of Nigeria (Men). Not only does he challenge us regarding our cultural and ideological perspectives. He also asks us to become aware of the pre-Christian foreshadowings of religious life.

We hope this volume enjoys a wide readership, especially from the members of diverse religious congregations, academics, and the larger faith community. May it encourage us to ask new questions – and even to ask old questions in new ways.

PART I

PRINCIPLES & EXPERIENCES OF THE RENEWAL

1

VATICAN II & MY RELIGIOUS LIFE JOURNEY

John Paul Szura, OSA

When I reflect upon the impact of the Second Vatican Council on religious life, what immediately springs to mind is how my own religious life journey dovetails with the broad sweep of Vatican II as a Spirit-inspired gift for Church renewal. Born September 21, 1940 as I was, every part, every aspect of the Council had its own providential effect upon me. Vatican II as a whole and in its documents and progression has accompanied each step of my religious life journey, and I pray that this grace will continue and endure.

I offer these following reflections in grateful memory of my religious life journey of more than fifty years and so will attempt a thumbnail sketch of the influence of the Second Vatican Council upon that journey of mine. Though it is my own journey that I am reflecting upon, I believe that my experience has significant points in common with that of many others who lived during the Council.

I will not attempt a full theological analysis of Vatican II document perspectives, teachings, or directives. While such analyses are helpful and necessary, I prefer at this time simply recalling with you the living impact upon my multi-year journey made by vital issues developed in the Council and through its documents. My thumbnail sketch will begin with Vatican II's liturgy renewal as a fundamental breakthrough, and then move to the Council's religious life renewal in the light of identity. I will follow with Vatican II on mission – offering side reflections supplementing this simple plan throughout.

Vatican II & Liturgy:
The Breakthrough of Renewal

I was a typical Chicago, Midwest United States Catholic in elementary school. Within three blocks of my home were five Catholic parishes, each with a thriving grade school and two with high schools. One Lutheran church shared our Catholic ghetto with us. My Catholic world felt no need for Church renewal.

Following without question or complaint the wisdom of Mother Church, we worshiped by listening passively to Latin words we did not understand. There was singing, but usually from a choir with much of it in Latin. Such was the Mass: holy, awesome, and mysterious. During Catholic high school, my worship experience stayed much the same. But in 1958 when I entered the Augustinian novitiate directly from high school, my experience did change — it intensified.

As clerical novices in the Order of Saint Augustine, we chanted divine office totally in Latin and separate from brotherhood-formation candidates who chanted the Little Office of the Blessed Virgin in English. Both our groups heard their own Latin Mass said by one priest without much more participation than would be found in a parish, except for more singing. Other priests on staff whispered their own private Masses at side altars with an equally quiet server. During my novitiate, Pope Pius XII died and was followed by Pope John XXIII, who on January 25, 1959 announced plans for an ecumenical council. I wondered why.

After novitiate, I began in 1959 four years of college concentrating on philosophy and followed by four years of theology studies for ordination. During philosophy, progressive faculty members and enthusiastic fellow students introduced me to the liturgical movement. I was also introduced to Pope Pius XII's foundational encyclical on liturgy, *Mediator Dei*,[1] calling for active participation in liturgy[2] while at the same time opposing the rash innovation of vernacular languages.[3] This encyclical proposed the new translation of the Psalms from the original texts into Latin as an example of how the Holy See promoted full liturgical participation![4] I questioned more and more how any liturgical language not understood by the people could be recommended as an aid for their participation in worship.

Toward the end of my philosophy years and into my theology studies for ordination, I kept up with news from the Council. It was clear that there arose within the Council conservative and progressive wings mirroring similar divisions within my Augustinian Order and differing sharply from each other on the directions the Church should take. In 1963 the fundamental direction for the Church to take regarding worship was set by the Council's *Constitution on the Sacred Liturgy*.[5]

The promulgation of the liturgy constitution profoundly renewed our community worship. Previously in our community there was a Mass for the formation students, a Mass for the brothers, a Mass for the sisters, plus private side-altar Masses celebrated by priests on staff. Now one daily Mass for all the several community sectors would be celebrated together, with each priest on staff either concelebrating or attending. We received communion under both species. The place of

---

[1] Pope Pius XII, Encyclical *Mediator Dei*, November 20, 1947.

[2] E.g., Ibid., 80.

[3] Ibid., 59, 60.

[4] Ibid., 6.

[5] Second Vatican Council, *Sacrosanctum Concilium*, Constitution on the Sacred Liturgy, December 4, 1963.

Scripture became more prominent, as Bible vigils began to be celebrated and Mass readings became richer and more varied. The vernacular became the worship language not only for Mass but also for community chanting of divine office. Community members from the youngest professed to the most academically accomplished Rome-trained faculty members sought dispensation to use the vernacular breviary because of "grave difficulty to pray in Latin."

The Vatican II renewal of liturgy also profoundly affected our religious life itself, for that life no longer appeared unchangeable and predefined. If the firm rock-solid, and seemingly eternally changeless, Latin Mass could be updated, anything could be renewed. New forms or styles of religious life became thinkable and open for discussion. If brothers and priests could chant divine office together, then they could eat together at the same table, relax, and play together in the same common room, and even share the same voting rights in chapter. By logical extension, other areas of Church life could be open to renewal. A new mindset replaced the old.

The controversy over reception of communion in the hand provides a striking example of this new mindset. In the years after the Council, an experimental custom arose regarding reception of communion in the hand, as an option to reception on the tongue. The United States bishops kept refusing to allow this alternate mode of reception, regardless of repeated requests and cogent explanations by advocates for its definitive approval.

However, many priests of diverse ideologies kept offering this mode of reception anyway. Finally, the bishops relented, and the practice was officially approved. We cannot know whether the persistence of numerous priests was holy disobedience or really a practicum on how a custom *contra legem* develops. Nor do we know for certain that the bishops' resistance to this mode of reception was broken down by its continued practice. But it cannot be denied that the Church's growing mindset of change contributed to this experimental custom enduring against the law and then becoming accepted by the law.

From discussions and by observations, I came to understand that my experience of the beginning of Vatican II Church renewal was quite common. Liturgical renewal cleared the way for Church renewal in other areas. All sectors of Church life are interrelated, so the renewal of the liturgy opened up all these other areas for their interaction. Liturgy is perhaps the activity of Church life most formative of our Catholic identity, the face of the Church we see most frequently, and the way that the Church most intimately touches us. So, the liturgy – where the Council began its work, or at least was seen and felt to begin it — was the place where the streams of Church renewal started to flow. The course of Vatican II would continue in a progressive direction.

The Council was announced in 1959, was prepared for during three years of intense work, opened its first of four sessions in October 1962, immediately adjourned as it struggled with opposing outlooks, and just as quickly reconvened. It produced no renewal documents, decisions or mandates even up to December 1962, when its first session ended. There were discussions and disagreements but no solid results to announce. The 1963 second session decision on liturgical renewal was the breakthrough that all other major renewal decisions followed. Thereafter, news of the Council's progress became not just interesting but also personally relevant and engaging. We who were involved in religious life became ever more deeply involved in Vatican II.

Two years later we were ready — and even eager — to receive the Council's *Decree on the Adaptation and Renewal of Religious Life*.[6] Our place within this culture of renewal demanded it.

---

[6] Second Vatican Council, *Perfectae Caritatis,* Decree on the Adaptation and Renewal of Religious Life, October 28, 1965.

Vatican II & Religious Life:
Our Identity Renewal

The Vatican II religious life decree became a matter of significant consequence for religious institutes and for their members it affected. As the Council's liturgy constitution *Sacrosanctum Concilium* gave to all the Church a divine worship that was worthier of celebrating, so its decree *Perfectae Caritatis* offered to many a renewal of religious life worthier of pursuing. The outcomes of both were crucial.

It can be conceded without question that the central and most necessary objective of religious life renewal must be a renewal of holiness within all institutes and among all their membership. Religious life demands it. The religious life decree demands it as well:

> *The purpose of the religious life is to help the members follow Christ and be united to God through the profession of the evangelical counsels. It should be constantly kept in mind, therefore, that even the best adjustments made in accordance with the needs of our age will be ineffectual unless they are animated by a renewal of spirit. This must take precedence over even the active ministry.*[7]

Charism

No matter how much we might need an ecumenical council to remind us of the obvious priority of holiness for all religious, we also needed the Council to give us an impetus to renew our particular institutional identities. We were not religious generically. Each of our institutes had its own character or founding spirit – its charism – and the Augustinian charism features common life, a key aspect of which is governance where the charism itself is sharply and existentially experienced for good or for ill.

---

[7] Ibid., 2e.

> *According to the same criteria let the manner of governing the institutes also be examined. Therefore let constitutions, directories, custom books, books of prayers and ceremonies and such like be suitably re-edited and, obsolete laws being suppressed, be adapted to the decrees of this sacred synod.[8]*

True as it may be that individuals faithfully seeking holiness may flourish in religious institutes governed under any system, in the world of real people a dysfunctional governance system can breed discord, resentment or other brutal obstacles to the peaceful serenity that nurtures sanctity and service.

At the time of the Council, some institutes did have dysfunctional systems of governance, though not necessarily because of malice or regulations imprudent in themselves. Some governance systems once good and necessary in past historical eras became dysfunctional in the present because of changes as the years and even centuries passed.

It was widely observed in my Augustinian order that our governance system needed updating. We are an international religious order of priests and brothers composed of many provinces. Our ultimate governance authority is a general chapter held every six years at which programs and policies are decided and our prior general with council is elected.

The ultimate authority in the provinces is a provincial chapter held every four years at which programs and policies are set. Just as the prior general with council implements the programs and policies of the general chapter, so too the provincial superior with council has the same responsibility on their level. Our governance system is basically well conceived and effective, but it had a dysfunction in the role of the provincial superior that ever more clearly appeared over time.

---

[8] Ibid., 3.

The provincial superiors in our governance system hold a great deal of power. Not only do they have huge responsibilities on a regional level, but in the general chapter their votes also play a major role in forming international programs and policies and in the election of the prior general. However, their own elections were problematic.

Provincial superiors were elected by the provincial chapter with a severely restricted membership consisting of the provincial superior and council with the priors and a representation from each house. But since our houses scattered over a region are of varied sizes, some houses being quite small and others large, the provincial chapter membership was hardly representative.

For example, if our high school community with thirty members would send its prior and an elected representative to the provincial chapter, then our parish community next to it with three members would likewise send a delegation of two to the chapter at which would be chosen the provincial superior, the province council and the local house priors. The province delegation accompanying the provincial superior to the next general chapter would be set there as well, and the process would continue to cascade down the years.

In past years this system may have been the best choice for community participation in governance, but with modern travel and communication possibilities, it would manifestly not be so today. Even if cronyism is avoided, the majority of a province was effectively left out of the wider community governance process.

Even though a dysfunction may be obvious and hurtful, reform may not come about easily or with little resistance. At times something from the outside may be needed to bring change. That something for us was the Council's 1965 religious life decree. Its words cited above led my order to its 1968 general chapter, which was convoked to renew our constitutions.

Our constitutions renewed by the chapter provided a more representative voting process for provincial superior. Each province member had one vote, regardless of their age or office, the size of their house membership or whether they would be priest or brother. Votes were secret and could be cast by mail. Moreover, brothers as well as priests could now vote in house chapters and could even be elected to province council. These governance reforms were not just political adjustments.

My order's growing interest in Augustinian spirituality led us to see participative governance as part of renewal, since that form of governance flows from a return to our charism so strongly mandated in the words of the decree cited below.

The adaptation and renewal of the religious life includes both the constant return to the sources of all Christian life and to the original spirit of the institutes and their adaptation to the changed conditions of our time. This renewal, under the inspiration of the Holy Spirit and the guidance of the Church, must be advanced according to the following principles:

a) *Since the ultimate norm of the religious life is the following of Christ set forth in the Gospels, let this be held by all institutes as the highest rule.*

b) *It redounds to the good of the Church that institutes have their own particular characteristics and work. Therefore let their founders' spirit and special aims they set before them as well as their sound traditions – all of which make up the patrimony of each institute – be faithfully held in honor.*[9]

My order's return to its charism was seen as doubly validated by Vatican II renewal. First, all religious institutes were called upon to return to their founding charism, and our charism of common life is essential-

---

[9] Ibid., 2, 2a, 2b.

ly that of the ancient Christian community of the Acts of the Apostles.[10] Second, the Vatican II religious life decree calls upon all religious institutes, regardless of their particular charism, to look to that ancient Christian community as an inspiration and example for their life.

Common life, fashioned on the model of the early Church where the body of believers was united in heart and soul (Cf. Acts 4:32), and given new force by the teaching of the Gospel, the sacred liturgy, and especially the Eucharist, should continue to be lived in prayer and the communion of the same spirit.

As members of Christ living together as brothers, religious should give pride of place in esteem to each other (Cf. Rom 12:10) and bear each other's burdens (Cf. Gal 6:2). For the community, a true family gathered together in the name of the Lord by God's love which has flooded the hearts of its members through the Holy Spirit (Cf. Rom 5:5), rejoices because He is present among them (Cf. Mat 18:20).[11]

Moreover, this ancient Christian community of the Acts of the Apostles is also recommended universally to priests as a model for poverty by the Vatican II *Decree on the Ministry and Life of Priests*.[12] A full treatment of this document would illuminate Vatican II perspectives on priesthood in general and on the priesthood in religious institutes in particular.

At the same time, it would contrast those issues with the essence of the Augustinian charism, which is religious but not necessarily priestly. In this area the full impact of Vatican II renewal has not yet been felt since our non-ordained brothers do not enjoy full equality with our priests, especially regarding appointment to positions of authority. This is a piece of our governance system not yet in accord with our charism.

---

[10] Acts of the Apostles, 2 and 4.

[11] *Perfectae Caritatis*, 15.

[12] Second Vatican Council, *Presbyterorum Ordinis,* Decree on the Ministry and Life of Priests, December 7, 1965, 17.

Worship is another aspect of our life where our charism is existentially experienced for good or for ill. We observed above the change from the varied sectors of our community celebrating their Masses separately to celebrating one community Mass together daily. The Council perspective confirmed for us that common worship was in accord with our charism just as participative governance was.

> *Liturgical services are not private functions, but are celebrations of the Church, which is the "sacrament of unity," namely, the holy people united and ordered under their bishops. Therefore, liturgical services pertain to the whole body of the Church; they manifest it and have effects upon it; but they concern the individual members of the Church in different ways, according to their differing rank, office, and actual participation.*
>
> *It is to be stressed that whenever rites, according to their specific nature, make provision for communal celebration involving the presence and active participation of the faithful, this way of celebrating them is to be preferred, so far as possible, to a celebration that is individual and quasi-private. This applies with especial force to the celebration of Mass and the administration of the sacraments, even though every Mass has of itself a public and social nature.*[13]

Scripture

As noted above, the Vatican II religious life decree saw Scripture and the institute's founding spirit as the twin bases for renewal. "*Since the ultimate norm of the religious life is the following of Christ set forth in the Gospels, let this be held by all institutes as the highest rule ... It redounds to the good of the Church that institutes have their own particular characteristics and work.*"[14] This aspect of the religious life decree reinforces, and is re-

---

[13] *Sacrosanctum Concilium*, 26, 27.

[14] *Perfectae Caritatis*, 2a, 2b.

inforced by, the Vatican II treatment of revelation and especially of Scripture itself in its *Dogmatic Constitution on Divine Revelation*.[15]

During theology studies for ordination, my eagerness to hear news about the Council on Scripture was like my eagerness to hear news about the Council on liturgy. Our progressive Bible professor not only taught Scripture courses enriched with modern scholarly perspectives, but he also entertained us with tales of intrigue in high places between biblical progressives and conservatives.[16]

I was as puzzled by conservatives trying to impede modern approaches to Scripture study as I was by conservatives trying to impede the vernacular in worship. I was also personally engaged in another issue concerning Scripture lodged in my memory from childhood years ago—the issue of Scripture and tradition.

In elementary school, my total environment was Catholic, but outside of school I played with Protestant friends. Sometimes passing the neighborhood Lutheran church, I wondered what made us different. Two explanations given me for our differences were Bible-based.

First, while Protestants interpreted Scripture as each individual may have read it, the Catholic Church possessed all revealed truth and so could tell us with certainty what Scripture meant.

Second, while Protestants had only the Bible as guide, we had tradition too. The Vatican II constitution on revelation brought healing truth to these perspectives that I had grown up with. Besides affirming the best of modern Scripture study methods, this document harmoniously integrated Scripture and tradition with the Church's teaching office.[17]

---

[15] Second Vatican Council, *Dei Verbum*, Dogmatic Constitution on Divine Revelation, November 18, 1965.

[16] Since modern approaches to Scripture often came to us from Protestant scholars, this played into issues of ecumenism. See the Council's November 21, 1964 Decree on Ecumenism *Unitatis Redintegratio*.

[17] See for example *Dei Verbum*, 9 and 10.

It is clear, therefore, that sacred tradition, Sacred Scripture and the teaching authority of the Church, in accord with God's most wise design, are so linked and joined together that one cannot stand without the others, and that all together and each in its own way under the action of the one Holy Spirit contribute effectively to the salvation of souls.[18]

My childhood understanding consistent with a "two font" theory of revelation – Scripture and tradition as two independent sources – was evidently not the understanding of the Council. Moreover, neither was the notion that the Church possessed all revealed truth in its fullness, for otherwise how would development be possible?

> *This tradition, which comes from the Apostles, develops in the Church with the help of the Holy Spirit. For there is a growth in the understanding of the realities and of the words which have been handed down. This happens through the contemplation and study made by believers, who treasure these things in their hearts (see Luke, 2:19, 51) through a penetrating understanding of the spiritual realities which they experience, and through the preaching of those who have received through Episcopal succession the sure gift of truth. For, as the centuries succeed one another, the Church constantly moves forward toward the fullness of divine truth, until the words of God reach their complete fulfillment in her.*[19]

These Vatican II perspectives on Scripture were widely assimilated into religious institutes – integrating Scripture more securely and intimately into our spirituality. This was true also in my order, the Augustinians, though with another consideration.

As modern developments in Scripture studies became more widely accepted, they seemed to give little place to patristic insights, including those of our spiritual father Saint Augustine. Providentially at that very

---

[18] Ibid., 10.

[19] Ibid., 8.

time, we were blessed with a renewal of Augustinian studies. This in turn gradually helped us value more deeply our founding charism as well as Augustinian insights into Scripture—the two bases of Vatican II religious life renewal. But the renewal of the Second Vatican Council and its impact on religious life must not end there. It must go out to others and to the world.

Vatican II & Mission

In 1961, in the midst of the final preparations for the Second Vatican Council and just one year before it opened, Pope John XXIII surprised United States religious communities with an extraordinary challenge. He asked them to set aside ten percent of their membership for missionary work in Latin America.[20] This was a remarkable request, considering that many of these institutes were not founded to be missionary in the first place. Nevertheless, many institutes did respond, and my Augustinian province was among them. We took on a mission in northern Peru.

This mission demanded generosity in personnel, administrative planning, initial financing, and long range financial support. The geographical area was large, with much rugged but varied terrain difficult to traverse. Its many people were poor, scattered over a wide area and confronted with overwhelming needs such as medical care, education, labor opportunities and simple subsistence.

Nevertheless, we did comply, and with an enthusiastic missionary spirit, a first fervor that later grew over time. Over time on the level of Church administration, this local Church grew into a diocese. Over time on the level of religious life administration, it grew into a vicariate of my province. But our missionary venture needed nourishment over time as well, for first fervors tend not to last if not tended to.

---

[20] Pope John XXIII, *Appeal of the Pontifical Commission to North American Superiors,* August 17, 1961. The pope delivered this appeal through then-Monsignor Agostino Casaroli.

Obviously, the Second Vatican Council's 1965 decree on the missionary activity of the Church[21] was not the initial impetus for our Peruvian mission. John XXIII's 1961 mission challenge preceded that decree by four years. However, the decree shows the Church's missionary spirit simmering in the Council from its beginning. *Ad Gentes* was the Council's reinforcing encouragement from 1965 and beyond, validating and blessing our 1961 beginning. In its decree, the Council proclaimed the Church as essentially missionary and sent to all people everywhere.

> *Divinely sent to the nations of the world to be unto them 'a universal sacrament of salvation,' the Church, driven by the inner necessity of her own catholicity, and obeying the mandate of her Founder (Cf. Mark 16:16), strives ever to proclaim the Gospel to all men.*[22]

The decree further encouraged mission to the poor.

> *But these churches, very often located in the poorer portions of the globe, are mostly suffering from a very serious lack of priests and of material support. Therefore, they are badly in need of the continued missionary activity of the whole Church to furnish them with those subsidies which serve for the growth of the local Church, and above all for the maturity of Christian life. This mission action should also furnish help to those churches, founded long since, which are in a certain state of regression or weakness.*[23]

Moreover, the decree recognized that a supreme goal of the Church's missionary activity in the mission area was "*Forming Christian Community,*"[24] which is our very charism itself.

The Vatican II mission impulse to others and to the world must send us further. Like many Catholic religious institutes, we have decided to

---

[21] Second Vatican Council, *Ad Gentes*, Decree on the Missionary Activity of the Church, December 7, 1965.

[22] Ibid., Preface, 1.

[23] Ibid., Chapter III, 19.

[24] Ibid., Chapter II (Article 3), 15 - 18.

associate ourselves as a non-governmental organization (NGO) with the United Nations. Analogous to the *Decree on the Missionary Activity of the Church* supporting our mission to Peru, the Vatican II *Pastoral Constitution on the Church in the Modern World*, supports our mission to the entire world.

> *An outstanding form of international activity on the part of Christians is found in the joint efforts which, both as individuals and in groups, they contribute to institutes already established or to be established for the encouragement of cooperation among nations. There are also various Catholic associations on an international level which can contribute in many ways to the building up of a peaceful and fraternal community of nations.*
>
> *These should be strengthened by augmenting in them the number of well qualified collaborators, by increasing needed resources, and by advantageously fortifying the coordination of their energies. For today both effective action and the need for dialogue demand joint projects. Moreover, such associations contribute much to the development of a universal outlook — some-thing certainly appropriate for Catholics. They also help to form an awareness of genuine universal solidarity and responsibility.*[25]

Postscript

The Second Vatican Council was, and remains, a Spirit-inspired gift for Church renewal. As weak human beings, none of us hears or receives it perfectly. That is true of myself as well, though it was my religious life journey I attempted to share with you. Let us give thanks for what we can hear and receive of it, reflecting on the words of Pope John XXIII spoken in his anticipation of this gift.

---

[25] Second Vatican Council, *Gaudium et Spes,* Pastoral Constitution on the Church in the Modern World, 7, 1965, Part II, Chapter V, Section II, 90.

In the present order of things, Divine Providence is leading us to a new order of human relations which, by men's own efforts and even beyond their very expectations, are directed toward the fulfillment of God's superior and inscrutable designs. And everything, even human differences, leads to the greater good of the Church.[26]

---

[26] Pope John XXIII, *Opening Speech to the Council* at Basilica of St. Peter, October 11, 1962.

2

WITH ALL DEVOTEDNESS:
WOMEN RELIGIOUS & THE RECEPTION OF
THE SECOND VATICAN COUNCIL[1]

Dianne Bergant, CSA

It has been fifty years since the issuance of *Perfectae Caritatis*, the Vatican II document on the renewal of religious life.[2] During that time, religious life has undergone radical changes. This is particularly true for women religious. Their lives and ministries were interwoven like a tapestry, so that even the slightest change reverberated throughout.

Many people maintain that a new form of religious life for women has emerged from this renewal.[3] They believe that contemporary religious faithfully exemplify *The Church in the Modern World*.[4] Others hold that the updating went too far and much of the former religious character of

---

[1] This is a revision of an earlier article: Dianne Bergant, "The Rebirth of an Apostolic Woman," *Ministerial Spirituality and Religious Life*, ed. John M. Lozano, CMF et al. (Chicago: Claret Center for Religious Resources in Spirituality, 1986), 73-90.

[2] For Vatican II documents, see *Vatican Council II, Vol. 1&2, The Conciliar and Postconciliar Documents*, New Revised Edition edited by Austin Flannery, OP. (Northport, NY: Costello Publishing Company, 1996).

[3] This is a central theme in Sandra M. Schneiders, IHM, *Buying the Field: Catholic Religious Life in Mission to the World* (Paulist Press, 2013).

[4] The Vatican II Pastoral Constitution on the Church in the Modern World, *Gaudium et Spes*.

the life was lost. They claim that the dearth in vocations is the result of the secularization of many contemporary women religious. Congregations and individuals went through this period of change in very different ways.

What follows reflects the experience of my congregation, the Congregation of the Sisters of St Agnes – simply known as the Sisters of St. Agnes.[5] While some of the members of my congregation might see things differently, I am quite sure that they would agree with the essence of what I am about to describe.

The Experience of Renewal

Contrary to some popular opinion, religious life before the Council often cherished and preserved what was best in the Church at that time. It is true that many did not enjoy a totally positive experience, but it cannot be denied that the life offered many opportunities for a deepening of religious sensibilities.

At the heart of our own religious formation was a healthy liturgical life. The rise and fall of Gregorian melodies, sung with the feelings that only centuries can define, frequently touched a hidden chord within the soul that echoed again and again even after the chapel had been deserted. The polyphony that served as sister to the chant sang of the harmony that was to be at the very heart of religious life. Everything was of a piece. Such music demanded vaulted architecture so that the waves of the melody might swell to their highest peaks. Thus, our convent chapel resembled a medieval cathedral.

Neither the music nor the building was intended to be merely an expression of art. They were meant to enhance the liturgical celebration. And what a celebration it was! There was a sense of belonging to some-

---

[5] We are a small congregation founded in 1848 to minister to the German speaking immigrants in Wisconsin. Well established in the Midwest, we also minister on the East Coast, in the Southwest and in Nicaragua.

thing bigger, something that encompassed the centuries and included other women who knelt there in their time as we knelt in ours. A sense of solemnity and reverence was created as graceful gestures performed sacred rites, elegant vestments denoted special events, and fragrant incense hung in the air long after the final "Amen."

Some may call this religious romanticism and nostalgia, and they might be correct. All of this does speak of another time and another place. Still, it was the Church of that time and that place; it was the liturgical life as we experienced it then; it was a formative influence in many of our lives; and it was good.

Another aspect of the pre-Vatican II period of religious life was our theological and spiritual instruction. We were blessed to have been grounded in the tradition of solid theology and nourished by the masters of the spiritual life. Still, the thinking of that time was seldom one of questioning or experimentation. It was neither cynical nor contentious. The Church seemed sure of its identity; its theology had endured; thus, it was considered trustworthy. The question that we asked was, "How can I be perfect?" not "What does it mean to be a Christian in today's world?" The Church was definitely built on a rock, and there was security in that kind of stability.

And then came the Council! Who would have thought that life could change so thoroughly and so rapidly? How did it all happen? Why did it happen in the first place?

Perhaps the last question can be answered first. It happened because a certain docility and obedience had always been a vital component of the very heart of religious life. Therefore, when we were called to enter into the process of renewal, we did so with the same willingness and openness with which we had responded to every other injunction from the Holy Father or the Congregation of Religious. Little did we, or anyone else, realize the sweeping ramifications of our response.

How did it happen? We were told that renewal was to take two focuses: a rediscovery of the original tradition or charism of the institute; and an in-depth examination of the authentic contemporary life of the members. We were commissioned to identify our founding charism and to see how we were manifesting it in our present circumstances.

This meant comprehensive study. The early writings of those who founded the congregation were examined. as were the political, social, and ecclesiastical circumstances of that time. It was no longer enough to know where, when and by whom we were founded. We were to discover the unique character or charism that gave us birth and meaning.

In addition to examining the founding period, it was important to trace how each successive generation understood this spirit and manifested it in its own circumstances. Once again, attention was focused on the Church and the society of the times. Hand in hand with the investigation of the past went the scrutiny of the present. Every aspect of contemporary religious life was probed.

We were asked to examine elements of our lives to critique and prioritize, to reaffirm or reject, to develop what was enduring or create something new. Everything that we had learned was to be questioned and reevaluated; everything that we had experienced was to be reappraised. True to the goals of Vatican II, our adaptation (*aggiornamento*) was to be grounded in the values on which we were founded (*ressourcement*).

This was an extremely difficult task to assign to women who had spent a lifetime learning to accept and obey in silence. Communication skills had to be developed, self-confidence had to be established, and mutual trust had to be fostered. There was often resistance from some who did not feel equal to the task, and unbounded anticipation from others who had felt repressed by forms of living they had experienced.

A life-style that had gradually developed over more than a hundred years, and to which we had been faithfully trying to commit ourselves, was altered almost overnight. This resulted in pain and confusion for members and sharp criticism from non-members. Many were disillusioned with the entire venture and left.

Eventually, the task of true renewal was viewed as a veritable refounding of the congregation, a rebirth. It is very important to understand something of this crucial period in the history of religious life, for it was the crucible through which our present-day members passed and within which many of their values were forged.

Unquestionably, renewal has not always been easy. Many mistakes were made; some valuable elements of religious life were lost, and others were replaced by features of lesser quality. Eventually, the dust settled and a new brand of religious life emerged.

Through it all we have acquired the art of communication without losing the ability to ponder and reflect. We have developed self-confidence while remaining sensitive to others. We have learned to balance assertiveness with docility, critical professional expertise with an unpretentious manner, and astounding versatility with fidelity to our original commitment. The transformation has not been perfect; there is always room for improvement. However, we are now post-Vatican II women religious.

The adaptation of the externals of our lives and the deeper renewal of our religious character were direct responses to the admonition found in *Perfectae Caritatis*:

> *The manner of living, praying and working should be suitably adapted everywhere, but especially in mission territories, to the modern physical and psychological circumstances of the members and also, as required by the nature of each institute, to the necessities of the apostolate, the demands of culture, and social and economic circumstances.*[6]

---

[6] *Perfectae Cariatis*, #3

After many years of study and experimentation, we rewrote our Constitutions, which received the approval of the Congregation for Institutes of Consecrated Life and Societies of Apostolic Life.

Believing that we had faithfully carried out the directives sent to us, we were both confused and saddened by the harsh critique recently lodged against us by that same Congregation. An official Apostolic Visitation of Institutes of Women Religious in the United States was launched in order to investigate the quality of our religious life. Like all other religious institutes, we were questioned regarding our canonical status, our properties, the age of our members, our ethnic profile, our living arrangements, governance and ministries, the character of our formation program and our common life, and our spiritual and liturgical life.

While we were troubled by the implications of this Visitation, we responded as we have always responded, with docility and obedience. We then took advantage of this external investigation to reflect internally and communally on some of the major issues that were the concern of the Visitation.

What resulted was a deepened appreciation of the life to which we had been called and of the commitment of the members of our congregation. Well aware of our declining numbers and the rise in our median age, we resolved to follow the lead of our founding sisters who placed the needs of ministry above personal concerns. This certainly meant judicious planning for an unknown future. However, we were resolved not to allow undue anxiety to determine that future.

Missionary Disciples

In his recent Apostolic Exhortation *Evangelii Gaudium*, Pope Francis reminds us that *"in virtue of their baptism, all the members of the People of God have become missionary disciples."*[7] Our experience of renewal

---

[7] *Evangelii Gaudium*, #120.

brought us to appreciate the fact that we are an apostolic congregation. Hence, our profession in this congregation simply reinforces our baptismal call to be missionary disciples.

One of the most acute struggles in our religious life today comes from tensions inherent in that apostolic self-consciousness. Previously, we sought to harmonize two seemingly contradictory aspects of life, the active and the contemplative. For the most part, our active life was devoted to good works and the service of others. Prayer was nonetheless a necessary ingredient of this life, for it inspired and strengthened us to act with courage and dedication.

The contemplative life, on the other hand, held prayer and interior union with God as primary, and everything else served that goal. We addressed this tension by prescribing times of prayer throughout the day. Apostolic demands that took us from this responsibility were avoided. At times, we called for more periods of prayer; at other times we felt summoned to more involvement in apostolic works. Both of these aspects of apostolic religious life are valuable, both are essential. Many of us are still trying to balance them and are achieving varying degrees of success.

Instructed by Vatican II to recapture the original spirit of our institute and inspired by the zeal of our early apostolic founders, we were awakened to a new self-understanding. We realized that we could no longer live a modified monastic life style; nor was it enough to increase our apostolic involvement. An entirely new world view was developing, one that insisted that the world should not be shunned. It should be transformed, and as religious we were to be a leaven in this transformation. Such a world view can only be characterized as apostolic.

It is difficult to distinguish between doing apostolic work and being apostolic. With so much of the world writhing in pain as it is, with children and women and men often living lives of desperation as they do, it is so easy to be overwhelmed by the needs pressing on every side and incapacitated by obvious limitations. The apostolic life has made tremendous demands on us.

Faced with these realities, we turned to the Scriptures with new questions. We sought new insights, and we found new inspiration. We have come to see that apostolic spirituality seeks to form Christ in the apostle, while apostolic ministry forms Christ in others. The primary focus is not on what we do as spirituality or as ministry, but on forming Christ as we do whatever is done. The circumstances of life wherein the spirituality is developed characterize the nature of the spirituality. Apostolic spirituality is characterized by response to the circumstances of a life that is apostolic.

What does it mean to form Christ? Is there a difference between forming Christ and continuing the ministry of Christ? What makes a life apostolic? What attitudes are essential if we are to be apostles or missionary disciples? Was not being sent in obedience enough? Was not patient endurance of the hardships of ministry evidence of 'imitation of Christ?' These are some soul-searching questions that face us today.

Such apostolic commitment is a formidable task for people who have been reared in a society that judges the value of an insurmountable undertaking by its relative success. When obstacles appear to be, when relationships become too demanding, when projects no longer guarantee a hundredfold, the values of our society seem to encourage us to redirect our energies and to embark on ventures that promise more for less. Contemporary life seems to offer neither the opportune time nor the place to expect wholehearted apostolic commitment. Yet this is precisely what *Perfectae Caritatis* and *Evangelii Gaudium* have mandated.

This new apostolic self-consciousness has also forced us to reevaluate our ministerial commitments. We were founded to serve the poor and the neglected, the marginal and the forgotten, those rejected by society or beyond the reach of Church agencies. We came to realize that the Spirit was calling us anew to these or to similar apostolic fields.

We came to realize that, like our early sisters, we too might have to leave the warmth and security of familiar surroundings in order to bring Christ and the Gospel to those who had no one to minister to them. This meant that, in some situations, the operation of well-established works was handed over to others, and some of our members ventured out into new fields as our early sisters had done.

This move has frequently brought us into conflict with people accustomed to the former roles of religious and resistant to new ones. It has catapulted us into social, political, and ecclesiastical arenas where, like those who preceded us, we might have to contend with structures at variance with the message of the Gospel. We might be *"afflicted in every way, but not crushed; perplexed, but not driven to despair; persecuted, but not forsaken; struck down, but not destroyed"* (2 Cor 4:8-9).

In the midst of this tension, we try to find strength in the conviction that we are responding to the call of God, a call that does not take us out of the world but situates us right at its heart – there to transform it by making Christ present through our presence. We do not see ourselves as set apart, but as purposefully involved. Our lives witness to an alternative way of living in the world, a way of righteousness and tenderness, a way of service and collaboration.

The notion of community has taken on an entirely different importance for us as well. No longer is it limited to common life with varying dimensions of uniformity. Now it is more the way we are bound together than how we live next to each other. Different life situations call for different life styles. The pressing needs of people cannot always be programmed and so schedules vary, complicating the issues of community prayer, community meetings, and community participation.

Once again tensions abound. While all members may be committed to apostolic ministry, some see community as the incontestable wellspring from which flows authentic ministry. Others believe that community serves ministry in a supportive manner. This tension has not yet been resolved and plays its part in the present anxiety of our religious life together.

What shape our apostolic life will eventually take is not certain, for this new self-consciousness is relatively young. One thing is clear: we are convinced of the appropriateness of the direction we have taken. We responded courageously to the challenge of Vatican II. We engaged our total membership in the renewal process. We believe that this entire venture is the work of the Spirit and, despite our mistakes and setbacks, we will continue on the path that lies before us.

American Women Religious

In the United States, the period of renewal after Vatican II coincided with both the women's movement and the civil rights movement. Many of the values of these other movements, and much of the energy that inspired them, influenced the way renewal of religious life unfolded. This was particularly true for women religious.

While it is impossible to talk about the typical woman because there is no single experience that is representative of all women, some aspects of this social upheaval were felt by all. For example, previously, women did not usually engage in social-activist movements. They simply accepted the clearly defined roles and models that were furnished for them. Women are now speaking out against discriminatory practices and points of view and are coming to a new self-consciousness.

A large number of women religious have also entered into this process of self-understanding. As similar as our involvement might appear to be, we have entered for reasons quite different from those of our counterparts. While many women became 'feminists' because they were disenchanted with society and the way society defined and treated them, our disenchantment followed rather than preceded our experience of self-definition. The self-study upon which we launched and our subsequent refounding produced an entirely new phenomenon, namely, post-Vatican II apostolic women religious.

Having been told that we could no longer be satisfied with the traditional pre-Vatican II definitions and understandings, we focused our attention on our own experience. Trusting in the ever-present Spirit of God and the integrity of our religious sisters, we defined our individual selves within the unique context of our congregation, thus altering the uniformity that had previously characterized us.

We agreed from the outset that the entire congregation was to be engaged in this enterprise. It was not intended merely for our leaders who would then communicate their findings and decisions to the rest of the community, who in turn would docilely accept these decisions. All of the members were called upon to examine, to critique, to discuss and then to come to consensus.

Most likely this could only have been attempted because we already had a certain common identity to which individual members had pledged themselves. The existing parameters of our vision, purpose and life-style facilitated honest discussion. However, we still had to be open and accepting in this discussion. We could not retreat from conflict and then hope to arrive at consensus. Simple adaptation was not enough. Superficial adjustments were rejected. The call was for a profound self-examination and subsequent self-definition, which would result in a new or revised way of life.

Nor was it sufficient to consider only some aspects of religious life and overlook others. Renewal demanded that the total religious tradition be scrutinized. Issues would be judged irrelevant only after they had been probed and analyzed. No predetermined scheme devised by a particular group within the congregation or provided by someone from the outside could be used as a guide for selectivity. Out of this experience was developed a self-confidence that readily rejects the slightest hint of discrimination to which women previously have been subjected. Consciousness-raising activities by discussion groups, workshops, unstructured associations of support have all contributed to a heightened self-awareness. We have taken hold of our lives and will not readily let go.

This ferment has thrust us, along with other women religious, into the forefront of some rather critical situations. Our new sense of purpose has left us dissatisfied with the image of 'the good sister' that so characterized us in the past. Though still docile, we are now more critical; though still unpretentious, we are now more discerning; though still self-sacrificing, we are now more judicious. Having discovered our own strengths, we are actively involved in movements aimed at enabling the powerless to discover theirs.

New ministries have changed us as well. We are now working in social agencies, political coalitions, and activities in developing countries. We have moved into leadership positions traditionally held by men. Some of our members serve as directors of diocesan departments, colleagues on theological faculties, and associate pastors. This has caused countless problems for us within the broader society and even within ecclesiastical circles.

Many people, women and men alike, are unhappy with, and even intimidated by, these developments. They see these changes as evidence of capitulation to secularism and the renunciation of religious commitment, when in fact they stem from disenchantment with stereotypes and roles that are no longer meaningful or that hamper the ministries to which we have committed ourselves.

Our experience of renewal and our theological study following Vatican II have led us to call for, and to pledge ourselves to, renewal in other quarters of the Church as well. Without necessarily moving out of our traditional spheres of influence, we have made significant contributions in areas of parish renewal, community development, continuing education, social action etc. We are persuaded that prayerful and prudent action can produce startling new opportunities "*to preach the good news to the poor ... to proclaim release to the captives and recovering of sight to the blind, to set at liberty those who are oppressed, to proclaim the acceptable year of the Lord"* (Lk 4:18-19).

In Earthen Vessels

The careful cultivation, daring experimentation, and painful pruning that have been described here all had a price and we continue to pay it. When, as daughters of the pre-Vatican II Church, we left home to join a religious congregation, we did not merely move from one locale to another, put aside one style of dress for another, and substitute one family unit for another. We literally left the world that we knew with its values and manner of life in the hopes of entering into a new way of living and acquiring a new world view. For most of us, the world we left was a good world, loving, challenging, supportive, and the transition that we underwent was not without great sacrifice.

Then with Vatican II, for a second time in our lives we were asked to leave the warmth and security of the familiar and to venture into uncharted waters. The pain that this created was twofold. We were threatened by both a sense of loss and a recurring fear. Much of the life to which we had committed ourselves, and for which we had sacrificed so much, was now but a memory. Many even wondered if their commitment had perhaps been a waste of themselves. The past was not only set aside as irrelevant, but it was even often ridiculed. Many members still grieve the loss of what they loved and feel that they must apologize for having loved what others consider worthless.

In addition to this, one of the most frightening aspects of post-Vatican II religious life is its uncertainty. There are few contemporary customs that presume to guarantee the kind of certainty and stability that earlier customs had often dared to do. Because we are often doing new things in new ways, we do not always have the assurance of knowing that we are right. True, ambiguity is a part of the post-Vatican II experience of every serious Christian, but by our consecration we have assumed certain added responsibilities that now weigh heavily on us.

We struggle with doubt and confusion about these responsibilities, and the criticism that comes from so many quarters often compounds our anxiety. We cannot always turn to an authority for direction as we did in the past. Blind obedience has given way to personal and communal discernment. A sense of security has been replaced by trust in God's loving presence.

Passing to another consideration, if the primary task of the apostle or missionary disciple is the transformation of the world, then a necessary ingredient of the apostolic disposition is patient endurance in the face of disappointment and failure. Apostles must face the possibility of being denied the security that often accompanies success. Gone is the myth that Sister can plant a medal of Jude, saint of the impossible, and a hospital will spring up in its place, or that the heavenly sound of nuns in choir will warm the heart of a hesitant benefactor. Identification with the poor and neglected, with the marginal and the forgotten does not guarantee that these needy people will open themselves to the ministry offered.

We frequently find that our commitment to certain projects and programs alienates us from 'respectable' Christians. As contemporary religious, we know that our struggle is against the structures of human greed and oppression. We also know that we are always vulnerable in this struggle. As apostles, we cannot withdraw; as Christians, we cannot compromise. We must be able to say with Paul: "*For while we live we are always being given up to death for Jesus' sake, so that the life of Jesus may be manifested in our mortal flesh*" (2 Cor 4:11).

Perhaps the heaviest cross that many of us endure is the sense of being misunderstood by the very Church that we have loved more than mother and father, more than husband and children. In the past, we may have been treated by some as school girls, as chamber maids, as an unquestioning labor force. Yet we continued to serve. Now we have become disenchanted with these roles, with the structures that supported them and with the theology that legitimated them. Yet we continue to serve.

All too frequently, our renewal has been criticized, our ministry has been thwarted and our commitment has been discredited. Yet we continue to serve. Is this ecclesiastical disapproval part of the birth pangs that often precede new life in the Church, or is it a legitimate response to the excesses of which we have been accused, and of which we might indeed be guilty? We are never quite sure.

Regardless of the very real challenges we face today, we strive to be staunch in our convictions, yet humble in our stance. We might not live to see the resolution of our conflict. We can only trust that our struggle has not been for naught.

In the meantime, we face soul-searching questions. In what ways might our celibate love bring new life to a suffering world? How is obedience to function in a collegial community? What forms should vowed poverty take in a congregation of professional women?

We continue in our searching because we have experienced God in the midst of all of the pain and excitement of the past and the ambiguity of the present. We are supported now by our faith in God's compassion, and we are convinced that whatever the future holds this same God will be there in righteousness and tenderness. It is to this same righteousness and tenderness that we continue to commit ourselves, with all devotedness.

PART II

EVANGELICAL COUNSELS & VATICAN II: UNDERSTANDING & LIVING

3

"WE HAVE LEFT EVERYTHING AND FOLLOWED YOU"[1] CHALLENGES OF BEING A RELIGIOUS IN TODAY'S WORLD IN THE LIGHT OF THE SECOND VATICAN COUNCIL

Francis Chidi Ezenezi

Introduction

When religious men and women make profession of the evangelical counsels of poverty, chastity and obedience, they essentially respond to a divine call allowing them to be singularly devoted to God and his service. Profession of vows, which constitutes the essence of religious life, is deeply rooted in their baptismal consecration, and expresses in a strikingly unique manner their commitment to Christ who emptied himself in obedience and humility to God.[2]

---

[1] Mark 10:28.

[2] See *Perfectae Caritatis*, Decree on the Adaptation and Renewal of Religious Life, nos. 5, 10 in *Vatican Council II: The Conciliar and Postconciliar Documents*, ed. Austin Flannery, OP. (New York: Costello Publishing Company, 1996). References to other council documents are also taken from this translation.

Certainly, the postconciliar experience of religious life has been marked with diverse feelings in several parts of the world. Second Vatican Council renewal seems to have provoked some exciting and enthusiastic responses, and the concrete implementations of some Council teachings on religious life during these fifty years have met with various challenging consequences. Animated by the same spirit of renewal initiated by the Council, our celebration of its fiftieth anniversary offers yet another unique opportunity to examine the Vatican II understanding of what it means to be a religious within the challenges of consecrated life in today's world.

I write not as a religious myself but as someone who, through many years of lived experiences with many members of religious institutes, has shared in some ways varied experiences of community life. I wish therefore to offer my personal observations in recognition of the profound meaning of Vatican II's theology of religious life – specifically with respect to the evangelical counsel of poverty and how it is lived within the North American and Sub-Saharan African regions – so as to appreciate its unique values and consequences in today's changing and challenging world.

In order to accomplish the intent of this reflection, I will first explore the Vatican II understanding of the evangelical counsel of poverty. Then I will attempt a comparative analysis of the geo-cultural contexts named above as well as their influence regarding evangelical poverty. Next, I will examine challenges and implications of being a religious in today's world, and finally suggest measures for an effective implementation of the renewal inaugurated at the Council.

The Second Vatican Council & the Evangelical Counsel of Poverty

The evangelical counsels which religious are called to embrace are fundamentally rooted in the Gospel and present a way of living out the Gospel in an unconditional response to God's love. They are 'counseled,' based on the New Testament understanding envisioned as a form of discipleship to which some, but by no means all, Christians are called (Mark 10:17-22; Matthew 19:16-22; Luke 18:18-23).[3] All Christians, nonetheless, are called to purity of heart following the example of Christ who surrendered himself in humble obedience to the will of his Father (Philippians 2:6-11).

The gift of self in living the evangelical counsels as vowed religious maintains within the Church the indispensable value of witnessing. The expression and public manifestation of the evangelical counsels serve as witness to the centrality of God's claim that the kingdom is the true realm to which all Christians belong (Philippians 3:20).[4]

The evangelical counsel of poverty is part of the religious profession, a special way of following Christ that gives a deeper expression of the individual's baptismal profession. An individual may bind himself or herself to a modest and frugal life, or even to directives of one's mentor or adviser in the use of acquired property, with an obligation either perpetual or temporary.

Generally speaking, evangelical poverty understood traditionally means that all resources are held in common. Also, generally speaking, community life expectations presume that work is taken on according to abilities while resources are shared according to member needs. Vowed poverty is thus characterized by a simple lifestyle which makes one poor in actuality and in spirit and fundamentally recognizes that all possessions are gifts from God.

Vatican II declares that voluntary poverty undertaken by religious is a life in imitation of Christ who became poor so that we may be rich. Re-

---

[3] Cf. J.P.M. Walsh, "Evangelical Counsels, "*The Modern Catholic Encyclopedia Revised and Expanded Edition*, 280.

[4] Ibid., 281.

ligious poverty, as the Council explained, is not merely obedience to superiors; rather it manifests itself in deed and in spirit (Mt 6:20).[5]

Evangelical poverty requires one to participate in a world of work and to share material goods and personal gifts of mind and heart with one's community and all God's people in the spirit of hospitality, detachment, service to the poor and commitment to justice. Religious men and women "should reject all undue solicitude, putting their trust in the providence of the heavenly Father (Cf. Mt 6:25)."[6]

Based on each institute's constitution and particular norms, members can for the sake of God's kingdom renounce their inheritances which are already acquired or those anticipated to be acquired. Religious, at the same time, should be willing to share part of their possessions with the Church and for support and assistance to the poor. The Council taught that, while institutes have the right in accordance with their respective rules and constitutions "to possess whatever they need for their temporal life and work," religious should strive to avoid any form of luxurious life and excessive accumulation of wealth and property.[7]

The reception of this Council teaching has found profound expressions within some magisterial documents. The present canonical discipline of the Church declares that the vow of poverty being undertaken by religious always involves a certain renunciation of rights. The independent disposal of any of these rights would be contrary not only to the vow but also to justice.

Moreover, *The Code of Canon Law* (1983) sees evangelical poverty as a vow taken "in imitation of Christ, who for our sake was made poor when he was rich." This vow of poverty signifies a life which is poor in

---

[5] See *Perfectae Caritatis*, no. 13. See also Pope John Paul II's Apostolic Exhortation *Vita Consecrata*, On the Consecrated Life and its Mission in the Church and in the World (Vatican City: Libreria Editrice Vaticana, March 25, 1996), nos. 21-22.

[6] Ibid.

[7] Ibid.

reality and in spirit, and a life in utter detachment from the acquisition of earthly riches. A vow of poverty as being made by religious expresses "dependence and limitation in the use and disposition of goods, in accordance with each institute's own law."[8]

The subject of evangelical poverty was also among the central concerns of the 1990 Ordinary General Assembly of the Synod of Bishops on the formation of priests in the circumstances of the present day. They describe evangelical poverty as "the subjection of all goods to the supreme good of God and his kingdom."

The Council fathers affirm that the only person who can understand and practice poverty is the one who can contemplate and live "the mystery of God as the one and supreme good." Practicing evangelical poverty, the synod fathers conclude, is "not a matter of despising or rejecting material goods, but of loving and responsible use of these goods and at the same time an ability to renounce them with great interior freedom, that is, with reference to God and his plan."[9]

In his Apostolic Exhortation *Vita Consecrata* (1996), John Paul II explains that the evangelical counsel of poverty is a proclamation that God is the sole treasure of the human desire and that poverty lived according to the mind of Christ is an expression of the total gift of the self. In this vow of poverty, religious profess their trust and dependence on the provident care of God and try to live their entire lives in imitation of God.

Evangelical poverty allows religious to witness pastorally to fraternal life inspired by principles of simplicity and hospitality towards the poor in imitation of the Lord who came to share the message of the Gospel with the most neglected of our society.[10]

---

[8] *The Code of Canon Law* (Vatican City: Libreria Editrice Vaticana, 1983), *CIC*, C. 600.

[9] John Paul II, Apostolic Exhortation *Pastores Dabo Vobis*, On the Formation of Priests in Circumstances of the Present Day (Vatican City: Libreria Editrice Vaticana, 1992), no. 30.

[10] See John Paul II, *Vita Consecrata*, nos. 16, 21, 90.

The World of the Religious
& Its Influence

In order to explore the challenges facing religious regarding the evangelical counsel of poverty, we will now focus on the contexts of our study, namely, some parts of the Sub-Saharan African and the North American regions respectively. This comparative analysis is required in order to discover the specific effects of these contexts on the actual implementation of the renewal initiated at the Council. In keeping with their vows, religious are often confronted with the challenging and changing world in which they are being called to exercise their various apostolates. These challenging contexts may take various forms and dimensions.

On the one hand, in many places of the Western industrialized world, especially in North America, there is a widespread individualistic culture with its various forms of indifference, as well as a materialistic and secularist mentality that harms not only the Church but all of society as well.[11] Individualism permeates almost everything we do. It is a basic assumption. It is like a cult. We worship the ego.[12]

On the other hand, the culture of communalism, which is prevalent in Africa, encourages interdependence and social coherence.[13] Concurrently this culture at times leads to dependence and even submission, subjugation and subordination of the individual to the institution and to those in authority. Such tendencies give room for the exploitation and appropriation of the common good by a few.

---

[11] Cf. Albert Nolan, *Jesus Today: A Spirituality of Radical Freedom* (New York: Orbis Books, 2006), 15-25. See also Pope Francis' Apostolic Exhortation *Evangelii Gaudium*, On the Proclamation of the Gospel in Today's World (Vatican City: Libreria Editrice Vaticana, 2013), nos. 61-62, 67.

[12] Ibid., 16. See also Robert Cardinal Sarah, *God or Nothing: A Conversation on Faith with Nicolas Diat* (San Francisco: Ignatius Press, 2015), 112-114.

[13] Ibid., 15-16.

Thus, Sub-Saharan Africa is afflicted by societal problems such as materialism and inequality as well, limitations of infrastructure, and scant social service.

Thus too, economic and social developments are hindered, leaving citizens mired in poverty.[14] This situation has resulted in a survivalist mentality among the people. In such circumstances, the struggle to accumulate more wealth among many individuals, in relation to seemingly meager resources, brings with it some elements of materialism and corrupt practices that encourage competition, struggles, and inequalities of various kinds and dimensions.

The realities of Western individualism and of African communalism have their varied impact on the ways the Church and the entire fabric of human society are perceived and understood. Such perceptions and understandings powerfully influence the ways the religious life practice of poverty is expressed and understood in our changing and challenging world. Here, some examples are needed for illustration.

Western individualism linked with the struggles to 'know oneself' or to 'take care of oneself' began many centuries ago.[15] This strong movement to 'know oneself' and to 'take care of that self' physically, spiritually and psychologically has influenced for several decades the way the evangelical counsel of poverty is embraced. The 'taking care of self' has contributed to more people living singly and acting for self, not always for the greater good of the community. Of course, self-care is not a bad thing in itself, but moderation is crucial for self-care to be healthy.

On the other hand, from the African cultural point of view, a person who is separated and isolated from the rest of the community would be regarded as very unfortunate. One cannot overemphasize interdependence, social coherence and reliance upon one another as inherent

---

[14] Cf. Lauren Ploch, "Nigeria: Current Issues and U.S. Policy, "*Congressional Research Service,* www.crs.gov (Accessed May 21, 2013), 1.

[15] Cf. Albert Nolan, *Jesus Today: A Spirituality of Radical Freedom,* 15-19.

values in African cultures. In Africa, we say: "A person becomes a person through other people." Thus, your identity depends upon your family, your friends, and your community who relate to you and to whom you relate.[16]

The cultural value of the African community can enhance the religious sense of communal living, and even encourage the authentic embrace of religious community life. However inordinate, excessive concern about one's biological family, to the detriment of one's commitment to God through the profession of poverty, may be an obstacle to a religious sense of community life regarding poverty itself. In other words, due to the impoverished situation of many African societies, living evangelical poverty may and often does face challenges from concerns for one's own extended family and the need to care for its members.

"We Have Left Everything & Followed You:"[17] Challenges of Being a Religious in Today's World

The use of the above biblical excerpt is an attempt to respond to Jesus' question to his disciples on the meaning of discipleship. Peter's response on behalf of the apostles highlights the reality of prophetic witnessing devoid of any distraction. Such a commitment made by the apostles reflected their unwavering trust in Jesus, whom they decidedly followed throughout his public ministry.

Similarly, when religious make such a commitment in response to a divine call through the profession of evangelical counsels, they imitate Christ who renounced everything in humble service and obedience to God. Such renunciation comes with various challenges as well.

In North America, one of the challenges is the emphasis that has been placed on individualism versus communal living — the problem of the

---

[16] Ibid., 15-16.
[17] Mark 1:28.

'me-generation' versus the 'we' syndrome. The 'me-generation' problematically sees life from the perspective of self-centeredness as self-fulfillment. Many people, especially young adults today, feel that, despite all this individualism, their egos have been silenced and suppressed. Thus, they continue to seek freedom to do their own thing, to express their opinion on issues and to assert themselves.[18] Such a strong tendency has influenced the way the evangelical counsel of poverty is expressed and embraced.

As mentioned above, the 'taking care of self' has contributed to more people living singly and acting for self but not always for the greater common good, thus making vowed poverty and religious life in general unattractive. Many religious communities in the Western world today have been left vacant with hardly anyone living in them. Many religious congregations in the Western world are suffering set-backs due to lack of vocations to religious life.

Our materialistic society with its struggles between 'wants' versus 'needs' is yet another challenge for all Christians, not just for vowed religious.[19] Sometimes religious find it difficult to make the distinction between what they essentially need in their daily life and things that are frivolous. This challenge is applicable to some religious in Sub-Saharan African areas such as Nigeria.

The evangelical counsel of poverty for some religious has indeed taken on a relativistic dimension, with blurred lines between what constitutes poverty and what does not. Today, many religious feel little guilt using what would be considered luxurious items. Today's secularized world and its way of thinking have led numerous religious to understand the evangelical counsel of poverty as putting into good use the good things of life. Instead of embracing a simple lifestyle, some religious are overly interested in acquiring the latest technological devices or expensive

---

[18] Ibid., 17.

[19] Cf. John Paul II, *Vita Consecrata*, no. 89.

cars or building modern houses for commercial purposes and for the use of their family members, no matter where and how such projects are financed.

For example, in Nigeria there is indeed a perceptible tendency of religious men and women going uninvited to events, occasions, and all kinds of celebrations with the intention of soliciting gifts and recognition. This has created an impression in the minds of some people that religious life is the most comfortable life. How then could someone refute the above impression concerning religious when people can see such a life of opulence surrounding them?

Toward an Effective Response to Challenges Regarding the Counsel of Poverty

The challenges which religious face today regarding the evangelical counsel of poverty can play a constructive role in deepening our awareness of the need to find plausible suggestions to address this situation. These challenges are serious and demand recognition and timely responses.

If religious respond poorly, these challenges can become debilitating crises or even a death-knell for many religious institutes, as we can see from their effects in both the Western and Sub-Saharan African societies. I will therefore examine some measures as effective responses to the challenges pertaining to the evangelical counsel of poverty.

Christo-Centric Ministry as a Paradigm

A call to embrace Jesus' ministry as a paradigm for the evangelical counsel of poverty for all Christians, and not only for religious, comes from his ministry being primarily directed to the Church as the 'Body of Christ.'[20] The ministry of Christ remains the ideal form of any Christian ministry.

Christ's ministry was not restricted to Temple and Synagogue worship. It extended far beyond these limits to involve all categories of people. His was a ministry which had profound expression in making the reign of God visible in all situations of human existence. This reign of God is clearly manifested in Jesus' attitude to human needs.[21]

Here, evangelical poverty, or poverty in spirit reconsidered in terms of service, is seen as a hermeneutical tool in understanding Jesus' ministry. John's Gospel tells us that the presence of Christ on earth is in solidarity with the fulfillment of this special desire of the human person. Hence, Jesus proclaims "*I have come that they may have life and have it more abundantly*" (Cf. John 10:10).

In the Gospel narratives, the people are the main reference point of Jesus' life. Without the people, we cannot appreciate or understand his everyday life. A great multitude from many places followed him (Mark 3:7). "*They brought to him all who were sick or possessed by demons. And the whole city was gathered around the door*" (Mark 1:32-33). And without the people, we cannot understand his denunciation of the powerful who "*load people with burdens hard to bear*" (Luke 11:46), and who "*are called benefactors*" while oppressing the people (Luke 22:25).

The ministry of the Church modeled after the example of Christ is a radical response to the Second Vatican Council's call for solidarity with humanity, as the Council fathers declared: "*The joy and hope, the grief and anguish of the men [sic] of our time, especially of those who are poor or afflicted in any way, are the joy and hope, the grief and anguish of the follow-*

---

[20] See Vatican II's Dogmatic Constitution on the Church, *Lumen Gentium*, no. 7.

[21] Cf. Pope Francis, *Evangelii Gaudium*, nos. 186-192.

ers of Christ as well."[22] Such a desire to respond genuinely to the circumstances of those who are poor and afflicted in any way became, amidst other things, the primary concern of Jesus in his public ministry.

Church is about people who have faith in Jesus Christ and are inspired by his life and vision for the world as well as by the desire to model their lives on the life of Christ. It is about discipleship and service. Thus, no institutional element in the Church exists for its own sake, but all are meant for the purpose of discipleship and should be seen by believers as valuable only if they facilitate discipleship or stewardship.[23]

Speaking of evangelical poverty, therefore, as an expression of discipleship and stewardship, one looks at how this way of life relates to the service of 'the people.' The poverty of Christ, whom the religious imitate, is demonstrative of self-emptying in other-serving.

During his time, Jesus stood among people as one who serves (Luke 22:27), for he was there not "*to be served, but to serve*" (Mark 10: 45). Jesus was deeply moved by the people's suffering. "*He saw a great crowd; and he had compassion for them, because they were like sheep without a shepherd*" (Mark 6:34). Matthew adds "*harassed and helpless*" (Matthew 9:36). He gives hope to this people of the poor and proclaims the good news of God's reign (Mark 1:14). And mysteriously, he tells this crowd of hungry and thirsty people, sick and naked, foreigners and prisoners, that he, the Son of Man [sic], the king, is one of them (Matthew 25:35-36).[24]

We can draw fruitful and useful impulses from Jesus' paradigm of ministry as clearly highlighted in the above citations. His poverty lifestyle and actions are at the service of the poor and the needy at all times.

---

[22] Vatican II"'s Pastoral Constitution on the Church in the Modern World, *Gaudium et Spes*, no. 1. See also Chris Lowney, *Pope Francis: Why He Leads the Way He Leads* (Chicago: Loyola Press, 2013), 41-88.

[23] See Humphrey Anameje, "Mission of the Laity as Mission of the Church -- Emergent Contemporary Theological Discussion,"*Bulletin of Ecumenical Theology, Vol. 19* (2007), 138.

[24] See Jon Sobrino, *No Salvation Outside the Poor: Prophetic-Utopian Essays* (Maryknoll, New York: Orbis Books, 2008), 115-116.

The religious evangelical counsel of poverty – on the path of renewal modeled on Christ – should focus on how the lifestyle and action of the members are at the service of the world.[25] Thus, as a ministering community, all the members have the responsibility to render faithful service to one another after the example of Jesus Christ, who, "*though he was rich, yet for your sakes he became poor, that ye through his poverty might be rich*" (II Corinthians 8:9). It is only in this paradigm of ministry that the religious vow of poverty becomes indeed evangelical to our contemporary challenges of the changing world.

Ongoing Formation for Bishops, Priests, & Religious

According to Pope Francis' Apostolic Letter inaugurating the celebration of the year of consecrated life, the event offers the whole Church an opportunity for thanking God for the gift of this way of life and in sharing in the life of these men and women. A deeper understanding of the meaning and implications of religious life are constituents of this sharing in the life of the religious.

Thus, given the important place of bishops, priests as well as religious in the entire mission of the Church regarding religious life vocations, particularly regarding the evangelical vow of poverty, a new approach to their ongoing formation must be a necessary, urgent task. The urgency of this responsibility is even more obvious in today's world, marked by spiritual disorientation and uncertainties regarding religious life vocations.[26]

The Council fathers made it clear that the successful renewal of the various religious institutes depends on the training of their members. The Council fathers recommended that ongoing formation, which consists of several aspects – religious, apostolic, doctrinal, as well as technical –

---

[25] Cf. Chris Lowney, *Pope Francis: Why He Leads the Way He Leads*, 109-135.

[26] Cf. Pope Francis, *Evangelii Gaudium*, no. 64.

should be given to non-clerical religious men and women after their novitiate.

Regarding other religious in active ministry, adequate training should be offered with due consideration and adaptation to the needs of the contemporary world. Superiors of religious institutes are to ensure that spiritual, doctrinal, and technical formation is provided to members and that other support is given for the enhancement of other forms of training.[27]

Since some religious communities have assignments in dioceses where bishops have responsibilities,[28] it is inevitable that ongoing formation for bishops cannot be overemphasized. Vatican II has maintained that the various forms of apostolate should be encouraged.[29] Since some religious cooperate with diocesan bishops in these apostolic works,[30] bishops should promote ongoing formation, not only for themselves but also for their collaborators, especially religious, to help them renew their life in accordance with their particular constitutions and norms especially regarding the evangelical vow of poverty.

Such involvement of religious in the ministry of diocesan bishops calls for a pastoral awareness on the part of the bishops. Thus, from the above analysis, the bishops' responsibilities are challenging and require serious attention to ongoing formation, which may pertain to the latest theological developments as they relate to religious and their various renewal programs.

This provision for ongoing formation is applicable to priests as well as to religious men and women. Ongoing formation of priests is required because priestly ministry is a service directed not only to themselves but also to others. John Paul II confirmed this in his 1992 Apostolic Ex-

---

[27] See *Perfectae Caritatis*, no. 18.

[28] See Vatican II's Decree on the Pastoral Office of Bishops, *Christus Dominus*, no. 3.

[29] Ibid., nos. 16-17, 27.

[30] Ibid., no. 27.

hortation *Pastores Dabo Vobis*: "This formation is demanded by his own continuing personal growth ... It is also demanded by priestly ministry seen in a general way and taken in common with other professions, that is, as a service directed to others."[31]

Since priestly ministry is directed to others, including religious, ongoing formation is needed to enable priests to be effective assisting religious in their renewal process. The same is true of religious men and women in a special way.

Religious, through profession of evangelical counsels, especially the evangelical vow of poverty, have been called and encouraged by the Council fathers to pursue ongoing formation. Each institute's superior is responsible for appropriate provision to be made for this formation with due consideration to the needs of contemporary society as well as the needs of the members of each institute. Superiors are also responsible for ensuring that directors, spiritual masters as well as professors are chosen and trained to serve the best interest of their institute as its members express their desire to live the demands of the evangelical vow of poverty.[32]

Formation Updating for Seminarians/Religious Students

Another way the Church can contribute to the ongoing process of religious life renewal regarding the evangelical counsel of poverty is to reconsider the formation given in major seminaries and other religious houses of formation for candidates to the priesthood and religious life. That such formation enrichment for seminarians and religious students could have profound effects on religious life renewal within the Church cannot be overemphasized.

---

[31] See John Paul II, *Pastores Dabo Vobis*, no. 70.

[32] See *Perfectae Caritatis*, no. 18.

In view of the anticipated life of evangelical counsels of religious men and women, seminary, study-house, and novitiate formation must be geared toward a meaningful encounter with the real world. Paul Lakeland rightly observes that the "seminary and ministerial training should be for ministry in the real world."[33] He further argues that present seminary formation systems require serious modifications in favor of genuine and authentic academic formation in Catholic higher education institutions without ignoring the spiritual formation of Catholic priesthood candidates.[34]

This argument equally applies to other houses of formation. There is good reason for ministry students and religious students to live together receiving spiritual formation. Nevertheless, since the academic preparation should be of a higher standard, it ought to be conducted, according to Paul Lakeland, in an atmosphere that is open, free and in contact with ordinary people in the real world.[35]

What then is the real world in the context of this study? It is a world where there is a widespread individualistic culture and a secularist mentality that affect not only the Church negatively but the entire society as well. It is also a world with a materialistic culture and inequalities of various kinds and dimensions. In addition, it is a world with its developmental challenges that have resulted in a survivalist mentality among the people.

This understanding of the world invariably has implications for how religious understand the evangelical counsel of poverty. The real world as the above description indicates is common virtually to all people, but unfortunately uncommon and unfamiliar for so many candidates for priesthood and religious life. Often candidates for religious ministry are protected from these realities and experiences, especially in Sub-

---

[33] See Paul Lakeland, *Catholicism at the Crossroads: How the Laity Can Save the Church* (New York: The Continuum International Publishing Group Inc., 2007), 111.

[34] Ibid.

[35] Ibid., 112.

Saharan Africa. Awareness through theological updating as well as through interactions with the rest of human society, will assist the seminarians and religious students in acquiring skills useful for real world ministry in the context of the vow and spirit of poverty.

Theological training oriented towards a pastoral response to real world demands can promote among seminarians and religious students a dynamic understanding of the spirit of poverty in acquisition and proper management of goods and services at their disposal. Such understanding of the real world will help to diffuse tensions which often arise while sharing community life in a world marked by various materialistic mentalities and tendencies. The people of God should also be made aware through basic catechesis of the appreciative attitude of religious towards the material world.

Basic Catechesis for the People of God on Consecrated Life & its Implications

As religious life is undeniably an important expression of the Church,[36] efforts should be made to inculcate the profound meaning of religious vocations to the entire people of God through basic catechetical methodology and other pedagogical means. The Council fathers elaborated on the need for this basic catechesis when they recommended that priests and Christian educators should seriously encourage vocations to religious life through suitable means of admission and frequently create awareness about the implications of such a life through proper teaching on the evangelical counsels.

In this case, special emphasis should be directed to proper catechesis on the evangelical vow of poverty. Parents are equally encouraged by the Council fathers to nurture and protect religious vocations in their children through basic catechesis in Christian virtues.[37]

---

[36] See *Perfectae Caritatis*, no. 25.

[37] Ibid., no. 24.

God's people should be made to understand the constitutive elements of religious life, the evangelical counsels of poverty, chastity, and obedience. They should understand too that these commitments are rooted in the religious' baptismal consecration and expressed in their loyalty to Christ who emptied himself in obedience and humility to God.[38]

They should be informed at the same time of the various challenges of the evangelical vow of poverty, especially the challenge of materialism *"which craves possessions, heedless of the needs and sufferings of the weakest, and lacking any concern for the balance of natural resources."*[39] This basic catechesis should include the response of consecrated life to materialism by the profession of evangelical poverty, which is expressed in active involvement in all activities that promote charity and show solidarity to the less-privileged, the marginalized and the most disadvantaged people of our society.[40]

Considering the two regional contexts of our study, this catechesis should focus on eliciting the support of the people of God in helping religious deal with the peculiar struggles of their vowed poverty relevant in their particular environment. For instance, families of religious men and women in Sub-Saharan Africa would see to it that they minimize the temptation for their relatives in vows to engage in material acquisition that panders to family dependence and expectations. On the other hand, those in the Western world should encourage their folks in vows to seek the beauty of sharing all things in common despite any individualistic enticements.

Another response to challenges to evangelical poverty should highlight the need to train future educators and leaders so that they may be able to eradicate the structures of oppression and promote initiatives that will show solidarity with the poor of our society. The people of God

---

[38] Ibid., nos. 5, 10.

[39] See John Paul II, *Vita Consecrata*, no. 89.

[40] Ibid. See also Pope Francis, *Evangelii Gaudium*, nos. 197-201.

should be encouraged to join activities of voluntary associations and humanitarian organizations in order to promote a fair distribution of international assistance programs and aid for the poor.[41]

Religious are called "to bear a renewed and vigorous evangelical witness to self-denial and restraint, in a form of fraternal life inspired by principles of simplicity and hospitality."[42] The Christian faithful should be aware that evangelical poverty is at the service of the poor and the most neglected of our society.

With this awareness, the people of God will be able to appreciate the core values of religious life and its implications regarding the evangelical counsel of poverty. With this understanding, they can assist religious without much distraction to live fully their renewed commitments to God through the profession of poverty.

Concluding Remarks

To meet the challenges of being a religious in today's world, one must be securely grounded in a poverty of spirit. This means recognizing that all I am and have comes from the Creator. Thus, one must be willing to share talents, time, love, and compassion in the service of God for all humanity without counting benefits accruing from such opportunities. The Church as the Body of Christ, as well as leadership and members of various religious institutes, should be people who appreciate and live in a spirit of poverty[43] – like the apostles who left everything and followed Christ with the ultimate intention of being at the service of God and humanity (Cf. Mark 10:28).

---

[41] Ibid.

[42] Ibid., no. 90.

[43] Cf. Chris Lowney, *Pope Francis: Why He Leads the Way He Leads*, 41-43.

4

UNTIL ALL HAVE ENOUGH:
VOW OF POVERTY & THE LATER IMPACT
OF VATICAN II[1]

Joan F. Burke, SND de Namur

Introduction

I was blessed to have entered religious life and received my initial formation as a Sister of Notre Dame de Namur literally during Vatican II. I entered in 196, two months before the Council opened, and made my first profession in 1965, the year of its closure. We were fortunate to have as our theology professors Jesuits from their theologate, which was about forty minutes away. This gave us the advantage of not only being steeped in the documents of the Council, but also being given a good understanding of how they reflected a theology that had been evolving for over forty years.

---

[1]An earlier version of this text was presented as a paper under the same heading at the "Vow Symposium" of the Sisters of Notre Dame de Namur held the 8th – 11th July 2004 in Springfield, Massachusetts as part of the bi-centenary of the congregation.

Perhaps one area of our lives as women religious, which demonstrates for me the profound impact of the Second Vatican Council on our self-understanding, is how we have come to interpret the call to live in our times the vow of poverty. Quite unlike the limited explanation of the vow in an earlier time, I see this vow today calling us to try both to model an alternative way of living and to restructure our world — so that all may indeed have enough. This has implications for all our ministries as well.

To trace this development, I would like to use the renewal documents (1968-78) and the 1990 Constitutions of the Sisters of Notre Dame de Namur. I imagine much of what I will describe here applies to other congregations of women as well.

Traditionally, the vow of poverty among us – up until the Renewal Years – was largely seen as a personal question and a matter of permissions, involving the obligations of 'common life.' This was spelled out in the Sisters of Notre Dame de Namur's *Constitutions of 1964*:

> *By the simple vow of poverty, the Sisters renounce the right to dispose freely of any temporal thing having a money value without permission of lawful superiors (Article 83). Religious poverty requires common life, that is, that each religious, out of fraternal [sic] love should live on goods held in common and should be content to receive the same as is given to all as regards food, clothing, furniture etc., without any exception for anyone ... (Article 90).*

Although the vow did have implications for what Americans call 'lifestyle,' we did not see it as touching our core self-perception as women religious, nor understand it in any larger social context with any impact on our ministries.

With the Renewal Years, a marked evolution began to take place. It brought to the fore a strong – and even central – social dimension of poverty for vowed religious. The seminal ideas for this marked shift can be found in the early renewal documents. Our collective thinking was naturally greatly influenced by the work of Sister Marie Augusta Neal, SND de Namur, the Harvard-trained sociologist who conducted the National Sisters Survey in the 1960s. Also, fo r many of us, the thoughts of Paulo Freire in his *Pedagogy of the Oppressed* (1970) helped us to see the importance of *conscientization* largely mediated for us through our sisters working in the Northeast Region of Brazil.

Following the canonical approbation of the *Constitutions of 1989*, the *Acts of the Chapter of 1990* set forth basic principles for the interpretation of the document, stating that the Constitutions were to be read and lived in the context of all the congregation documents since the Renewal Years:

> *These principles, we accept as valid for our lives, emerge from the values and spirit of the Acts of the Renewal Chapters, culminating in the Acts of [the General Chapter of] 1984. We see these documents as our common heritage, as documents which flow from our experience and form the developing structures which facilitate mission. These documents will continue to inspire and guide us in our living out the mission and charism of our Congregation.*[2]

Ground Well-Prepared

Women religious in Europe were well prepared for Pope John XXIII's "throwing open the windows" of the Church by the Scriptural and liturgical movements of the 1950s and 1960s, and in the United States by the concerted effort at the same time to educate sisters.

The Sisters Formation Conference was founded in 1954 to respond to the need to update the theological-religious training and the professional education of women religious. Marie Augusta Neal later documented the seminal impact of this in her book *From Nuns to Sisters*:

---

[2] p. 26.

> *Of [women religious] living and working in the United States in 1966, only 5 percent had entered with a [college] degree. Only 20 percent had fathers whose occupation was classified as professional, and only 6 percent of their fathers and 3 percent of their mothers were college graduates. Yet, in 1967, 68 percent of the sisters themselves had, at least, a college education and by 1980, that number was 88 percent, with 68 percent having advanced degrees.*[3]

These statistics indicate that American women religious in the 1960s were very well prepared to welcome Vatican II and seriously study its output. Their education had opened them to understand its importance for effectiveness in ministry. I remember how we 'devoured' the Council documents for years, and discussed in the community their implications, and I can still now relive the hopes they stirred in us!

Documenting a Revolution

Our first Renewal Chapter took place in 1967-68. The meeting itself was preceded by a period of intense drafting and discussion of a wide range of position papers which explored what we saw as the significance of the Vatican II documents for the living of religious life. We also took seriously the Council fathers' request to return to our roots. And, fortunately, this was just at a time when we had greater access than ever before to the then-recently translated writings and letters of our Foundress and Co-Foundress and of many of their colleagues.

I remember particularly vividly how more aware we became of the importance in our tradition of living in the 'liberty of the children of God.' This had been tested in the early struggles of the first sisters to live into their vision, in spite of great resistance on the part of some members of the hierarchy. This conflict led the Foundress St. Julie Billiart to leave Amiens, France, where she had founded the congregation

---

[3] Marie Augusta Neal, *From Nuns to Sisters* (1990), 32.

in 1804, to seek refuge five years later in the Diocese of Namur, Belgium. Namur remains our Mother House.

The documents issued at the end of the renewal chapters presaged a marked shift that was to impact almost every dimension of our lives: community living, ministry, relationship with the people we served, our relationship with the institutional Church, our self-perception. What Sandra M. Schneiders later would call another historical era of religious life – that of "ministerial religious life" – was beginning to take shape.

In this chapter, I will try to track, through a careful reading of our internal documents, how this transformation resulted in a very different understanding of religious life. Our perception of the vow of poverty changed and came literally to take on a global perspective.

Even our earliest renewal documents suggested that the sisters were aware of the significance of the journey they were being called to embark upon:

> *The problem of evangelical poverty is one of such depth and importance that only a long-term period of meditative reflection, research and experimentation will enable us to respond with integrity to the mandate of the Council fathers concerning revitalization of Christ's counsel to be poor.*[4]

As pointed out by Sr. Marie Augusta Neal in *The Just Demands of the Poor: Essays in Socio-Theology*, between 1960 and 1970 a major shift occurred in the Church's elaboration of its theological position on human development and ministry. The primary focus of the Church herself moved from ministry with the poor aimed at alleviating the results of poverty – the longstanding goal of human service – to

---

[4] *Interim Directives 1967-68*, Directive 1.

eliminating its causes. This change was a recognizable shift in its post-Vatican II position.[5]

This evolution is clear in the Church documents of the decade: John XXIII's *Mater et Magistra* ("Christianity and Social Progress"), 1961 and *Pacem in Terris* ("Peace on Earth"), 1963; Paul VI's *Populorum Progressio* ("On the Development of Peoples"), 1967 and *Octogesima Adveniens* ("A Call to Action"), 1971; and the Synod of Bishops "Justice in the World", 1971. The impact of this quickly developing body of social teaching of the Church on SNDs and other women religious would be profound.

The *Acts of the Special Chapter of 1969* testified to a discernible desire to search for and live into a new self-understanding. This was clear in the very first section of the document on the "End and Spirit:"

> *Rooted and founded in love, inspired by the courageous faith of Mary's "Yes," we want to be ready to bring the Gospel to all those whom we can reach. To do this effectively, we want to live as simply as possible. To do it relevantly we want to respond to the most pressing needs of our day by influencing human behavior and institutions towards justice and charity. In order to further this quiet revolution on as wide a scale as possible, we need to listen to the voices of the world, and to collaborate generously with other persons and organizations who serve the family of man [sic].[6]*

The reference in the section on the "Apostolate" was even more explicit:

> ... *we will prepare ourselves to present so effectively the social doctrine of the Church, whose light is truth, whose object is justice, whose driving force is love, that we help form mature persons filled with Christ's concern for the needs of men [sic] and determined to*

---

[5] Sr. Marie Augusta Neal, *The Just Demands of the Poor: Essays in Socio-Theology* (New York: Paulist Press), 104-09.

[6] *Acts of the Special Chapter of 1969*, p. 2.

exercise their power to influence and shape the society in which they live (Gaudium et Spes, 59; Mater et Magistra, 226).[7]

In the Directives of this same document of 1969, one of the proposed lines of policy made the direct link with the importance of the structural underpinning of justice: "We strive consistently to teach the central Christian values and to motivate those we serve *to help build structures consistent with justice and charity in the societies to which they belong.*"[8]

Another Directive reflected Paul VI's insightful observation that "development is the new name for peace,"[9] and noted the importance of collaborating with groups beyond ourselves: "... *We also stand ready to cooperate with other international groups seeking for mankind that development which is the new name for peace.*"[10]

Also, in the document is the suggestion that sisters recognize that their experience of belonging to an international congregation itself was a valuable resource in their lives of ministry. Directive 31, which addressed the "Ministry of Reconciliation," stipulated:

Inspired by faith in Christ and the belief that all men [sic] are called to be one in him and among themselves we, Sisters of Notre Dame, will strive to find concrete means to promote a world vision of redeemed humanity opposing all selfish nationalism and provincialism of outlook, so that we may be true mediators and ambassadors seeking the promotion of international peace and unity; the international character of our congregation can become a resource for promoting such peace and unity.

---

[7] *Acts of the Special Chapter of 1969*, p. 4.

[8] *Interim Directives 1967-68*, D. 4, p. 7.

[9] Paul VI, *Populorum Progressio* (1967).

[10] *Interim Directives 1967-68*, D. 30.

Significantly, the first major papal documents after the Second Vatican Council were the publications of Paul VI on the challenges of the global social reality, especially the growing inequality and world poverty. *Populorum Progressio* ("On the Development of Peoples") argued that economic justice was essential for building world peace, and that every person as every nation had a right to integral human development. His letter *Octogesima Adveniens* ("A Call to Action"), 1971, which marked the eightieth anniversary of *Rerum Novarum*, challenged every Christian community to consider its social reality and read there the "signs of the times" and act on behalf of justice.

This was a sequel to the Council's emphasis on the "local / particular Churches:" Council documents *Lumen Gentium* ("Dogmatic Constitution on the Church") and *Ad Gentes* ("Decree on the Missionary Activity of the Church"). In the same year the Synod of Bishops, in the introduction of their outcome document "Justice in the World," boldly asserted, "Action on behalf of justice and participation in the transformation of the world fully appear to us as a constitutive dimension of the Gospel."

Living into the Renewal Years

The tumultuous socio-political context of the 1960s and 1970s — the youth revolts, Vietnam War, the development of Liberation Theology in Latin America — touched many women religious who were working with youth and congregations whose members were engaged in various countries of South America.

The Sisters of Notre Dame de Namur serving in the Northeast Region of Brazil were particularly impacted by the oppression suffered by the impoverished peasants and the landless peoples among whom they were living and working, as well as by the writings of Paulo Freire. Many orders of women in the Northern Hemisphere were also becoming aware of the growing number of African and Latin American members who began to share their particular perspectives and challenges.

Given this context, the SND de Namur *Chapter of 1975* fittingly chose to write for the congregation a Mission Statement which put justice squarely at the heart of the call of the disciples of Jesus: "... Any ability we find in ourselves, by which we may influence other groups or individuals in their action, should be exercised in favor of 'the poor, the dispossessed, the powerless of this planet'."[11] The Statement ended with the questions: To what extent does our consecrated life possess a prophetic dimension, calling us to denounce unjust structures, and to announce by our own lives the values of the Kingdom? By using the expression "the poor" rather than "the materially poor," are we denying a real dimension of our life and mission? Besides working "on behalf of the poor," are we willing to "stand with the powerless."[12]

In part two of the same outcome-document of the *Chapter of 1975* were strong policy guidelines:

> *That in decisions about the use of our material resources (money, contributed services, property) priority be given to programs which serve the poor and/or which have a high potential for changing oppressive structures."*[13] *"Conscious of the congregation's responsibility to use its resources to achieve the goals of social justice, each government unit will determine an effective method of using in the interests of social justice whatever financial power it may possess.*[14]

Three years later, when the congregation reassembled and drafted the *Chapter Acts of 1978*, another dimension was added under the rubric of "Towards a Further Understanding of Mission:"

---

[11] *SNDdeN Chapter 1975*, Part One, p. 16.

[12] Ibid., Part One, p. 18.

[13] Ibid., Part Two, p.18.

[14] Ibid., Part Two, p. 31.

> *Inherent in our developing understanding of mission is the belief that God, who continues to speak to us in diverse ways today, calls to us with a special insistence through the voices of the dispossessed and the materially poor as they attempt to organize themselves to claim their rights as human beings.*[15]

All of these developments are found in the *Constitutions of 1989*, which were the summary outcome of the Renewal Years.

Interestingly, what had been posed as a question in 1975 now was integrated into the "End and Spirit" of the congregation:

> *Through our developing understanding of mission, we search anew in each time and place for ways to spread the Gospel and to take our stand with the poor of the earth. According to our tradition, in all our ministries, we value education as fundamental in bringing about the reign of God.*[16]

Strikingly, in Article 68, the vow of poverty is directly linked to the mission of the Sisters of Notre Dame de Namur in a way that demonstrates the essential social context and dimension of the vow:

> *Our poverty is related to mission and calls us: to evaluate our lifestyle and ministries from the perspective of the poor, allowing ourselves to be challenged by them, to choose to live with less until all have enough, to incorporate the concerns of the poor into our prayer and ministries, to contribute, in whatever ways we are able, to the building of an economically just world in which all persons can live in dignity.*[17]

For many of us today, the expression that best explains the vow of poverty is the above-quoted phrase: we are called "*to choose to live with*

---

[15] *SNDdeN Chapter Acts of 1978*, section B, p. 12.

[16] *SNDdeN 1987 Constitution*, C. 14.

[17] Ibid., C. 68.

less until all have enough." The mission intent of Article 68 is elaborated further in the following Mission Directive:

> *In our decision-making we give priority to situations in which we can: respond to the needs of the local church, promote Christian values by educating for justice and peace, accompany the poor as they work together to exercise their rights as human beings, work towards the alleviation of the effects of poverty, work towards the elimination of the systemic causes of poverty and oppression.*[18]

Testing Grounds

The 1980s were the last decade of the Cold War and of living in the "shadow of the nuclear threat." The major powers of the United Kingdom and the United States had conservative governments in the persons of Margaret Thatcher and Ronald Reagan.

Towards the end of the decade, a major change was in the air, with the Soviet Union President Mikhail Gorbachev calling for *glasnost* (openness) and *perestroika* (restructuring). In 1989, the Berlin Wall was torn down, which signaled the coming end of the Cold War. The anti-*apartheid* was increasingly weighing on the South African regime. The rest of the continent was suffering under the weight of externally imposed "Structural Adjustment Programs" (SAP) which led to deep economic crises.

In this period, however, conferences of bishops were taking the call of Paul VI seriously to try to address the most pressing socio-economic issues of their people. The United States Bishops published three very focused pastoral letters: one on peace in a time of the arms race (1983); another on pastoral concern for increasing Hispanic population (1984); and yet another on the impact of the United States economy on the poor (1986). In tandem, the local theological developments on the dif-

---

[18] Mission Directive, D. 5.

ferent continents began to be more readily available, largely through the publications of the Maryknoll-sponsored Orbis Press.

Offering a critique of both the liberal capitalist and the socialist models of economics were the writings of Pope John Paul II: *Laborem Exercens* ("On Human Work"), 1981; and *Sollicitudo Rei Socialis* ("On Social Concern"), 1987. Consistently he pointed out the growing gap between the North and the South and called for solidarity of commitment to the common good of all. The dynamism of the Polish Pope created a great enthusiasm initially and sense of engagement, especially among the young. He courageously spoke and wrote of the need to re-assess structures in terms of justice.

It was in this context that the congregation came together for its first Chapter in 1990, after submitting the year before its revised Constitutions for the approval of the Roman Congregation for Religious and Secular Institutes (CRIS). This fact left the membership much freer in choosing the focus of its deliberations.

Interestingly, I found that the concluding document closely echoed what was quoted above as the Mission Statement of 1975. The *Chapter Acts of 1990* reaffirmed the option for the poor and the call to work to change unjust structures: "… as Sisters of Notre Dame, we wish to re-commit ourselves to the poor and marginalized and to the creation of structures in the world which will bring about justice and peace."[19]

Increasingly, many sisters moved into ministries which more directly served the materially poor and the marginalized; others took up advocacy work. Many had moved into these kinds of work from their earlier engagements in schools, which – although initially started for the materially poor often – were serving more children of the middle classes. Gradually, some moved back into formal education, but specifically for the impoverished, since education for these groups was so lacking or deficient.

---

[19] *SNDdeN Chapter Acts of 1990*, p. 25.

One particular ministry which the congregation adopted at the end of this period was advocacy at the United Nations on behalf of those served by the sisters throughout the world. This advocacy would be accomplished through our congregation as a non-governmental organization (NGO) accredited by the UN and headed by our full-time UN representative.

A Time of Great Hope / A "Shift of Gravity"

During the decade that followed, the global realities became palpable in their wide-ranging impact on the lives of the sisters. The 1990s saw the collapse of the Soviet Union, the end of Communism except for China and a few smaller countries, the phenomenal growth of the Internet, the Rwandan genocide, the release of Nelson Mandela from prison, and the abolition of *Apartheid*. The growing areas of the congregation shifted to Africa and Latin America in the Southern Hemisphere.

Members were still becoming aware that Vatican II ushered in the era of what Karl Rahner called 'World Church.' The congregation also was beginning to experience a coming "shift of gravity." This was the very expression that one of our former superior generals, Mère Josepha de St. Francoise, had commented to me on the eve of my first visit to sisters of the congregation in Africa.

The economic crisis in Africa and other parts of what was then referred to as the "global South" deepened, even as the inequality gap in the North became more manifest. In 1991, John Paul II issued his encyclical *Centesimus Annus* ("100th Anniversary of *Rerum Novarum*, 'The Condition of Labor'"), in which he reaffirmed the centrality of the human being as the heart of an economy.

He particularly criticized the dehumanization effected by the market economy, which was structured to serve money interests before that of human beings. He also looked to the larger global reality and called for a new order of governance that would challenge the excesses of national sovereignty. The Pope argued the world order needed to be refashioned to promote the common good of all.

When SNDs met again in 1996, the Chapter Acts challenged the membership: "We commit ourselves to educating ourselves about structures that cause poverty and work to change them."[20] The Congregation Mission Statement drafted by the General Government Group in 1999 stated unequivocally: "Each of us commits her one and only life to work with others to create justice and peace for all."

Three years later the same General Government Group referred back to the challenge of self-education (*Acts of the Chapter of 1996*) and how it would impact ministries when they wrote in their *Triennial Report* (1999), "A Time for Saving and a Time for Giving Away." It is true that we cannot change our ministries or their focus overnight, but as the Chapter directed, we can begin to educate ourselves "*about structures that cause poverty and work to change them.*"

Even that is not an easy commitment to make or to keep. It involves taking time to read about the issues, to raise questions within ourselves and with others and then to challenge those who are in a position to change laws and structures. It also invites each of us personally to examine how we engage with others and to ask if there are unjust structures even in our places of ministry.[21]

In their *Report to the Chapter of 2002*, the leadership group of the congregation identified three specific ways in which they had tried to foster among the sisters the broader collaboration mentioned above in living out the Chapter of 1996 Directive on the Poor: "We have ... persevered in our efforts to obtain NGO status at the United Nations as

---

[20] *SNDdeN Chapter Acts 1996*, D. 37.

[21] SNDdeN General Government's *Triennial Report (1999)*, p. 10.

members of an international congregation so that the voices of the poor with whom we work can be heard."[22]

With our encouragement, the congregational offices have responded to the Chapter Direction. The Justice and Peace office, in collaboration with the Communications Office, provides on the Internet information about today's society, especially about the poor of our world, and the Congregational Resource Planning Committee has established guidelines and investment policies to respond to the needs of the poor.[23]

The above themes were echoed in the deliberations of the first two General Chapters in the new century. The first in 2002 underscored how the commitment to social justice was directly related to the charism of the congregation: "Impelled by Julie's passion that everyone experiences the goodness of God, we commit ourselves to help to create a more just and loving world."[24] And then one of the Chapter Calls of 2008 stated, "We yearn to deepen our fundamental commitment to stand with our sisters and brothers who live in poverty and accompany them in their struggle."[25]

Stretching Now for the Way Forward

What can be said about the unfolding direction for the sisters today, after having this changed perception of their vowed commitment? The congregation is now preparing for its next General Chapter. The following is a gleaning from the proposals that have surfaced for the international meeting to consider as major focuses for discussion:

---

[22] SNDdeN General Government's *Report to 2002 Chapter*, p. 4.

[23] Ibid.

[24] *SND General Chapter 2002*, C. 4.

[25] *SND General Chapter 2008*, p. 2.

Mission and Ministry

- Acting to change structures of inequality to empower those who are living in poverty
- Being communities of charity and simplicity in solidarity with the poor
- Deepening our commitment to acting on the calls of the 16th General Chapter, especially on human trafficking and the environment
- Making systemic connections
- Strengthening our mission to people who live on the margins of society through education and through a greater sharing of our resources
- Placing even greater focus on our mission with people who are poor or living on the margins of society
- Deepening our understanding of global issues: the environment, immigration, human trafficking, technology, quality of life, etc.
- Identifying the causes of policies and practices that keep people in poverty and addressing them in all possible ways
- Identifying and addressing systemic causes of poverty and injustice in our own cultures
- Promoting through education dialogue, non-violence and cooperation between nations, races and religions
- Giving shape to our spirituality through a clear preference for the poor, today's people in need.

Care of Earth

- Feeling responsible for future generations by caring for the environment every day and acting as good managers, instead of as owners of the universe

- Working toward a sustainable global society founded on respect for nature
- Engaging with interest groups in reflection-action-reflection to assess the effects of environmental destruction on people, land and resources and act on a specific issue
- Studying how environmental concerns contribute to human exploitation and impact those living in poverty.

Women in the Church and Society

- Initiating structures for reflection and action on our issues as women within the Church and within our world
- Challenging unjust structures in the hierarchical Church
- Living with courage our prophetic role in the Church
- Expressing indignity and opposition to human trafficking, sex tourism, abuse of power and exclusion of women.

Besides the question of poverty, increasingly the issues of the environment and women in the Church and society are major concerns and are seen in the context of justice. The latter two issues need to be addressed ever more directly and with depth by the Church herself. For example, Pope Benedict XVI made a valuable contribution to seeing the question of the environment in terms of an intergenerational justice in his *Caritas in Veritate* ("Integral Human Development in Charity and Truth"), 2009, nos. 48 and 49. Pope Francis issued his powerful and influential encyclical *Laudato Si'* ("On Care for Our Common Home") in 2015.

A burning issue for me, which I personally would have expected to figure more dramatically in the list above, is the inequality which continues to grow and mark all our societies and the larger world community. Has it now become an un-worded assumption across the globe that there is a deeply embedded structured injustice of the unfettered greed of the few and powerful, which results in the consequent impoverishment of the masses who are exploited and rendered voiceless?

I have no doubt that, in the era of Pope Francis, this reality will be clearly identified and condemned, and that we will be forcefully challenged to search with others for a strong Gospel response to the plight of our sisters and brothers. In a very short time, the witness of his life and his "walking his talk" have been a cry that has found an echo in so many peoples across the world.

Obviously, the work is not done. What I have chronicled above, however, does trace how we as a congregation since Vatican II have increasingly seen as central to our mission both an identification with the poor and a strong engagement with others in working to change the systemic causes of poverty in our world. For me, these are directly linked with our vow of poverty: *"choosing to live with less until all have enough."*

This suggests as well a deep underpinning in a spirituality of universal solidarity. This challenges the religious to relate to others as sister and brother, especially those living in poverty, and to try to see the world from their perspective. Like that of Jesus, the first question always would be, "What is it that you seek?"

PART III

RELIGIOUS LIFESTYLE

5

RELIGIOUS COMMUNITY LIFE: THEN & NOW

Theresa Eke, DC

If we live by the truth and in love, we shall grow completely into Christ, who is the head by whom the whole Body is fitted and joined together, every joint adding its own strength, for each individual part to work according to its function. So the body grows until it has built itself up in love. (Ephesians 4:15-16)

Introduction

Religious life is a unique way of life. One of the features that make it unique is that of a common way of life that angles into the spiritual, apostolic, and social life. Its uniqueness is further highlighted by living these common aspects in community where individuals, generally unknown to one another prior to entry, gather together under one institution, and in smaller or larger groups, believing to have heard the same call from God.

The Webster dictionary of the English language defines community as "a body of people living near one another in social relationship" or "a body of people with a faith, profession or way of life in common." This second definition better describes the community of religious men and women, whose uniting force is the common faith, common profession, and common way of life they share. The idea of community points to a group of people sharing a common lifestyle animated by a shared vision.

In the history of Christianity, Jesus always called people first to be with him, and then to help him carry on the mission for which the Father had sent him (Cf. Matthew 4:19; Mark 1:17; John 1:39). The "*come and see*" of John and the "*come with me*" of Matthew and Mark were not a mere trial invitation but a "live-in" experience, an invitation to see where the Master "lived" and to spend "the rest of the day with him."

This 'spending' of time with Jesus was always in company. In the Gospels, the disciples were called in twos or in groups (Cf. Luke 10:1). When eventually Levi alone was invited (Cf. Matthew 9:9; Mark 2:14; Luke 5:27-28), there was already an existing community into which he was inserted. Thus, the basic way of following Jesus is in community, be it the universal community of the Church or the particular community of the religious/consecrated life.[1]

Nevertheless, there have been among the disciples of Jesus men and women who were inspired by the Holy Spirit to follow Christ in solitude as hermits, while others founded religious communities. These hermits generally lived by themselves, but history as well as experience shows that these hermits, though living solitarily, welcomed disciples, people who came to them for teaching and spiritual direction.

At the end of the Second Vatican Council, the Church called out for an "up-to-date renewal of the religious life." This demanded both "a constant return to the sources of the whole of the Christian life and to the primitive inspiration of the institutes, as well as their adaptation to the

---

[1] Diarmuid O'Murchú, *The Prophetic Horizon of Religious Life* (London: Excalibur Press, 1989), 127.

changed conditions of our time."[2] This call was holistic. The consecrated persons were called to renew themselves spiritually, apostolically, and communally.

Certain habits, attitudes, and behaviors that were not characteristically evangelical – or perhaps had been incorporated into the life following the particular desires or spirituality of certain leaders – deserved to be shed. Other practices that were rather outdated, and which did not impact on the core of the faith and religion, needed to be discarded. This was the call of the Second Vatican Council. To this call most religious congregations responded with great zeal and vivacious devotion.

This chapter first discusses religious community life in the preconciliar era, highlighting its peculiar model with some characteristic features and implications. It then examines religious community life in the postconciliar period with its problems and prospects, and sets forth how individual personality differences, group dynamics, and styles of leadership might impact the quality of the common life in religious institutes. It is hoped that this chapter, in some small way, informs and forms the readers on the value of community life within the context of the legacy left by the Second Vatican Council after its fiftieth year, and it poses a challenge or two for further reflection.

The Foundational Element of Religious Community Life

The basic element in any community is relationship or relatedness. This is true of the religious community. A core revealed truth of Christianity is that God is love. Thus, the person who lives in love lives in God, and God lives in that person (I John 1:4f). Love is God's deepest essence and love *ipso facto* connotes relationship.

---

[2] "Perfectae Caritatis,"in *Vatican Council II, Conciliar and Postconciliar Documents*, Austin Flannery, ed. (New York: Costello Publishing, 1975), #2.

The theology of the Holy Trinity presents the relatedness of God and the Godhead in relationship. It is this dimension of divine relatedness that provides the theological foundation for community in the monastic and religious life, and that constantly challenges the religious to individual and corporate conversion.[3] Consequently, like the community of the triune God, the religious community is, before anything else, about relationships and relatedness.

The mystery of religious community and its beauty lie in its nature as both 'chosen' and 'given.' It is chosen in so far as the intending member is never forced into relationship with the particular religious group. It ought to be voluntary. It is also given, in so far as nobody, at least in the traditional form of religious life, chooses whom to live with. The individual is believed to have been called by God and he/she freely responds and chooses a particular religious congregation where members were, prior to entry, largely unknown to one another.

It thus becomes a faith community in which everyone in the group believes and accepts that they have been called individually and assembled by God for a common mission. It is always hoped that, through this group experience, the individual members will reach their personal fulfillment and maximally develop their potentials.

Models of Community Life

There are basically two forms or models of religious community life, although these have been lived in multifarious styles. These are the traditional and the progressive models of community. To a certain extent, the traditional model seems to correspond more with the preconciliar way of religious community living, while the progressive model appears to correspond more with its postconciliar forms. History and

---

[3] G.A. Arbuckle, *Out of Chaos: Refounding Religious Congregations* (London: Geoffrey Chapman, 1988), 130.

experience have, however, shown that each era has some elements of the various models in them.

Preconciliar Era:
Traditional Models of Community Life

Prior to the Second Vatican Council, the structure of the religious community life was basically uniform. Members did the same thing nearly at the same time, including such personal things as bathing. The use of the bell was something that reminded everyone of the 'voice of God' and, from rising to retiring to bed, members knew where and what each one did or should be doing at a given time. If they went out, they did so in pairs or in larger groups and with the expressed permission of the superior.[4]

Without judging intentions, it would have been very difficult in preconciliar times to measure correctly one's level of maturity in terms of living the values. It would be rather difficult to say definitely whether people were more compliant than they were convinced of the values they proclaimed – or more fearful than they were free. To be a 'good religious' then was almost, if not completely, about observing the rules. Freely choosing and acting according to one's conviction or belief was not seriously considered.

The traditional model of religious community is founded on the model of the family. The consecrated persons gather together to form a family of believers with common vision, goals and ideals. The religious family thus becomes the individual's 'spiritual family' as distinct from the 'natural family' with biological relationships. The individual joins others who have made a similar commitment of service to be a sign of support and encouragement, even though members may be involved in varying ministries. Thus, members live together in community to

---

[4] Cf. Sandra M. Schneiders, *Selling All: Commitment, Consecrated Celibacy and Community in Catholic Religious Life* (New York: Paulist Press, 2001), 308-309.

give witness to common goals of service, simplicity of life, and prayer as they strive to actualize together the charism of their founders or institutes.

There is a relational background from which one enters into the 'supernatural' or spiritual family. This background is the natural family.[5] Prior to the Second Vatican Council, entry into the religious community meant a complete severance of the affective relationship between the individual and the natural family with the intention of facilitating total self-giving.

The members of the religious institute, having been called into the same family and professing the same values, gather in the name of the Lord (Matthew 18:20) to collaborate in a common mission and to promote God's kingdom on earth through their witness of life.

However, religious community, being a spiritual and supernatural family, cannot be expected to function exactly like the natural family, which is founded on blood ties. Regardless of the mimicking of the natural family by the presence of a 'mother superior' or 'father superior' who acts as head of the family, the local community is generally constructed on faith. The superior is a representative of God in whose name members have gathered, and who they believe has brought them together.

Religious community cannot therefore be built on exclusively natural love or natural relationships. Christian love is something we must have for everyone and of itself cannot form a community. But once given the ideals, purposes and means of the institute, divine love is the bond which absolutely will give life to these ideals, purposes and means.[6]

---

[5] *Perfectae Caritatis*, #15a.

[6] Dominic Hoffman and Basil Cole, *Consecrated Life, Contribution of Vatican II* (Bombay, India: St. Paul's Publications, 2005), 316.

Having said this, one needs to realize that mere profession of love – natural or divine – and the ideals cannot hold a community together without clearly defined rights and responsibilities of its members. Thus, rules and regulations, or some form of structure, must be put in place. It is these that make a traditional community largely conservative and give it its basic characteristics such as the severance of affective ties, common ownership of temporal goods, structure, and uniformity.

Severance of Affective Ties

The decision to enter a religious order, especially in the preconciliar period, occasioned semi-total or total cut from family and friends. The religious very often was disallowed to participate in family joys or sorrows such as weddings or funerals. The desperate homesickness of some members of the community was greeted with admonitions, denials, or exhortations to sacrificial self-transcendence.[7]

Inasmuch as this approach has its spiritual merits, the emotional hangover or residue can only be imagined. It also lasted many years after. An elderly sister often recounts how she was denied permission to visit her ailing father or to attend his funeral – the reason being that she was still in formation. Fifty years down the line, she still talked about it with deep emotion as though it happened yesterday.

Friendships outside the community, and even within it, were discouraged. In fact, one's affective needs or attachment should be to Christ alone. It is expected that prayer, discipline, and mortification should take care of one's needs for affection. The discouragement of affective ties with the world imposed upon religious was intended to strengthen resolve to offer oneself totally to God in chaste living.

This is not just a preconciliar phenomenon, but something expected of every consecrated person, though in reasonable measure. It does not

---

[7] Sandra M. Schneiders, *Selling All*, 203.

have to be drastic; but, for one to really commit oneself to the religious family, there needs to be some level of emotional detachment from the natural family and friends. Consequently, formation programs ought to have contents and processes that will equip the individual to live more serenely this affective detachment.

Common Ownership of Temporal Goods

In imitation of the early Christian community, religious communities, practicing the traditional or conservative style of community-living, own things in common, so that "no one may be in want" (Acts 4:32-35). Disparities and inequalities are to be minimized; they live together in radical solidarity, loving each other with a love that is willing to share everything for the sake of those in need.[8]

In the preconciliar traditional religious community, practically everything was in common, and some members of the community lived to tell the story. They laundered all their clothing in common, and as one moved to another stage of formation, one left her clothing to those after her and inherited clothing from the preceding group! All this was aimed at helping the religious to arrive at some degree of self-emptying and denial, which is synonymous with evangelical poverty.

In this age of technological revolution, there are still some institutes, both contemplative and apostolic, which maintain strict communal ownership of temporal goods including telephones. Recently in one community, the sister responsible for the group did not see the reason why individual sisters should have phones, until one of them was involved in a road mishap and the rest of the community had no way of knowing where she was or what had happened to her until very late. To make matters worse, it happened in a country where the police response to accident cases/victims is rather very poor. Discretion and

---

[8] Peter McVerry, "Blessed, Broken and Shared," *Religious Life Review*, vol. 51, #277 (Nov./Dec., 2012), 353.

responsible use of relevant material things are what the religious are called to embrace in the light of the renewal of religious life.

Structure

This was a basic feature of the traditional model of religious community. A certain amount of structure is necessary to form a community. Duties and responsibilities are shared and there was one among others who ensured that the structure was maintained. A plan of activities was drawn encompassing details of times for prayers, meals, community exercises, visits and every aspect of the community's life.

Both structure and schedule were symbols of the religious consecration to God through the evangelical counsels; specifically, they were practical effects of obedience.[9] It was not permissible for a member of the community to have her meal in isolation or, as is mostly seen today, to eat at one's convenience. The time stipulated must be adhered to no matter what work one had at hand. Obedience indeed was better than sacrifice! Thus, as a family, members ate together, prayed together, and played together.

In the wake of Vatican Council II, some religious men and women had difficulty, in varying degrees, adjusting to a more flexible life-style. Some institutes were more open to change than others. In many cases members were ready and willing for change, but the leadership was not. Conversely in some rare cases the leadership was ready for renewal and adaptation, but members were not.[10]

In both cases, there was noted the phenomenal exodus of many religious from various institutes. Some gathered to live out their vision

---

[9] Hoffman with Cole, *Consecrated Life, Contribution of Vatican II,* 31.

[10] The Sisters of St. Joseph of Peace serve as an example of one of those congregations whose leadership teams were open to give up rigid structures, but most members were not ready for it. Consequently many members left, but others adapted to the new situation.

and convictions under a new foundation, thus beginning several religious institutes that we have today.

Uniformity

In preconciliar times, uniformity went beyond the same color and style of habit, to embrace uniformity in posture, movement, and even the manner of holding up the breviary and hymnbook, or the cutleries while eating. All this was included as part of the formation program. It was as though the individuals passed through a mold and eventually all got shaped the same way.

Inability to fall in line simply spelled lack of vocation. An older sister recounted how a novice, whom they considered very good and attentive to the needs of others, was asked to leave the congregation because "she did not have enough religious decorum." She tended to 'shake' her body while walking!

Implications of the Traditional Model:
for the Individual, the Group, & the Church

Psychological Implications

This traditional model, which was totally hierarchical, had a lot of psychological implications. In the first place, there seemed to have been a lot of need-deprivation. Psychologists have established that when human needs are not met at the basic level, they could cause some developmental retardation at the emotional level.

Fran Ferder, a psychologist and author, posited that when individuals have had their human needs adequately met, they will be able to create a life-giving, freeing environment for others, because those needs no longer have the motivational force they once had.[11] Where there are

---

[11] Fran Ferder, *Words Made Flesh: Scripture, Psychology, and Human Communication* (NY: Ave Maria Press, 1988), 88.

such persons, there is the possibility of dialogue, individuals are open to healthy relationships, and there is positive energy flow. Where you get people with needs-starvation, they generally exude negative energy. There may be fear, anxiety, mistrust, and inability to let go of familiar and learned behavior, among other negatives.

In over-structured communities, the vision of the group was articulated by the leader(s). Security and trust were the central values: if you trust the leader, there is security in the system. Dependency was also valued. The individual members did not take initiative toward their ministry, house duties or personal matters. Most of the thinking was done by the leader – the one with that role. Consequently, power comes through role status.[12]

For members with the psychological need of *abasement* (poor self-esteem), *succorance* (affective dependence), or *submission* (deference), this model would be quite suitable, so they might not experience the internal tension that comes when one's needs are being frustrated. On the other hand, members who have the need for *autonomy, change* or *order*, would go through a lot of internal stress within the community.[13]

In 2013, I was invited to mediate a conflict that erupted in a particular community as a result of a style that some members described as 'oppressive.' The aggrieved felt they were being treated like children and

---

[12] The Craighead Institute in Scotland has identified four styles of organization which more or less match religious community life styles before Vatican Council II and after. These are the hierarchical model, the swamp model, the wheel model, and the integrated model. Whereas the hierarchical model corresponds with the traditional model of religious community life generally lived in the preconciliar period, there has been a sandwich of the swamp, the wheel, and the integrated models in the styles of religious community life mostly adopted in postconciliar times. Cf. *www.craighead.org.uk* accessed September 17th 2014.

[13] Cf. L.M. Rulla, *Anthropology of the Christian Vocation, vol. II* (Rome: Gregorian University Press, 1986), 29-31. Rulla extensively employed the work of H.A. Murray on needs and attitudes as presented in Murray's book, *Exploration of Personality*, 1938.

so were given no space to make 'adult decisions' regarding their personal lives allowing them to live out their consecration joyfully.

While they complained, there were some members of that same community who expressed shock at the reaction of these aggrieved members. They could not see the reason why anyone would raise any issue concerning the way things were going since they have come to live a life of 'sacrifice.' In managing this conflict, it was not necessary to work at anyone accepting the other's standpoint, but to bring all to appreciate the lens from which each party saw life, and to make an adult decision to accept those differences while checking high-handedness.

Social Implications

One of the social consequences of this traditional model with a hierarchical structure of leadership is that everyone tends to look up to the one person. There is very little reference-power or a model outside the one with the role. One's relationship with the superior, and not one's personal commitment to the vision, defines one's inclusion or level of belonging to the group. Every member rallies around the one with the role of leader. If one wants to initiate something, it must go through, or come from this one individual that is the legitimate superior.

Nevertheless, this model may be appropriate for the beginning of a group, such as when new members arrive and are being introduced to the life, or when the group is in crisis. But it need not continue forever. There comes a time when individuals have to become 'adults' and take responsibility for the choices they make.

Spiritual Implications

Some consecrated persons who lived both before and after the Second Vatican Council say that they felt more connected with God and with the value of self-donation then than they do now. For some who initially struggled with obedience without dialogue, when they accepted to submit, they did so joyfully and eventually made it their own choice. Yet for others, they suffered as long as the system remained that way. They felt deprived, humiliated, treated like children and, although they followed the rules for various reasons, they confessed that they felt "suffocated." Amidst all this, many remained and many bolted out the door once they had the chance!

Postconciliar Era: Progressive Model of Community Life

As the wind of the Spirit, the air of freshness, blew into the religious institutes, some members flew out of it. Why? Were they unsure or untrusting of the incoming change? Did the past hold more promise for them than the unexplored, unknown future? Was the renewal rather a walk to freedom and liberation from the shackles of an obligatory life style? We may never know for sure.

What about those that remained? Why did they remain? It is possible that they found the renewal more comfortable and freeing. It may also be that they believed in the values they professed rather than worried about the style of living them. It could also be that they believed in the promise that the future held – trusting that everything is grace and that they would follow Christ in the consecrated life however its expression. Perhaps some did not even know why they remained, and may not have cared. Again, we may never know for sure. Perhaps all of these possibilities applied.

Sharing with and listening to some consecrated persons who lived through the preconciliar and postconciliar periods,[14] I discovered that many who remained or returned saw value in the life they lived. They lived to bear witness to the constancy of God who promised to be with

---

[14] Two religious women who had left their respective communities after the Second Vatican Council, but returned some years later following the formal process of readmission into their respective congregations, shared their particular experiences with the contributor of this chapter.

the disciples until the end of time (Matthew 28:20) and they wanted to be part of the fulfillment of that promise in their own chosen vocation.

One of the religious women who shared her experiences of former times declared her belief in the presence of the Holy Spirit in both eras and believed too that the future held some promise whose fulfillment she wanted to be a part of. Some who left and returned claimed that, after staying awhile in the 'outside world,' they consciously reclaimed their vocation and wanted to bear witness to its 'sacredness' and 'royalty.'

In order to continue to live out the values of the consecrated life after the Second Vatican Council, many religious institutes, following the clarion call for renewal, got to work. Constitutions and statutes were revised, guidelines and directives were drawn up – touching on various aspects of the consecrated life – and community life style was no exception.

It took many institutes years to agree on certain issues, and many times this was done by trial and error. In effect, there was some degree of change in the style of community living according to different institute adaptation. All these hold their promises and pains as members strive to build up the body of Christ through an evangelical witness.

Styles of Progressive Model of Community Life & their Characteristics

Since Vatican Council II, there have been many adaptations of religious community life. Basically, there are two forms of the progressive model of community life which some have identified as: *Community of Faith* and *Community of Choice*.

Community of Faith

Many religious congregations that still wish to live the group form of the Christian faith-community adopt the traditional style of community life with some variations. The basic feature of this sort of community is that members 'find' themselves in the same community without having to make a choice of where and with whom to live.

Just as they receive their vocation at the point of entry into the congregation of their choice as a gift, so they receive their placement into one or other of the congregation's local communities, taking into account the influence of personality dynamics and leadership styles on group life. These leadership and personality styles often determine the community dynamics and atmosphere as subsequent sections reveal.

The Wheel Model of Community[15]

In the wheel model, local communities are created with members who live together under the leadership of a 'legitimate' leader. In most cases, the leader does not exert an absolute authority as seen in the pre-Vatican II period or in some modern institutes that still adopt the hierarchical model of community.

There seems to be more room for dialogue and communal discernment. The *horarium* (daily schedule) may become somewhat less rigid, and members may not be expected to be home at the same time, but they keep the community informed of their plans in most cases. Members may travel alone or with non-members of the local community.

The pivot of the community is the vision articulated by members. The leader stands at the center to point members to the vision and to call for communal discernment, hence the nomenclature 'wheel' model. Here, boundaries need to be clear but have the ability to change, unlike in the hierarchical or triangular style of community living. Since people are committed to the vision of the group, there is interdependence.

---

[15] The 'wheel model' of community is so called because members operate as though held by a hub which is the leader of the group who points to the group's goal or mission.

In fact, this is the ideal form of community life many yearn for but no one has yet perfectly attained. Sometimes those who practice this style experience lapses depending on the personality and leadership style of the 'person in charge.' The appearance or reality of such a community could be the same as in preconciliar time, assuming a sociological form where members are 'bound' by the rule to share things in common even when some of these rules are unnecessary and have no moral implications.

A leader with a hangover of psychological and emotional needs may use the members of the religious community to satisfy them. Thus, an affectively dependent leader may adopt a laissez-faire style of leadership, or may indulge the members with the conscious or unconscious desire to gain their approval or their affection. This also happens where the leader has some degree of ego-weakness or low self-esteem. The person may feel overwhelmed by the responsibility entrusted to her, or threatened by the members whom she perceives as stronger or better equipped, and so allow values to be compromised.

On the other hand, where the leader's need for power or domination is central,[16] there may be undue imposition and high-handedness. In such a situation, members live as in the preconciliar era but with a greater degree of dissatisfaction and pain, since they have experienced or witnessed a different way of being community in postconciliar times.

Beyond psychological influence, socio-cultural background can also exert some influence on the style of leadership an individual adopts. Religious of international congregations may observe the difference in style of leadership of an American and that of a European or an African. Sometimes this may be a source of internal or external conflict for some members, who experience these two forms of leadership but mistakenly expect them to be the same. Generally considered, an American

---

[16] The definitions of these needs and their strength in relation to the Christian vocation can be found in L.M. Rulla's *Anthropology of the Christian Vocation, Vol. II*, 405-407.

leader of a religious community will tend to be more liberal than the Sub-Saharan African counterpart, more because of socio-cultural background than personality.

The Integrated Model of Community

Another form of the progressive model with a group-living tilt to the 'wheel' model is the 'integrated model' of community. Here, members hold the vision of the congregation and give unity, motivation, and clarity to what the organization is about. Each one is part of the whole, and their interconnectedness arises from the common vision which is owned by everyone. Thus, the mission, and not the leader, becomes the point of reference.

Power comes through inner authority, and understanding of membership, and is connected to the integrity with which each part of the organization lives out the mission. The leader of the community works for the implementation of the common mission and does not become the center of the congregation or its mission.

The result of this style is a clear identity and a deeper commitment in terms of working to fulfill the mission collectively agreed upon. Other people can engage with the congregation as a whole, even if it is represented by one or more members in a given place and time. More importantly, new members can easily join the group.[17] They build community, sharing laughter and tears. Their inclusive attitude promotes community bonding. Like the wheel model earlier described, many institutes have yet to embrace this community life-style in its entirety.

The Swamp Model of Community

In some congregations, there is rotational non-elective coordination of its local activities according to the method chosen by the particular lo-

---

[17] Cf. Dominic Hoffman with Basil Cole, *Consecrated Life, Contribution of Vatican II,* 318f.

cal community members. Everyone takes a turn to coordinate for a stipulated period of time as may be decided by that particular group.[18] Where this form of community leadership is adopted, the coordinator or leader has not got much executive powers. The members have the freedom to do what they wish and how or when they want to do it. This demands a high level of maturity, which includes affective or psychosexual maturity and a great sense of responsibility for one's actions or choices.[19]

Sometimes, there can be unclear boundaries; there may be a vision but it may not be well articulated. The value of freedom or independence may be overemphasized to the detriment of the common mission and vision. The leader spends a lot of time walking around the swamp and changing the goal posts, since members are so busy in ministry or in their own affairs that they neither listen to nor even hear the leader.

The organizational structure here is 'swamped' and power comes from individuals or pockets of groups who feel they must be listened to. If the congregation is not careful, the essence of community life may become eroded. Thus, people may live together but not bear witness to the Christian religious life.

This is in fact the struggle that the leadership-teams of some congregations contend with. However much individual wellbeing and freedom are important, the common vision and mission of the congregation need not be sacrificed at the altar of individual wellbeing. Granted that a lot of personal and communal growth in values, principles, and prac-

---

[18] Members are placed by the institute's leadership in a local community, but they may decide on how they want to share power within the group and this affects how life is shared in community.

[19] Cf. L.M. Rulla, *Anthropology of the Christian Vocation, Vol. II,* 321f. An international missionary congregation of women with communities in Africa, Europe, and the Americas has practiced this model in some of their communities in the last decade. In line with their founding charism, they attempt to epitomize in their own community the dignity of womanhood and promotion of their rights which they were founded to pursue.

tices has taken place with the post-Vatican II renewal, some aberrations and abuse of freedom have also surfaced as exemplified in the section that follows.

Community of Choice

In modern times, terms such as 'community of choice' or 'individual community witness' have emerged, and some congregations, willingly or unwillingly, have either adopted or carefully avoided such styles of religious community life.[20] In these communities of choice, the needs of the individual rather than that of the congregation are central.

There is a congregation of women in Europe which has battled for a dozen years with sisters choosing who to live with and where to live and work – believing that whatever they do promotes their charism and founding spirit. This pattern contrasts with the community of faith where people go where they are sent and learn to live with those they meet or who meet them.

Multi-institutes Community

Certain ministerial or personal needs have arisen in recent times, leading to members of religious institutes living outside their own congregations. In this regard, some religious decide to live together as members, even though they are of different institutes. They may share some times in common during the course of the week and undertake their individual apostolate or ministry, but they are not strictly tied to one another as in a homogeneous and traditional community.

The emotional ties are not very strong, and so tensions and conflicts are equally reduced. The likely causes of tension sometimes are the bills to which members make individual contributions. This conflict is often

---

[20] Sandra Schneiders in *Selling All* outlined some forms of religious community life in modern times with their advantages and challenges, 316ff.

resolved amicably or by voluntary withdrawal from the group, since there is no strong binding force.

The structure here is largely swamped as the vision may not be well articulated, and independence is of higher value. There may be many interest groups, and so boundaries are constantly expanded. Experts from different walks of life may be welcomed into the community and inclusion into the community may be one-on-one and not on group bases.

There is almost no call to commitment except commitment to individual ministry. Influence of members is largely through influence groups, through the experts, reading of articles, doing of workshops or making a particular retreat.[21]

Co-habitation

Some Religious in the postconciliar era have opted for 'coupling' in a non-sexual sense, as a way of living out their vocation. Generally, two religious who may be from the same or different congregations may decide to come together, find a ministry in the same area and live out their religious vocation.[22] Here, there is some form of exclusion, as a third person's presence is largely unwelcome. The comfort and welfare of the 'couple' are paramount and whatever or whoever seems to threaten these is generally blocked out.

The two can make untold sacrifices to keep their space and keep each other happy. Programs are planned to accommodate both, and invitations to functions for only one of the 'couple' that exclude the other are largely unthinkable.[23]

---

[21] The Craighead Institute suggests that this way of living community and those in it are in adolescence. It seems to be a reaction to being treated as a 'child' in the hierarchical model of community!

[22] S. M. Schneiders, *Selling All*, 240

[23] Ibid.

Individual Habitation

For some individuals, living in group or with another person can generate a lot of negative energy which does not favor personal growth and does not facilitate good interpersonal relationship. Such individuals, though belonging to a recognizable group, choose (they are not asked) not to live with anyone. Even when such persons meet religious of other congregations in their educational or ministerial area, they do not initiate or accept the offer of sharing habitation.

Sandra Schneiders of the Sisters, Servants of the Immaculate Heart of Mary (IHM), and professor emerita of theology and New Testament studies, in the work already cited, would consider this a deviation rather than a form of community life, since the individual may choose to marginalize herself/himself.[24] Such persons own themselves and whatever they have, as their deeds may all be done in theirs or their family's name. They hardly participate in their congregational affairs. Financial and any other form of accountability is generally lacking, and they may expose themselves to dangerous relationships and situations.

Sometimes though, the absence of such persons may bring relative solace to other members of the community because of the tension such people create in group situations. The onus here is on the discernment/formation process to ensure that extremely dysfunctional persons are not admitted to the religious community where mere living with diverse personalities is already a challenge.

Alternative Community

In the wake of modern information technology, many religious have adopted what some have termed an 'alternative' form of community life. In this case, the religious have other persons with whom they share life outside the legitimate members of the community within which

---

[24] Ibid., 336.

they reside. This alternative community is formed mainly through social networks such as Facebook, Viber, Twitter, Skype and other chat-networks. Recently, at an inter-congregational meeting, the question of community life in modern times was raised and some religious men and women shared how they have formed these alternative communities.

Generally, it begins like a 'fling' and then the addictive nature of cyber drags the person deep into the so-called 'alternative community.' Members begin to take their phones to meals and recreation. Rather than engage in meaningful discussions or be present to the 'live' community members, they fiddle with their phones, chatting with invisible (or physically absent) friends!

One of the handicaps of this form of 'community' is that the members often do not have a common goal or mission. The inability of an individual to relate with persons he or she can physically encounter in an adult-to-adult way is covered up by his or her popularity in cyber-relationships. Commitment to religious community life and its value is consequently lost to the individual.

These so-called 'alternative' ways to religious community-living do not bear much evangelical witness to the *Sequela Christi* (following Christ). They are rather aberrations and, as noted earlier, they form some of the challenges that face religious community life in the twenty-first century. So, where do we go from here?

Conclusion:
Putting Things in Perspective

Amidst all the challenges facing the religious life in modern times, the religious must have their priorities right. And what is having one's priorities right? The following of Christ!

Short of this, any group of men or women with a common goal is, at best, a committee of friends or a social club. What gives the religious community its primary identity is Christ, and gathering in order to bear witness to the reign of God's Kingdom of love should be central to their vision.

There are obvious positive elements in one living by himself or herself, or with another person such as a friend, colleague, or religious of his or her choice. There is, for instance, the reduction of tension, more relaxation, and easy consensus on matters. However, it must be wondered if this way of living the religious community life really bears as much Gospel witness as the 'community of faith' earlier described. Hoffman and Cole maintain that when members of a religious community separate themselves from the local community, they often involve themselves in situations where they have little time left for the essentials of religious life.[25]

Modern people are often seeking an alternative to the materialistic and over-industrialized world in which we live, and to a very great extent they look at religious life to offer this alternative. Is it not ironical that at times religious men and women, rather than offer this alternative, eagerly borrow the very thing their counterparts in the world seek to get away from? The saying that the garden is always greener on the other side of the fence seems to hold true here. Perhaps it is an invitation to evaluate the religious way of life and adopt such values that best lend credence to the call to bear evangelical witness. This in fact was intrinsic to the renewal called for by the Second Vatican Council.

Fifty years after Vatican Council II and its call to renew the religious life in its different dimensions, religious institutes and their members still struggle with this renewal. In fact, many think that renewal has been proposed but not actually practiced. As we have tried to show in this chapter, there have been various attempts at the renewal of the community aspect of religious life, and these have gains and losses.

---

[25] Hoffman and Cole, *Consecrated Life, Contribution of Vatican II*, 314.

It is obvious that the style of community life in the preconciliar period laid more emphasis on the community than on the individual members. The common good, whatever would promote the institute and keep members together and not diminish the integrity of the group, was upheld even if this did not do much for the development of the individual as a person. The individual's needs and emotions were less considered. The status-quo was maintained, and the religious had to abide by the rules, no matter their nature, to be considered good religious.

Today, religious community life has taken varying styles. Certain community practices that promoted fraternity have become obsolete. Often, to avoid conflict and its consequent process of reconciliation and forgiveness, religious opted to live alone or with persons of their choice – thus, avoiding the mystery and divine choice that make religious communities a sacramental reality.

Religious life is presently at a crossroad. Religious men and women therefore must heed again the call of the Lord, and choose from the old and the new styles of religious community living what gives more life to its members and bears greater witness to Gospel values – returning to the community's sources, but also adapting to the modern world as the Council decreed.

This is what the Lord says: *"Stand at the crossroads and look; ask for the ancient paths, ask where the good way is, and walk in it, and you will find rest for your souls"* (Jeremiah 6:16).

6

LIVING & THRIVING IN RELIGIOUS COMMUNITY IN THE LIGHT OF CONTEMPORARY SOCIAL CHANGES

Christiana Calice Matris (Ngozi) Idika, DMMM

Introduction

Like any other way of life, religious life, especially community living, is impacted by times and places with their varying phenomena and dynamics. In no other time is this reality more true and severe than our contemporary twenty-first century. Living and thriving in religious community endure adverse effects of the many and diverse dynamics of this age.

Two examples of how community living is impacted by the effects of this contemporary time are: 1) the role of the individual in the community; and 2) the realization of personal freedom, versus authority and the vow of obedience. Inadequate handling of these issues has resulted in these aspects of life being set at odd against each other. This situation creates visible conflicts in religious communities that sometimes threaten the continuous existence of religious life.

Drawing on the grace of the fifty-year anniversary of the document on the renewal of religious life and the celebration of the year of the consecrated life, I attempt in this chapter to take us through some of these challenges facing a healthy and purposeful living of the religious community life in the light of the contemporary values of freedom and the individual.

The aim of this chapter is to consider this problem in the light of the changes that characterize the society of the twenty-first Century. These changes are like forces shaping both individuals and their experience of the religious life and the challenges to the question of authority and followership, abdication, and delegation of will, and the vow of obedience.

This chapter discusses this tension between authority and obedience, that is, the tension between the challenges to the vow of obedience and the claims of authority. It aims at offering different perspectives on a possible reconciliatory approach, an approach which neither sacrifices religious obedience on the altar of secularism and anarchy nor merges into the absolutist self-elevation of authorities as divine or divine apparatus on earth.

The Individual & Community

One of the major challenges and questions of these contemporary times is that which is provoked when the role of the individual comes into conflict with the individual's place in the community. This conflict can be summed up in the following questions:

- Is the individual swallowed up in the community?
- Does the community assume priority over the individual?
- How should the individual relate to the community and how should the community relate to the individual?

- How can a particular religious retain her personality, talents, and gifts, and at the same time be integrated into the community?
- How does the concept of 'We' of community relate to 'I' of the individual religious?
- How can authority in religious life foster the growth of the individual religious?

The contemporary changes are also affecting religious life and the community because, though the religious are not of the world, nevertheless they live in the world. Thus, the relation between the individual and community is also assuming a growing concern in religious life. A closer look at this development manifests an imperative if ever community life would continue to strive and to fulfill its goal of helping individuals realize their personal vocation and the collective vocation of all the children of God.

Indeed, in most religious institutes, it seems there is a growing number of depressed, unhappy, low self-esteemed religious, especially among institutes of women religious. We also witness what seems like gradual decay in community life – increasing human depreciation, wastage of human resources, talents, and gifts in the form of depression, and other health hazards and preventable deaths. On some occasions, sick members are left to care for themselves or given over to the care of their families. The consequences are a disconnection from community and constant conflict with relevant authorities over earnings and possessions.

Therefore, some religious perceive the 'We' of community or common life as a threat to their self-actualization. Indeed, though the community strengthens the ego, individuals could also face dangers within a collective experience (Honneth, 2012, 203). So as to deal with this growing tendency that can destroy community, this present contribution attempts to look at these developments and to propose a solution.

Recognition as a Basis for an Individual-Community Relation

Recognition for the German social and critical theorist, Axel Honneth (1996), is an acknowledgement and as well an affirmation that responds to the emotional needs of love, self-understanding, personal autonomy, and unique abilities of individuals. The absence of recognition could affect an individual's participation in the community. Thus, *"it is through being recognized as a particular human being that each gains status within a community"* (Shibutani, 1961, 218).

Status means a person's standing in a community as identifiable regarding rights, duties, privileges, and immunities that she enjoys by virtue of her membership (Ibid). *"Having status then enables a person to anticipate the manner in which she will be treated"* (Ibid). The anticipation also conditions to what extent an individual religious cooperates in the community and becomes well fitted into the common life.

This implies that the individual is not completely lost. To be recognized as a particular human being entails an acknowledgement of the particular gifts, talents, and capabilities with which an individual religious is endowed. Within this ambience, it is not enough that gifts, talents, and capacities are acknowledged and affirmed, for there is also a demand for the enhancement of these talents and gifts according to the person's capacity.

Noteworthy is that this is not simply because of its emotional or physical consequences. Rather, the vow of poverty also demands that each and every talent must not be wasted because it will be accounted for (Matthew 25:14-30). In a situation where individual religious are being stretched beyond their capacity directly or indirectly, or their gifts and talents are not maximized, a result could be emotional and psychological breakdown. Such a waste of human resources seems to be contrary to the vow of poverty. Thus, recognition of individual members of a religious community is essential to living out the community life and keeping the evangelical vow of poverty as well. An additional consideration is tension reduction between the individual religious and community.

According to Pope Francis, consecrated men and women must make it their task to create a space wherein each person could become himself or herself so as to realize his or her gifts. This space would be where she or he could express herself or himself and become fully co-responsible (Cf. *Letter to all Consecrated People*, Expectations, 3). Recognizing individuals and their specific talents and affirming them belong to the essential elements of community formation. Consequently, recognition is a driving force of community formation, because recognition reconciles individual members of a community or group as well as the individual and the collective.

According to Martin Buber, the Austrian-born Israeli Jewish philosopher famous for his philosophy of dialogue predicated on the I-Thou relationship (Buber in Moore, 1996), anyone who could not say 'Thou' would as well not be able to say 'We.' Recognition makes one be at home with the other. Being at home with the other implies that an individual can come to terms with her individuality within a group. Thus, her individuality can be realized through her membership, and her membership through her individuality. The integration of the individual into the 'We' community takes stages characterized by intersubjective recognition.

Recognition as a Human Need

Human needs are a powerful source of explanation of human behavior and social interaction. According to this need theory, the instincts for survival are a necessary part of the human person. When people feel deprived of their needs, the feeling of deprivation often leads to tension because, unlike interests or wants, needs are ontological and non-negotiable. This, of course, applies to consecrated persons.

Human needs include clothing, food and shelter, as well as good health, feelings of acceptance and belonging, justice, love and care. Psychological health and mental stability, cooperative disposition, and sense of commitment are vulnerable to both material deprivations and disruptions in the social nexus that are necessary for the religious to feel belonged.

The need for recognition by its vital nature shares something in common with the basic needs of food, clothing and shelter yet differs from them in a distinguishable way. Food and shelter belong to the category of existential needs while recognition is axiological in character. While existential needs respond to subsistence, human persons need more than mere subsistence, because lower animals also subsist. Axiological needs are value oriented and affect issues of worth within the person as a religious.

Recognition is the need to be confirmed by others in what one is and what one could become. It further affects the inner capacity to confirm others. Very often this mutual and reciprocal affirmation and capacity are left undeveloped. A religious as a human being is endowed with possibilities because he or she participates in the constant creative power of God, not only by being the image of God but also through the action of the Holy Spirit. Without the affirmative 'yes' we cannot speak to the other, and individuals are abandoned to the dread of loneliness and unhealthy solitude.

The religious needs confirmation because human beings as such need it. An animal does not need to be confirmed for it is what it is unquestionably. It is different with human beings. A religious is a human being sent forth from the natural domain of species into the hazard of the solitary category. She is surrounded by the air of chaos which came into being with her. Secretly and bashfully, a religious watches for a 'yes' which allows her to be and which can come only from one human person to another. It is from one religious to another that the heavenly bread of self-being is shared (Buber in Moore, 1996).

Hence, the warm gratitude and praise, a smiling approval, a hearty congratulation, a rich applause from significant others add pleasure and joy to the life of a religious. These make her strong, brave and courageous. The religious expects recognition of her merits and wants to be loved, appreciated and accepted for who she is and often feels dispirited when this fails to come about. The 'yes' of the other helps a religious to face the uncertainty and insecurity of life. The 'yes' helps the religious to give constantly her own 'yes' to God and the rest of humanity. There is also the danger of false affirmation or confirmation, whereby, in order to be confirmed, one pretends or plagiarizes his or her identity, lives a false life, and never becomes a decided religious.

Pope Francis made evident in his letter that the community should be a place every member experiences space where they could be accepted and loved. Psychology admits that recognition, esteem, and praise are essential to the progress and well-being of the human person, and that they contribute to a person's relation to self. The way a religious understands her community identity depends on her consciousness of herself as a member of a religious institute.

Besides the deprivation of needs manifesting that a religious has not been granted due recognition in the community, non-recognition or withdrawal of recognition could also manifest the abuse of a religious by another, or of a member by relevant authorities, through what can be categorized as bullying.

Psychologists generally understand bullying as "*a repeated oppression, psychological or physical, of a weaker person or group by a more powerful and advantaged person or group*" (Rigby 2007:15). Most of our actions reveal whether we are bullies or not. Such actions like opening others' letters or private files, entering rooms without the owners' knowledge, screening phones and computers, seeking information about the other, either for use as a constant control over her or for the sake of manipulation, all show one as a bully.

Bullying can destroy religious consciousness of the community. Non-recognition or withdrawal of recognition could sometimes manifest itself in withholding rights, information or anything else that the other religious needs so as to maintain power over the person. One can bully another through banging of phones on people. One can also do that through verbal expressions and calling of names, which reduce the self-esteem and the dignity of the other.

Non-recognition or withdrawal of recognition of a member by another member or authority could show itself in the silent treatment as if the religious has little or no significance. It also shows in the spread of rumors, unwelcome looks, giggling, mocking, humiliation, judging before hearing, and other forms of negative behaviors that reduce a person to the status of an object.

The consequence is a persistent tension in the willing integration of the individual religious into the 'We' of community. For one thing, humans can trample, jump, walk over other obstacles, but the being of another person is impenetrable and challenges one's existence. According to the German philosopher Gottlieb Fichte, the presence of the other summons one to responsibility and this coincides with Christ's demand that we should love our neighbor.

By being autonomous, a religious is distinct and unique. Through self-consciousness, she recognizes this uniqueness in the presence of the other, and she can distinguish herself from the other and the group. She can identify her distinct power of being, but as she is becoming conscious of herself, she is becoming also aware of the other as distinct and unique. Simultaneously, she is also becoming conscious of the inter-subjectivity of her being – that her self is only a reality in the presence of the other. She becomes conscious of the ontological but latent struggle that can occur between her and the other in the community and the community itself as a whole.

She becomes aware that the way out is not resistance, challenge, or withdrawal. She becomes conscious that the solution to retaining her particularity, and her membership as well, is not to reduce herself, nor to reduce the other. She becomes conscious that the solution is neither to become assimilated nor to assimilate the other, neither to destroy the other nor allow herself to be destroyed by the other. Rather, she becomes conscious of the need to grow together with the other and the community.

She can achieve this through communication. In communication, she seeks through dialogue to understand and to know and enters into a relationship with the other. In knowing the other, a new power is created, a creative power, the power of synergy, a power of being of the community. At this point, she transcends her ego – the constant self-reference, the 'I.' Then the religious can say 'I am' because 'We are,' and the community could say 'We are' because 'she is.'

Participation in Collective Intention

Another way through which the individual religious becomes integrated into the community is through participating in the collective intention. The notion of collective intention could be, of course, problematic, but in religious life that would not be the case. The reason is that religious communities or congregations are institutes of consecrated life with aims and purposes, spirit and charism, as well as apostolate.

Moreover, belonging to any such group requires primarily deliberation and choice made by the relevant individual. A community concept expressed as a 'We' somehow expresses a collective intentionality. That means when one speaks of a congregation from a 'We' perspective, what is implied is that the spirit and charism, as well as the apostolate of the congregation, express a collective intention. Thus, the intention of the individual should somehow be reconciled with the collective intention.

Hence, one's particular choice, work, actions, and behaviors would have to correspond with what it means to belong to a congregation with all that is entailed. This seems problematic in some cases where to belong in the first place was never a choice, such as when one is coerced or born into a group. However, it is different when voluntary choice is at stake.

Take, for instance, the profession of the vows whereby the candidate vows to live in accordance with the way of life identical with a particular congregation. By this single act, the candidate has expressed a collective intention, or rather has participated in the collective intention. One may argue that this intention existed prior to the person's entrance, but this does not seem to be cogent. The candidate, the individual, had other alternatives, other congregations, and the collective intention expressed in the constitution had been made known to the individual in the formative process.

Consequently, by accepting and making profession of vows in the congregation, one has accepted to subsume her intention into the collective. One may as well ask how the individual's intention is contained in the collective intention. The constitution describes the role of the individual. Hence, the collective intention expressed in the apostolate, spirit, and charism does not undermine the personal identity of the individual since, having expressed through the vows the willingness to be part of the collective intention, the person contributes through her particular gifts and talents to the realization of the collective intention.

Thus, there is no 'We' without an 'I' and there is no 'I' without a 'We,' in so far as community life in the context of religious life is concerned. For instance, one cannot be and not be a sister of the Sacred Heart at the same time. A member of the Sacred Heart Congregation is that precisely by the participation in the collective intention expressed not alone by the vows, because the vows cut across every institute of consecrated life, but in living the vows according to the spirit, charism and apostolate of the congregation.

Belonging & Obligation

The community concept generates commitment because it expresses belongingness. Consequently, to belong is to have rights as well as obligations. The 'individual-community' relation is a relation of rights and obligations.

We may ask how belonging to a group generates obligations. Rights include such categories as entitlements, prerogative, and advantages which a person enjoys by virtue of belonging to a group or by membership in the group. Obligations, on the other hand, refer to duties, commitment, and responsibilities that one morally owes to her group, or which are morally binding on a religious by virtue of her membership. The idea of morality suggests what ought to be the case, all things being equal. Such obligations are independent of any personal inclinations or self-interests.

An interesting thing about belonging and obligation is that very often an individual religious does not feel or have a sense of belonging. Maybe she does not enjoy the rights and status of membership, her sense of obligation thus being affected. However, because obligations are moral and binding, religious are expected to fulfill them all the same.

Interestingly too, the relevant persons whose duty it is to grant individual religious the corresponding status as members are equally under obligation to do that. The obligation is binding on both sides and is independent of personal feelings or perceptions.

For instance, a religious according to the Canon is entitled to her needs by virtue of her membership. The expression is not conditional. Also from the Canon and constantly, a religious is bound by the virtue of her membership to live in accordance with the demands of her membership. This is also unconditional. Nevertheless, to achieve this, the relevant constitutions should also consider the reason behind the statutory, since laws are made and expressed in universal terms.

The point is that the sense of belonging raises in the individual religious a feeling of obligation. The task of the congregation is to create this sense of belonging that makes the individual religious willingly integrate herself into the community. The 'We' concept of community expresses joint commitment that gives the religious institute a substantial unity, a unity perceived by members, without whose appropriate understanding unity cannot be. This perception underlies the individual identification with the community in the sense of pride or shame over a group's action.

That can as well be individually oriented. It is interesting that when an individual sister does something bad, one rarely hears among outsiders about the person as a particular individual. It is often expressed through the group identity such as the congregation to which the perpetrator belongs or even in the form of 'this Reverend Sister.' Therefore, a joint commitment based on the perception of unity places responsibility on an individual religious, so that she would be an embodiment of a community identity. It implies that she carries within not simply her personal identity but also the identity of her religious institute.

'I' & 'We' in Christ & the Eucharist

Being at home in the religious community in its comprehensive form necessarily entails that members actualize their individuality through their membership and at the same time actualize their membership through their individuality. They are simultaneously individuals and members of the community. Importantly, it is because religious life has its basis in the mystery of Christ's life that the individual–community relationship finds its root in Christ, who is the second person in the Trinity.

Very often Christ uses 'I' to refer to himself as an individual person. However, he does not use it without some reference to his Father. 'I' and my Father are one (John 10:30). 'I' came to do my Fathers' will

(John 4:34; 6:38). The 'I' of Jesus is not an egoistic 'I'. Rather his is an 'I' that is already in communion with his Father and the Holy Spirit.

In the teaching of the Catholic Church, the life of community or communion derives its existence from the Trinity. Jesus gave us an example to follow, calling us to walk in his footsteps. The 'I' of the religious should be in communion with the rest of the members of the community. The 'I' of a religious should find its meaning and place in the 'We' of the community.

Ultimately, the Eucharist is at the heart of this communion between the individual and community. The individual members of religious institutes are like individual grains and grapes that form the bread and the wine respectively. To be fitted into the community, to be integrated into the community, and for the 'I' to be in communion with the 'We', the grain and the grapes must be well processed.

This can be done first by the intersubjective recognition of the individual members, second by their participation in the collective intention, and third by the growing consciousness of their rights and obligations and willingness to engage in joint action. More important, to be fitted into the community requires the disposition of members to be processed by Christ.

Christ gives us His Body and Blood so that what we are – the grain and the grapes – may become what we eat: Eucharistic people, people of praise and communion, a perfect host, the Body of Christ. To be separated because of one reason or the other is to be unprocessed. To be isolated, estranged, neglected, rejected, or abused is to be unprocessed. The danger is that the host will be rough, and there won't be perfect communion, perfect unity, and community.

Religious themselves must understand and appreciate the importance of being together, because they have to make that decision themselves. Any coercion or force creates a dysfunctional relationship wherein individual religious may at first be willing to cooperate for a time, but afterwards become disconnected. It is important that religious develop the conviction and understanding so as to respond with joy to the demands of common life. Otherwise, they will be lifeless and dry. People may be physically there, but they are really absent. The joy that Pope Francis talks about in both *Evangelii Gaudium* and his letter to the consecrated people is not artificial joy but one that flows from a heart filled with God of communion.

Freedom & the Vow of Obedience

Among the three evangelical vows, the vow of obedience has assumed the roles both of a paradox and a dilemma, so that we can call our situation today a crisis of authority and obedience.

On the one hand, Scripture warns that Christian obedience is owed to God and not to a human being, and that the law of God is written in the human heart. In that case, it is better and rewarding to obey God rather than a human being, or, in other words, one must act according to one's conscience.

On the other hand, authority claims to draw its legitimacy and power from God, such that resistance or disobedience to such authority is a disobedience to God. Moreover, through the vow of obedience, religious submit themselves in faith to those superiors who take the place of God (*Perfectae Caritatis*, 14).

Given the concepts of right, will, and freedom, the act of submitting oneself to another is perceived to be a denial of human freedom, right, will and autonomy. For some, obedience strips one of human agency,[1] responsibility, and accountability. According to such an understanding

---

[1] Agency is a concept used in philosophy and sociology to refer to the capacity of an agent to act in the world. Human agency is a form of positive freedom because it entails choice and action, freedom to choose and to act according to one's moral dictates or convictions.

of obedience, this vow can hamper personal growth and self-actualization.

In view of these perspectives, both in theory and in practice, authority and obedience become conflictual. Some serious questions consequently follow.

- What does it mean to obey?
- Should one always obey, even when what is commanded contradicts one's conscience?
- To whom is obedience due – to an authority, to the constitutions or to God? Is the vow of obedience an abdication of will?
- Through the vow of obedience, does the individual religious give up her right or her ability to reason and judge actions and events?
- Does obedience make a religious less free and less responsible?
- How can there be accountability and human agency if obedience is understood as an abdication of will?
- How does one understand dialogue in the context of command and obedience?

These and many more questions demand answers if the core element of religious life is to be maintained.

Additionally, the changes going on in contemporary societies are impacting consecrated persons, whereas their life should challenge society (*Vita Consecrata*, 63). One witnesses today an increasing resistance against authority. The resistance is not unconnected from the growing awareness among the religious of their individuality and self-conception, which are continually shaped by the modern world. Thus, the crisis of authority and obedience is rooted in the understanding of authority and obedience and in the increasing influence exerted on religious by a changing society.

Authority & Obedience: Analysis of the Crisis

Considering an insufficient understanding of religious obedience and an exaggerated notion of authority, we can admit a growing crisis in our understanding of authority and obedience which puts the vow of obedience into jeopardy. The link between obedience and the rest of the vows makes the crisis volatile.

The year of the consecrated life seems to offer an excellent opportunity to address this growing crisis, if the identity of the consecrated life would survive. Moreover, the impact of the modern world on the religious (Cf. *Novo Millennio Ineunte*, NMI, 51, *Fraternal Life in Community*, 1), makes it essential and thematic.

The first point of crisis is to be found in the notion of authority and the understanding of human freedom and autonomy. The notion of authority in concept is problematic. Authority is an office, not a person. However, it seems that the office and the person in the office of authority are identical. This has a consequence when looking at the conceptualization of religious authority. However, before getting into that, authority as such requires our attention. Authority may be defined as the power to give orders, make decisions, and enforce obedience. Thus, authority is associated with power.

There is a pervasive disagreement on the notion of power and how it works. Many theories are of the assumption that power has a substantive causal feature that plays a central role in human social and political life. Power is diffused not concentrated, embodied and enacted rather than possessed, discursive rather than purely coercive. It constitutes agents rather than simply being deployed by them. Power is ubiquitous and invisible but can be embodied in those who exercise it. It can also be visible in action because it has a relation to force. Hence, it seems to be present in every encounter (Gaventa 2003:1).

This corresponds to the analogy of the struggle between two kinds of consciousness in the philosophy of the German thinker Georg Wilhelm

Friedrich Hegel (1971, 117). One also finds such an analysis in the German Protestant theologian Paul Tillich, who claims that power is "the dynamic self-affirmation of life overcoming internal and external resistance" (Tillich, 1954, 37).

In the thought of the French philosopher Michel Foucault, where there is power there is resistance. Thus, power is repressive, demanding compliance and obedience, and it is conflictual (Foucault, 1980). The power to make decisions or enforce obedience could be repressive, and once there is repression, there is always a corresponding resistance because the object of repression has power and struggles to overcome external or internal resistance to its existence.

At this point, one discovers the conflict between authority and obedience as such. In other words, any attempt to resolve it must interpret power in relation to authority. The secular idea of authority as the power to coerce a subject to comply or to obey seems to replicate itself in the understanding of religious authority. Consequently, religious authority is presumed to be the power to bring religious persons to compliance and obedience. The unexpected effect is the resistance from the relevant religious subjects.

The crisis begins when the power of authority encounters resistance from the subject. Since power is a relational force, when it becomes repressive, the logic of resistance results in a process of action and opposing reaction. However, power itself is not the problem because it can also produce positive effects. The question is how religious authority can bring their subjects to obey, through the positive effect of power.

Again, on the other side of the crisis are the values of autonomy and freedom. Autonomy is conceived as the capacity of an agent to be its own lawgiver. In that case, an individual is free and autonomous to the existent that he or she cannot be coerced into obedience to another's law or command. This concept of human freedom derived from the notion of autonomy is most central to the crisis of authority and obedience in modern society.

The events taking place in civil society are also gradually creeping into religious life. The growing sense of individualism's claims of rights and freedoms is also gaining ground in religious congregations, thus challenging religious authority. A consequence is that religious authority and religious obedience become conflictual. The crisis of authority and obedience in religious life seems to be more consequential and entrenched because of the claims of religious authority to a divine origin and the consequences of religious obedience.

Authority in religious life, like every authority in the Church, claims to derive its source of power and legitimacy from God. The most preferred source of such a claim is found in Paul's letter to the Romans:

> *Let everyone be subject to the governing authorities, for there is no authority except that which God has established. God has established the authorities that exist. Consequently, whoever rebels against the authority is rebelling against what God has instituted, and those who do so will bring judgment on themselves* (Romans 13:1-2).

In verse five of the same chapter, Paul added "*You must be obedient, therefore, not only because of this retribution but also for conscience's sake.*" It is not clear what Paul meant by "*for conscience sake.*" It is a common saying that "if conscience does not condemn one, then no one brings the person to any retribution." The saying is dependent on the understanding of conscience as the seat of reason and rationality. Moreover, it is believed that the conscience is the voice of God.

Does the conscience always conform to what an authority commands? Besides, the teaching of the Church on conscience makes the crisis of authority and obedience more pronounced when the issue of conscience arises. The Church teaches that human beings have an obligation to obey their conscience because there is a law that is laid upon them deep inside their conscience. *Gaudium et Spes* maintains that their dignity lies in the observance of this law and by it they will be judged (*Gaudium et Spes*, 16).

Following the logic, if human beings must answer to their conscience, then obedience to the conscience takes priority over obedience to a human being. Furthermore, the crisis gets sharper when obedience is said to be owed to God and not [man]. The point then is not the source of power and legitimacy of religious authority but that the bearer of authority is simply a human being who is vulnerable and weak.

Further, Paul's claim was over-generalized, as it cannot be every authority that is meant but only some authority. Some instances in the Scripture contradict Paul's over-generalization about authority that has yielded the crisis of authority and how those who bear authority in the religious life understand their role.

In Acts 5:29, Peter and his group resisted the orders of the authorities to stop preaching in the name of Christ. Peter boldly said to them: "*'Obedience to God comes before obedience to men.*" The crisis is that the men Peter and the other apostles refer to in this passage are authorities, and in fact, religious authorities.

So where is the difference? Are there times when one should or should not obey, or is there some authority one should or should not obey? If all authority comes from God and resistance to authority is a resistance to God, but obedience to God comes first before obedience to man, one observes that there is an endemic crisis of authority and obedience even in religious circumstances.

Furthermore, Jesus as the model of religious obedience also lived under human religious and political authority. The Gospel recorded his constant conflict with the religious leaders. His focus was his Father's will. Meanwhile, the Pharisees are supposed to be the custodians of the law. During his passion, his bold words to Pilate speak of Jesus' disposition to authority. Pilate claimed to have authority over him and demanded that he tell him what truth is. Jesus said to Pilate (if one can give a non-exegetical interpretation), "*you have no authority over me, except the one given from above*" (John 19:11). Jesus may be referring to his death that is the will of his Father, not necessarily saying that Pilate's authority comes from God.

The above discussion on authority is to demonstrate the critical conflict between authority and obedience. However, it does not mean that there is never obedience to authority in any relevant sense. The argument seeks only to unfold the crisis inherent in the conception of authority that necessitates human authorities' claim to be divine apparatus on earth.

Nevertheless, since all about religious authority and obedience are technically rooted in the Scripture, which is the Word, it cannot be the case that there would be a contradiction. Moreover, whether God speaks in the depth of the human conscience or he commands through a human authority, it is evident that there must be something that reconciles them. In other words, the voice of conscience, the command of an authority, and God's Words in the Scriptures revealed to the human person must reconcile with each other, since it is God who is at the center of them. Hence, the question of priority – God, human being, or conscience – does not arise if authority and obedience are very well understood.

The crisis of obedience in the religious life is connected not only to the crisis inherent in the religious concept of authority or the human conscience as the primary lawgiver. It is connected also to the notion of freedom and autonomy. Freedom and autonomy are among the most discussed issues in the societies of the modern era. The crisis of obedience as it relates to freedom and autonomy has a philosophical root. However, this does not rule out some theological development of the idea of freedom, which somehow informs its philosophical development.

The creation narratives of the book of Genesis assert that God created human beings and gave them freedom, a gift he expected they would use to choose life rather than death. God gave human beings not only freedom but also made them master of all that he created (Genesis 1:26-29). Modern Western philosophy takes its concepts of person and freedom from Christianity.

The notion of autonomy is mostly linked to the German philosopher Immanuel Kant, whose philosophy bears some Christian features. Consequently, the place accorded to the human person in creation became exaggerated. Kant thus made the human person an 'end' and the source of authority and of laws that must be legislated over the person. The Kantian moral subject declines external influences other than reason.

Thus, for Kant, the individual acts freely and voluntarily only when he or she obeys no other person but self. The consequence is that any authority that would command obedience from the autonomous individual must be legitimate and its legitimacy depends on the consent of the individual.

Hence, in Western philosophy human freedom is praised as the most worthy and sacred inheritance of humanity. It is conceived as the final hinge on which humanity turns and the highest possible summit that does not allow itself to be compromised or impressed by anything. For existentialists like the French Jean-Paul Sartre, humanity is condemned to freedom. The problem is not the necessity or foundational relevance of freedom, but how best to understand what one means when one speaks about human freedom.

In contrast to this pathological view of freedom, Axel Honneth (2014) observed that these individualistic understandings of freedom as a human value are creating a process of personal individualization which is decisively shaping the thought of Western industrialized societies. In that, the individuals' detachment from pre-given social forms bears a character of the present age.

Thus, as the sense of individual freedom constantly gains ground in modern societies, it is simultaneously mutating in religious life. The result is that religious are becoming increasingly conscious of their individualism to the extent that both authority and community life are seen as a threat to that individual conception of oneself.

Therefore, when an exaggerated concept of authority and insufficient understanding of freedom encounter each other, there occurs a crisis of authority and obedience. The centrality of obedience to the life of consecration makes this crisis a threat to the character of religious life. There is a need to reconceptualize authority and obedience. This is necessary because Vatican II, realizing the consequence of an inadequate conception of authority and its exercise from the perspective of the history of the Church, recommended a change in how authority relates to its subjects.

According to the Catholic theologian John W. O'Malley, the spirit of Vatican II introduced new vocabulary in the authority – subject relationship. It introduced words like dialogue, cooperation, and friendship, in place of words of threat and intimidation, words of surveillance and punishment, words of a superior speaking to an inferior that characterized authority – subject relationship before Vatican II (John W. O'Malley, 2010).

On the other hand, while the Church acknowledges the value of human freedom, it warned that

> *one must also keep in mind that when freedom tends to become arbitrariness and autonomy of the person, independence from the Creator and relationships with others, then one finds oneself before forms of idolatry that do not increase freedom but rather enslave"* (Faciem tuam, Domine, requiram, 2).

This is true not only for religious obedience but also relevant in society. Freedom, when individually absolutized, becomes only a possibility. Real freedom is freedom realized with and through others. Hence, it becomes an imperative that authority and obedience must be reconciled in a way that the vow of obedience is not sacrificed at the altar of secularism, and authority does not itself trend towards assuming divinity.

Most religious institutes maintain that God is the source of authority, and their leaders participate in that authority. By the vow of obedience, a religious conforms her will to that of Christ who was obedient to the Father even unto death. By the vow, the religious dedicate their will to God, and by the virtue of religion obey their lawful superiors when they give commands that are in accordance with the respective constitution. This obedience must take the example of Mary. Also, in the spirit of Vatican II, authority should be exercised in dialogue, communion, and participation. The question that arises is how we understand dialogue, communion, and participation.

The kernel of the crisis of authority and obedience in religious congregations finds its root in how dialogue is understood, how those with authority and subjects of obedience participate and experience communion in the process of decision-making.

Authority & Obedience in Dialogue

The notion of dialogue seems to be misunderstood in its relationship with obedience. This misunderstanding sees dialogue as a consultative process which is necessary only so that the order would be determined by the subject in the case where the individual's subjectivity is the point of departure, and he or she must in the relevant situation be the ultimate decision maker. The concept of dialogue itself rejects such conclusions, and the emphasis on the authority having the final decision rejects this conclusion as well.

Of course, the consideration of the individual in the first place has a role to play in the exercise of authority, and the form of religious obedience is not anthropocentric but God-centered. Religious obedience is owed to God. Nevertheless, both in its form and matter, obedience is constituted by dialogue and is not an addition to it.

Dialogue according to Martin Buber is an encounter. In an encounter, the encountering parties become present to themselves. In dialogue, Buber argues, realities become part of each other because differences negotiate themselves. It means that dialogue is not about who wins or who loses but how to achieve a point of connection while retaining differences.

An essential part of a dialogue is listening. According to *Faciem tuam, Domine, requiram*, 5, obedience is also listening. Listening is a disposition and an attitude, but it is not a passivity in the one who listens. This is where the aspect of participation becomes relevant. A passive listener cannot be co-responsible. Obedience does not make one irresponsible. The subject must make the command her own for it to be virtuous. There must be something a subject brings to the table, and this is what is commonly known as his or her will.

From the time when a religious professes vows, she or he has responded to the call of God to hand freely over to him that gift he gave to the individual from creation. However, the vocation of the religious is not a one-moment event. God keeps calling and remains in continuous communication with the religious. This continuous communication is the eternal dialogue of love founded on communion. Significant then is the aspect that speaks of communion as also necessary in "superior-member" relationship.

The constant communication, in which the call of God is daily renewed, is a dialogue between the religious and God. Hence, in listening to the superior, the religious is not passive but participates and constantly responds in various ways and through various gestures in order to reach the goal – the fullness of God's will. The will of God unfolds in history, and John Paul II's movement of incarnation points in this direction.

Dialogue is a process that can take place only between two relational beings. It is an 'I–Thou' relation. A passive listener is no longer a 'thou' but an 'it.' Here, it is not about subjectivity but about otherness, the other being to whom Jesus commands radical commitment. Thus, it becomes relevant that the dialogue in a superior-member relationship is not based on subjectivity but intersubjectivity. Radical obedience does not include the objectification of the subject of obedience; otherwise, it would be unnecessary for God to ask for Mary's consent to be the mother of his only begotten Son.

In the cases of Jesus and Mary, from whom radical religious obedience finds meaning, there was a process. The dialogues that took place in the Annunciation and the Garden of Gethsemane were moments of reconciliation of will, and there was a negotiation of differences. Indeed, before the FIAT, there were questions and answers; before "*not my will but your will be done*" (Luke 22:42), there was "*Father I wish that this cup should pass me by.*" (Luke 22:42). For Mary, it was not clear how a virgin could conceive without a man; for Jesus, to carry the sins of the world would be too much for one man, so maybe there could be other options. However, in both cases, they submitted to God's will reinforced by love rather than anything else.

In the incident of the finding in the temple, before Jesus left with them, there was an encounter. Dialogue is an encounter and a process of entering into the reality of the 'thou.' Jesus invited his mother to enter into his reality telling her that he should be about his Father's business. Jesus entered into Mary's reality as he knew the pain of losing and searching for him for three days.

In entering into each other's reality, truth is revealed, and common perspectives are shared in order to reach a common goal. As Mary was the human authority to whom Jesus was entrusted, his radical question to his mother was not a misdirected one meant for insult. At that moment, Jesus learnt more, and Mary realized more who her child was. It was a moment to reveal more of themselves to each other.

Dialogue is an essential part of the reconciliation of human will with God's will; otherwise the joy of obedience would not be complete. Obedience to God alone does not contradict obedience to the human authority. According to *Faciem tuam, Domine, requiram*, 12, "Authority is at the service of obedience to the will of God."

At the beginning of his papacy, Benedict XVI remarked,

> *My real program of governance is not to do my will, not to pursue my own ideas, but to listen, together with the whole Church, to the word and the will of the Lord, to be guided by Him, so that He himself will lead the Church at this hour of our history (Faciem tuam, Domine, requiram, 12).*

Benedict XVI used the term to "listen together." One may say that his German roots influenced him. The German word for obedience is *Gehorsam*. This word is rooted in two other German words, *hören and zussamen*, the former meaning to listen, the latter meaning together. Thus obedience in the German context means to hear together. It means to hear together, first listening to each other and then to God, what God has to say. Reducing or eliminating the constant increase in the crisis of authority and obedience in religious institutes requires that authority not be at the service of itself but rather of true obedience to God. Authority works with the individual religious to discover what is the will of God at the particular point in time.

To listen together is to be present to each other. Very often one notices that, after consultations, discussions or meetings, people take what is not said home and leave behind what is said. The reason is that many people seem not to listen to the other, but rather they listen to themselves. They are full of what they want to say to the other and consequently are unable to hear the voice of the other.

To listen means to be present, to empty oneself of previous prejudice and stereotypes. Sometimes, religious go into a dialogue with an authority having their mind already made up, to obey or not to obey. In like manner, authorities may invite a religious for a dialogue with already made up minds. In such situations, there is no dialogue.

Dialogue is a route to a decision. Already made decisions cannot be a product of dialogue. To listen is to be open to questions and answers, open to affirmation or contradictions; these are all part of a process that creates a living spirit of dialogue and communion. Dialogue is not possible where there is power asymmetry, for the atmosphere of tension will be unleashed wherein the repressed takes the position of resistance.

The French thinker Paul Ricoeur understood and extended the German Protestant theologian Paul Tillich's claim that power should be collaborative rather than oppressive or repressive and thus counter-productive. The positive effect of power in an authority-subject relationship should not be power-over. Power-over generates crisis and sometimes violence (Ricoeur, 1990).

Violence could be physical, emotional, or psychological. An authority could be a victim of psychological violence as well as a subject. As a result, it becomes an imperative for 'happy authority' and 'happy obedience' to transform their power-to-act both as an authority and as a subject to power-in-common and power-of-productivity.

Power-in-common results when, on the one hand, the power of an authority to bring subjects to compliance is not repressive, but allows the subject in dialogue, participation, and communion, and, on the other hand, the subject cooperates rather than resists. Power-in-common thus is the power shared with others. It is the power to act as a community that shows the desire and disposition to live together. This form of power is necessary to build a religious family. Power-in-common generates power-of-productivity. Power-of-productivity is creative and produces good effects (Ricoeur, 1990).

The goal of dialogue in a superior-member relationship must be to listen together, to speak to the 'thou' and not to an 'it.' We read in *Faciem tuam, Domine, requiram*:

> [O]bedience is an attitude of a son or daughter. It is that particular kind of listening that only a son or daughter can do in listening to his or her parent, because it is enlightened by the certainty that the parent has only good things to say and give to him or her. This is a listening full of the trust that makes a son or daughter accept the parent's will, sure that it will be for his or her own good (5).

A significant point in the document is that a religious listens like a child to her parents, with the full trust that the authority meant good to her. Trust becomes essential for obedience. Most of the crisis of obedience witnessed in some religious institutes arises when a particular religious could not trust the intentions of some particular authority. It can also be the case that the lack of trust might result from a perception. Perception could be, as it has at times been the case, wrong, and moreover whether right or wrong, it has consequences. Thus, authority should be at the service of God whom she represents and should build the atmosphere of trust to facilitate in the religious person the willingness to obey.

Furthermore, the document points to another essential element that is very often neglected. It is the analogy between religious authority and parents. That means authority exercises an analogous parental love in bringing the religious person to respond to the will of God.

Finally, there is of certainty nothing in what an authority commands that evidently bears witness to whether it is the will of God or not or whether the intention of the authority is for all intents and purposes for the good of the religious. Indeed, authority is human, could pervert justice, abuse office, or use office to victimize. In such cases, one also witnesses a crisis of authority and obedience. This is where the question of conscience comes in, for St Paul admonishes that one should obey for conscience sake. "For conscience sake" refers to consistency, since what the conscience commands, so long as it is not in error, is that one should always do the right thing and shun evil. So long as there is no evil in the content of the command, one is expected to obey so as to be consistent with the way of life one chose.

In the Gospel, Jesus was confronted by some persons asking him about the rightness or wrongness of paying tax (Matthew 22:15-22). Jesus told them to give to Caesar what is Caesar's and to God, what is God's. He had no intention of placing God and Caesar at the same level. His intention was not to affirm Caesar's authority. Thus, in his letter to the Romans, St. Paul included paying tax as a sign of obedience to authorities. One can say that both Jesus and Paul were interested in people being honest and consistent with their choice.

Religious are expected by the vow of obedience to be consistent with their choice. Simultaneously, because authority is at service of obedience to God's will *(Faciem tuam, Domine, requiram)*, it is the authority's responsibility to facilitate in the religious the desire to be consistent and the joy of fulfilling the demands placed on them by their choice.

The crisis of authority and obedience is a real problem for many religious institutes because it affects the at times most difficult of all the vows and could put the other vows into crisis. Its central role, whereby it controls the chief obstacles to perfection, pride, and self-will, make the crisis a threat to the central character of religious consecration. Hence it becomes necessary that religious subjects and those in authority should make dialogue a reality and provide space and time for those who obey and those who command for the salvation of their souls and the glory of God.

PART IV

THE WAY FORWARD:
QUESTIONS & PROPHECY

7

RELIGIOUS LIFE IN THE POST-VATICAN II ERA

Robert Dueweke, OSA

Is Religious Life Obsolete & Coming to an End?

Statistics seem to demonstrate this trend. There is decline of membership in religious life because there is a decline in overall Church membership. The 'unaffiliated' category is growing every year. The reasons for the decline and perception of the Church's irrelevancy are many and complex. Some causes for the exodus of the faithful are the sexual abuse crises, patriarchy, issues of gender and sexual orientations, women's ordination, authoritarianism, closed-mindedness, and arrogance. Attitudes toward the institutional Church will effectively affect attitudes towards religious life, for both are intertwined with each other.

A new consciousness is emerging where one does not have to be a Christian and follow regulations of an institution to promote the common good and to be compassionate toward one's neighbor. People are making responsible decisions. Those decisions clearly exclude the Church. So, is religious life obsolete?

How we approach the question and what other questions are asked are important. What we do with the answers to those questions will depend on the courage of the one who becomes aware of new possibilities. Such possibilities emerge as an invitation to go deeper into the inquiry.

- Why is there decline in religious life?
- Those who join, are they seeking nostalgia and a refuge or God and a mission?
- Do the evangelical counsels make sense today?

Some adherents are convinced that religious life should never change; others claim that change gives life to the organization. These attitudes often clash and create a crisis in orientation. The basic question is: are we able to face the situation and dig below the surface to see what underlies it?

Leadership of the diverse expressions of religious life has already manifested concern over the crisis and relevancy of the consecrated life style. Among these Church leaders is the Swiss abbot Martin Werlen of the Abbey of Einsiedeln and Fahr, and his appeal for Church reform in *Embers in these Ashes*. He wants to wake up the Catholic Church by asking questions and bringing to light the contradictions and dishonest patterns of behavior of the Church.[1] What is at stake is religious life as a "believable sign of our times."

In a study on religious life, several collaborators offer insights and optimism in *A Monastic Vision for the 21st Century: Where do we go from here?*[2] It is clear that, if monastic life is not changed and updated, it will have nothing to say to the questions of future generations. In the introduction, the Cistercian Dom Bernardo Olivera writes with clarity what

---

[1] Martin Werlen, *Embers in the Ashes: New Life in the Church* (Mahwah, NJ: Paulist Press ebook edition, 2013), Chapter 2.

[2] Patrick Hart (ed.), *A Monastic Vision for the 21st Century: Where do We Go from Here?* (Cistercian Publications, 2006).

options must be thought through and considered for implementation. Benedictine Joan Chittister identifies this time of crisis as *"crossover points"* in history. She strongly believes that *"only religion can possibly stop the violence being used in its name."*[3]

In *The Basic Inspiration of Religious Life,* the Augustinian Tarcisius van Bavel reminds us that we are moving into a new period in religious life, and we should not forget the original inspiration is about *"forming a personal bond to Jesus, following him."*[4] But because this inspiration is a calling for all people, it should not be exaggerated as a *"distinctive character of the religious life."* The Jesuit Pope Francis echoes the same theme of renewal and updating in his writings like *Joy of the Gospel* (*Evangelii Gaudium,* 1-2) and the apostolic letter *"To All Consecrated People on the Occasion of the Year of Consecrated Life."*[5]

Purpose

The purpose of this reflection is to examine the crisis and trends of religious life from a phenomenological perspective in its broadest terms and in the light of the words of 1 Peter 3:15: *"Always be ready to bear witness to any who ask you of the hope that lives in you."* This pericope will serve as a leitmotiv for further reflection in three points:

- Part 1 - a subjective inquiry into the *hope that lives in you;*

- Part 2 - a consideration of the vision of the Second Vatican Council, *to bear witness;* and

- Part 3- the quality of appropriation of the Council fifty years later in religious life, *to any who ask you.* Is anyone 'asking?'

---

[3] Ibid., pp. 92 and 101. Kofi Annan is quoted: "The world cannot find peace without the cooperation of the religions of the world"(101-102).

[4] Tarcisius Van Bavel, *The Basic Inspiration of Religious Life* (Villanova: Augustinian Press, 1996), 44, 86-87.

[5] Accessed on April 8, 2016, at *https://goo.gl/1YdJG7.*

I will briefly expand on each point.

Considering the present state of affairs with religious life and the Church in general, Part 1 encompasses the question: Are the scientists, poets, politicians, economists, atheists, believers, Christian and non-Christian asking about the *hope that lives in you*? If not, why? Are religious of congregations even concerned with this question and its connection with the secular world and the violence people experience? Are member religious asking questions? Or is one drifting along knowing that the institution will provide basic needs and security and provide comfort?

We will use Bernard Lonergan's cognitional process of understanding to explore these questions. In other words, emphasis will be given between the *hope that lives in you* and the person as the reflecting subject with the desire to know.

Lonergan's ideas can assist us in uncovering what underlies issues and the great questions. He is identified by one of the bishops as the "*peritus* (expert) of the *periti* (experts)" and the "intellectual vitality released by the Council." But one can greatly benefit from Lonergan's thought without being a 'Lonergan specialist' or a theological scholar. Many of his insights can be quite readily appreciated and appropriated, as they regard why we question, how we approach wonder, the possible effect of bias upon us, and what authenticity really demands of us.

Reflection on religious life requires a correct understanding of the Vatican II context. In brief, the *Constitution on the Liturgy* (*Sacrosanctum Concilium*), which established the aims of the Council, foresees a Church that is primarily Eucharistic in nature and structure. This is a paradigm shift similar to the scientific revolutions. In Part 2, we want to explore what is at stake with religious life in the postconciliar era of the twenty-first century. Does religious life highlight the Eucharistic Church that Vatican II imagined? Has it adapted, developed, and appropriated that vision, or has it been compromised? Is there 'shift' or 'drift?' New questions are pondered regarding obstacles and future possibilities. In our consideration of relevant questions and conciliar context, we will examine once more our present situation through the lens of what Lonergan calls "Foundations."

However, there remains an older reactionary paradigm of the preconciliar Church that is hierarchically structured as the primary model of Christian witness in the world. This paradigm – called the 'reform of the reform'[6] — refuses adjustment to the newer vision and maintains an identity that is primarily institutional, clerical, sexist, and patriarchal. The reintroduction of the Latin Mass as Extraordinary Form and the new English translation of the *Roman Missal*, based on the new rules for interpretation from *Liturgiam Authenticam*, are examples of this recalcitrance.

Part 3 will examine this clash between these two paradigms and the extent that religious life is caught in the conflict. We will use Lonergan's notion of 'Dialectic' to understand the conflict and its root causes as well as the conditions for making the 'shift' to the new Eucharistic paradigm.

Many people are anxious about the future of their institutes and wonder how to navigate the waters of these confusing times. The best approach is to face the situation intelligently and with integrity. Lonergan highlights the tension of inquiry for understanding and reflection, and an awareness of what it means to be an 'authentic and creative' person in the time of change.[7]

Following these cues, the structure of this essay is: 1) the reflecting person as authentic and creative; 2) the 'foundation' paradigm of a Eucha-

---

[6] Vatican spokesman Father Federico Lombardi, speaking for Pope Francis, tells us it is better to avoid this expression with reference to the liturgy as it may at times give rise to errors. *Comunicato della Sala Stampa della Santa Sede: Alcuni chiarimenti sulla celebrazione della Messa,* July 11, 2016.

[7] See Bernard Lonergan, "Healing and Creating in History" in *A Third Collection*. (Mahwah, NJ: Paulist Press, 1985), 100-109.

ristic Church established by Vatican II and how religious life is understood within that paradigm; and 3) the conflict between old and new paradigms (dialectic) and questions confronting religious life and the conditions for a 'shift' to the new paradigm.

We will conclude by pointing toward new terrains in which religious life is Eucharistic and can give effective testimony to following Christ, which is the *hope that lives in you.*

PART I
LONERGAN ON THE REFLECTING PERSON:
"HOPE THAT LIVES IN YOU"

Authentic Christian living begins with an inspiration, an inner experience, motivated by a profound "unrestricted desire to know" marked by wonder and awe and not with dogma or doctrines. It is the relationship with someone or something that drives one forward. Augustine was aware of this deep inner impulse when he wrote in his *Soliloquies* a theme for the later history of monasticism: "Let me know myself, let me know You, O God."[8] Pope Francis speaks of this relationship with the person of Jesus in the opening lines of "Joy of the Gospel." Doctrines have their roots in the inner experience.

Symbols Disconnected from Ordinary Life

Hence abstract ideas about God and the Christian way of life are formulated from a basic experience of encounter and relatedness. In other words, life comes before doctrines. Misunderstanding occurs when doctrines are uprooted from the experiences. A pastoral problem today is that symbols, sacraments, and rituals are disconnected from everyday living. From a recent study of the Pew Forum and the Center for Applied Research in the Apostolate, about forty-five per cent of Catho-

---

[8] Augustine, full text: "O God, always the same, let me know myself, let me know you. This is prayer." *"Deus semper idem, noverim me, noverim te. Oratum est."* (*Soliloquies* 2.1.1.)

lics do not believe the sacraments are essential to the faith, *never* participate in the sacrament of reconciliation and do not believe that Jesus is really present in the Eucharist.[9]

Cognition Process & Misguided Attitude of "Knowing is Looking"

People no longer ask questions because the desire to know has faded away from conscious awareness. Christian life, with its worn-out patterns, becomes like a woodchip curling around a center that does not exist. It is vital to recover that 'center,' for it is from there that one *bears witness*.

Lonergan's 1957 classic work *Insight*[10] can shed light on recovering the 'center' and that *hope which lives in you*. Naturally, the whole of Lonergan's thought on the operations of the mind and understanding cannot be treated here in its totality, but some indicators can be pursued regarding how one comes to know through experiencing, inquiring and reflecting – the cognition process – and how this is important for religious life.

---

[9] Statistic from the Pew Forum and CARA studies in Kathleen Hughes, *Becoming the Sign. Sacramental Living in a Post-Conciliar Church* (Mahwah, NJ: Paulist Press, 2013), 74.

[10] Bernard Lonergan, *Insight. A Study of Human Understanding,* Collected Works of Bernard Lonergan 3, edited by Frederick E. Crowe and Robert M. Doran (Toronto: University of Toronto, 1992 [1957]). The aim of this almost 800-page work is to guide the reader to become aware and reflect on one's own inner process of understanding and how one comes to know anything. Once the process is understood, then there is a kind of template for understanding other fields of knowledge. All human beings experience wonder and awe, have a desire to know, ask and answer questions, receive insights and new connections, verify the results, make judgments and decisions. This set of operations in one's consciousness is common to everyone. Lonergan's aim in this work is delineated on pages 22 and 769.

Knowing is not Looking[11]

Lonergan writes about what is going on in the knower as subject who wants to know, or what the thinker is thinking. How do those operations occur and what patterns of experience happen that give rise to inquiry? A basic approach begins with learning to 'see' and not just 'look.' 'Seeing' asks questions for understanding; 'looking' is unreflective and more like empty entertainment. When one sees the stars, the snow falling to the ground, or the dogwood in the first bloom of the season, one pauses and wonders at what is seen. This experience provides a kind of awakening that the stars, snow and budding trees want to communicate with us as though they possess a certain kind of intelligence all their own.

But if I turn to myself and reflect on my capacity to wonder, I come to an awareness of an inner depth that is not empty space, but a kind of presence and I ask 'why?' Searching for answers to the 'why' leads me to insight and then to more questions. Why do the stars twinkle? Why does snow sparkle? Motivated by the experience of wonder, I begin to be more attentive and inquire about life that surrounds me and is within me (Cf. Rom 5:5).

Capacity to Wonder & Desire to Know:
the 'Authentic' Person

The capacity to wonder is what makes humans distinct from other animals. Dogs and cats do not wonder why it is raining outside or question why bells and nametags dangle from their collars. Animals respond to stimuli and instinct in an unconscious manner rather than wonder about String theory, black holes and if there is meaning, purpose and direction in life. Human beings have a different capacity that

---

[11] See "knowing and looking" in the index of *Insight* for page references (845).

is conscious: humans have the gifted ability to be captivated by awe and Eros, which are linked to the pure, unrestricted desire to know.

If one is attentive to the desire to know, one begins to ask questions for understanding and for critical reflection. Here I address the reader to pause and to become aware of what is going on inside you when serious questions are posed to you. Why do I wonder? What does this mean? How is it related to other things? It is clear that knowing is not 'looking.' For example, a person can 'look' at the Evening News, which is not the same as 'to know' or 'to be informed.' Being informed entails asking questions, making connections and looking for insights. It is a dynamic process of reflection that begins to ask questions from different viewpoints, and there are insights into the experience or issue at hand.

Once there is clarity and no more questions on the issue, then a judgment is made: "Is it so? True or false? Yes or no?" At this point, a decision is put into action. Lonergan calls this action the work of the 'authentic' person. This is particularly important for the discussion on the paradigm-shift in Part 3 below.

Bias: Derailment of the Knowing Process

The object of the knowing process is to come to a judgment. But that process can be truncated by other motives that are opposed to the unrestricted drive to know. The reader is surely aware of how many times people make judgments without having all the data or facts. Underlying emotions and interests influence the judgments. These motives emerge when the cognition process is affected by bias, because bias fails to follow the cognitional process. Lonergan speaks of several kinds of bias in Chapters 6 and 7 of *Insight*: dramatic bias, egoist bias, group bias, and common-sense bias.

Bias occurs when one refuses to consider all the data at hand or the necessary questions to be asked and makes rash judgments based more on personal self-centeredness or group shortsightedness than dealing with the insights and new questions from the process of inquiry. This refusal to be attentive is the "flight from understanding" Lonergan refers to in the "Preface" to *Insight.* The person *prefers* not to understand. When one, as the unauthentic person, does not attend to the experiencing, inquiring, and reflecting *process,* then the accumulation of bias judgments will contribute to the "cycle of decline."

Inner Experience & Knowing Reality

Thus far we have stressed the need to ask questions which touch on the *hope that lives in you.* If this inner experience is ambiguous and abstract, the quality of the hope and witnessing will be dubious. For the religious person, it is not enough just to ask questions; one must go to a deeper reality. I invite the reader to make an experiment. Take and hold in your hand a pencil, cell-phone, or any object. Say the word 'it' several times; repeat it over to get a sense of its reality as it is. Say 'it,' 'it,' 'it' ... Get a feel for the sense of the object.

Then turn your attention from 'it' and say 'you.' Repeat it slowly and consciously several times, 'you,' 'you,' 'you.' You might sense a shift that this 'you' is somewhat responsible for the 'it.' The 'you' becomes a 'You' and there is a sense of reality and interconnectedness with things around you; "everything suddenly becomes overwhelmingly personal." The 'You' is connected to the notion of 'following Christ' and becomes the *hope* that is within. The *hope* is a 'You.'

Religious life & the Eucharistic Church

In our present reflection we have to ponder whether religious life promotes creativity and authenticity as a focus among its members. Do religious gravitate toward the 'You' that is within and live from that center? Some wonder, in the era of diminishment, if religious life concentrates too much on self-preservation and on the externals of its life style rather than taking seriously their capacity to attend to the experiencing of the data, inquiring about the causes and implications, and reflecting and making decisions from these experiences. The challenge is to move from institutional anxiety to a community of individuals who are attentive to and want to follow the 'You.' Are congregations ready and capable of giving voice to the knowledge of the *hope that lives in you?* This is the question.

To answer this question, we need to go beyond what Vatican II says about religious life in *Perfectae Caritatis* and Chapter VI of *Lumen Gentium* to the radical call to follow Christ in the overall dynamic of the Council itself and to foster expression of a Eucharistic Church. To know this is to attend to what the Council wanted, to what Lonergan calls "Foundations" in *Method in Theology,* before jumping to conclusions on how *to bear witness.*

PART II
FOUNDATIONS: VISION OF THE COUNCIL
"TO BEAR WITNESS"

Three Dynamisms of the Vatican II Paradigm

Keeping in mind Lonergan's process of knowing, or cognition, the vision of religious life must be taken within the whole context of Vatican II to which I refer as 'dynamisms.' The temptation is to hunt through the text of the *"Decree on the Adaptation and Renewal of Religious Life"* for answers and not see the broader horizon that the Council set forth for conversion and reform of structures. This broader horizon is the 'foundation' from which trends are taken into consideration.

There are three dynamisms or trends at the Council: *aggiornamento, ressourcement, and rapprochement.* These dynamisms constitute a new paradigm in the Church's self-understanding and mission in the world. The greatest impact of the new paradigm is with the understanding of the laity and the role of the bishops. Aside from the updating of the rules and constitutions, the structures of religious life in general have not adapted to the paradigm. In fact, the reverse has taken hold in the era of the 'reform of the reform' in the pontificates of John Paul II and Benedict XVI. That era is far from over, in spite of the presence of a Pope Francis.

When Pope John XXIII convoked the Second Vatican Council, he made it clear that it was a *pastoral* Council, with the purpose not to correct errors in doctrine and condemn heresies but to have a discerning attitude of openness to the movements of the Spirit in the Church and in the world, which he called *aggiornamento*. The underlying dynamic of all the discussions is a fundamental openness to the unknown and unfamiliar.

A dimension of 'being open' to future possibilities involves another dynamic of 'returning to the sources,' or *ressourcement*. This trend is an invitation to ground oneself in the tradition, or a foundation. The return to the sources of wisdom accumulated over the centuries is a way of proceeding forward. This spawned a tremendous interest in research and new translations of the great texts of spiritual founders and the early Church.

The last dynamic trend is 'approaching the other who is different' or *rapprochement*. No text, constitution or decree from the Council spoke specifically about *rapprochement;* rather it is that fundamental attitude that penetrated the texts, especially on how the Church relates with the world (*Gaudium et Spes*), communicates with other non-Christian traditions (*Nostra Aetate*), collaborates ecumenically with other Christian churches (*Unitatis Redintegratio*) and listens and works together with the laity as partners in the mission of the Church (*Apostolicam Actuositatem*). These three dynamic trends form the framework against which religious life in its varied dimensions must be analyzed. Congregations ought to evaluate themselves with the criteria of *aggiornamento, ressourcement,* and *rapprochement.*

Aims of the Council & the Link between Liturgy & Ecclesiology

Before moving on, there is another factor about Vatican II that must be identified and brought into our awareness: the aims of the Council itself. The opening paragraph of the "Constitution on the Sacred Liturgy" (*Sacrosanctum Concilium*) identifies the goals:

1. Renewal with 'increasing vigor'
2. Adaptation of the structures to modern times
3. Ecumenism
4. Evangelization

After identifying these goals, the document immediately declares: "The Council therefore sees particularly cogent reasons for undertaking the reform and promotion of the liturgy" and "structural revision of liturgical rites" (Nos. 21 and 23). This is very important. The manner in which the liturgy is celebrated and understood will point to a way of being Church. In other words, liturgy and ecclesiology are intimately connected and they give expression to each other. This link is often not recognized by liturgy planners or by those who discuss the mission of the Church.

Liturgy was adapted to represent the Church it wanted to see realized. According to the brilliant liturgist Ralph Kiefer (1940-1987), the repositioning of the altar to face the assembly is the major change effected. The change says something about a shift in the Church's self-understanding from the institutional as the primary model to that of a *sacramental* community on the move and a real presence of the living Christ in the world. Where the traditional church was FOR the people, the new paradigm is calling for a living Church OF the people.

The ecclesiology found in the "Constitution on the Sacred Liturgy" – based on baptism and the common priesthood of the faithful -- is profoundly Eucharistic. Every time the community gathers for liturgy it is being a Eucharistic church and it is the "work of Christ himself" (Nos. 5

to 10). The community lives as an expression of "full, conscious, active participation" (No. 14). The intent is to do this not just 'spiritually' but in reality as *communion, participation and dialogue,* and this includes the structures as well. We might pause and ask ourselves if religious communities have explicit structural expressions of "full, conscious, active participation" within the institutional church. What would those structures look like?

Polarization in the Liturgy & Ecclesiology

The connection between liturgy and ecclesiology is an insight that has developed over a century through the Liturgical Movement in Europe and the United States. Upon closer examination, one discovers a different kind of ecclesiology in the "Dogmatic Constitution on the Church" (*Lumen Gentium*), especially with the "Preliminary Note of Explanation" at the end of the document, which highlights in contradictory fashion a preconciliar structure and hierarchy. The difference is striking and palpable. The tension and polarization in the Church today is between an understanding of Church as Eucharistic and one that is of the "Preliminary Note." With the last two popes, the vision of that "Preliminary Note" has been elevated to a higher status, while themes like the 'People of God' and the 'priesthood of the baptized' have been reduced in significance. This shift and contraction to the idea of a 'reform of the reform' should cause one to wonder how a Eucharistic Church fits within a structure that sees itself as monarchical. One only has to examine the negative impact of the new English Latinate translation of the *Roman Missal* based on the hermeneutics of *Liturgiam Authenticam.*

From Polarization to Communion, Participation & Dialogue

The way to view this apparent contradiction and confusion is to be aware of its source. The Council has opened many doors and there are a multitude of interpretations. One must decide where one is going to stand in the interpretation of what it means to be Church in the world and how that Church celebrates its liturgy and prayer. Hopefully, communities can move beyond polarization toward a greater reception of the Council, one that is committed to the horizon of *communion, participation and dialogue*.

What does this discussion on Vatican II have for religious communities and the meaning of *to bear witness … to the hope that lives in you*? The act of bearing *witness* involves the horizon of *communion, participation, and dialogue.* The horizon of this new paradigm is an open-system that is willing to engage the unknown with courage and to risk being influenced toward greater change. The vision that is witnessed is one of companionship, hospitality and compassion. Individual religious and communities need to ask questions and to probe deeper into issues to see where they are with bearing *witness* to this new horizon.

A person or organization has the right to critique others only if they themselves accept self-criticism. The criterion for change is: Christ and the world with all its complexities or the Order's founders and supposed safety net and survival of closed institutional structures. Some areas for change might be simplifying forms of authority and its relation with communities and each person, examining the symbols and customs, searching for new ways to live together, and discussing new forms of living traditional values, such as poverty, celibacy, fasting, austerity, silence, solitude and fraternal correction.

Each religious must ponder the questions and decide where to stand in relation to the invitation to follow Christ: in creativity or in comfort; in authenticity or in conformity. As Church membership dwindles and religious orders diminish, it is no longer a luxury to postpone honest inquiry that confronts the situation as it is so as to move beyond 'praying for vocations' and implementing complex marketing strategies. The Jesuit General Pedro Arrupe speaks to this congregational hesitancy.

In all these experiences and encounters [in the countries of the third world] I am continually overcome by a concerned feeling of urgency. Do not we Christians hesitate too much and too long? Are not our plans often too long-term and do they not play safe too much? Surely, we stick too readily to what is guaranteed and tested, and our courage deserts us too rapidly when we face open-ended and risk ventures. I do not want here to speak up for aimless panic. But if according to Scripture we are called on to read the signs of the times, then included in that today is essentially a feeling for the closeness of our deadlines and a readiness to act quickly.[12]

Where do we go from here? As we compare these two paradigms, we see the necessity for a 'shift' or conversion in oneself from one horizon to another. Our focus in the next section is on the nature of this 'shift' as the reception of the Council and whether or not religious communities have appropriated the 'shift.'

PART III
DIALECTIC, PARADIGM SHIFTS:
"WITNESS TO ANY WHO ASK YOU"

To understand the Church situation and religious life as well in the post-Vatican II era, we will apply Lonergan's concept of 'Dialectic' to the present reality. In *Method in Theology,* dialectic means to analyze the conflicts and the root causes that underlie them. The most that we can do is try to understand better the nature of the conflict and find a handle on how to move with it toward a resolution. Thus, the dialectic is between two paradigms: the new paradigm of Vatican II and the older paradigm of the 'reform of the reform.' We will explore these two paradigms and the 'shift' required to move from one to the other. Integral to the shift is the unique role of religious life to be 'provocative' within

---

[12] From an address given by Arrupe in the Paulskirche at Frankfurt in 1976 and cited in Johann B. Metz, *Followers of Christ. Perspectives on the Religious Life* (Mahwah, NJ: Paulist Press, translated 1978), 79-80.

its communities and the institutional Church by raising important questions and encouraging conversion. We will conclude by pointing to possible future directions.

Eucharistic Paradigm in the Dialectic

Most of the details of this paradigm have already been worked out in Part 2: Foundations. Briefly, the theme that marks this paradigm is the Church's self-understanding (horizon) as a Eucharistic Church and the reform of the liturgy reflecting that identity. Ecclesiology and liturgy are connected. Vatican II is a Eucharistic paradigm.

The challenge today is to revisit how the changes in the liturgy, such as moving the altar away from the wall and using the vernacular for the language of the ritual, all reflect a change in relationships between the faithful and hierarchy and in the understanding of ministry, Church and world. A key phrase from the document on the liturgy is "full, conscious, active participation" in the liturgy (SC 14). But such active participation does not stop with the liturgy; it ought to overflow into the structures of the parish and diocese at all levels. The identity of the Church is not based on gender or hierarchical class, but on baptism and the common priesthood of all the faithful. The Jesuit Robert Taft says that the "Liturgy is the Christian life in a nutshell." The role of the religious orders and congregations must reflect this new identity of "full, conscious, active participation" and the Church as Eucharistic.

The Eucharistic Church is a dynamic reality that is constantly moving and evolving. It is a living reality of engagement. As an event, the Council vibrated with significant attitudes that characterized itself as one of creative openness (*aggiornamento*) always finding its ground in the sources of tradition and wisdom (*ressourcement*) and a willing engagement of approaching the 'other' that is different (*rapprochement*). Religious communities – in their formation programs, governance and ministry -- ought to embrace these same attitudes of openness, return to the sources of their original inspiration and engagement of the new, the strange and the unknown. Five decades later this image of an inclusive Church did not resonate well with the Church of the older paradigm.

Clash between Paradigms

From the beginning the sessions at the Vatican Council struggled to be unified in thought and in task. Different camps emerged immediately around various premises: Does doctrine change? Is collegiality dangerous? What are tradition and the meaning of 'the world?' Each camp had its own interpretive horizon. The seeds of division sprouted immediately after the Council and the attempt to implement adaptations and changes in Church life. Religious communities were also caught up in this struggle as they attempted to study and update their rules and constitutions. The clash exacerbated itself to such an extent that real polarization between the conservative and progressive camps effected breakdown in dialogue. Still, conservatives call for a 'reform of the reform' and progressives find themselves more in the minority and many leave the Church completely. In spite of the progressive calls for reform by Pope Francis, the clash between a conservative ideology and a movement for change becomes more toxic.

The division of fundamental attitudes in the Church between pro- and anti-Vatican II mindsets is found in the conciliar documents. We already mentioned that the document on the liturgy points to a Church that is Eucharistic and encourages "full, conscious, active participation" on the part of all the baptized, not just in the liturgy, but in its style of life and mission in the world (Cf. 1 Cor 12:12-31). The body of Christ is represented in the sacrament on the altar and the *Totus Christus* on the earth. This image of Church is more inclusive and involves all the faithful and not just hierarchy, clerics and vowed religious.

Where does one find a statement about the 'reform of the reform' trend in the documents? I propose that it is the "Explanatory Note" attached to the end of the Constitution on the Church (*Lumen Gentium*). This note, regardless of what the constitution says, reinforces the hierarchical structure of the Church as the primary structure. This addition nullifies the inclusive nature of the Eucharistic Church set out in the constitution on the liturgy.

The image of Church in the "Explanatory Note" finds its expression in the nostalgia of the liturgy that privileges Latin as the 'sacred' language for worship. The hierarchy is the ecclesial center and the faithful do not ask questions and are mere observers with the crumbs of pious devotions curled up in a privatized spirituality. Eucharist is for adoration: *look at Jesus as Jesus looks at you.* Augustine's Eucharistic theology of *receive what you are, be what you receive* is strange language in this paradigm. In this closed liturgical environment, there are only altar boys who look like 'miniature clerics' (Italian: *chiericetti*), and girls are prohibited in the sanctuary. Women wear veils and bells are rung at the consecration. This paradigm image of Church, to which many religious are attached, is gender-specific with power belonging to celibate male clerics -- situations without theological justification. It is an image that does not connect well with the world of the twenty-first century.

In 2007, when Pope Benedict XVI issued the Apostolic Letter *Summorum Pontificum* that permitted the Latin Mass as the "Extraordinary Form" of the liturgy, the old ecclesiology of the pre-Vatican II era was re-established as a legitimate form for being a Church community. This is precisely where the clash occurs and reverberates in religious communities. As in the time of Augustine and the Donatists, the Catholic Church has two 'altars' and parallel and opposed churches. Time will tell how this situation will move forward.

What are some of the underlying factors to the clash between these two paradigms? The issue is over the question of continuity. Critics of Vatican II claim that the Council failed to be one of continuity with Church tradition. Nevertheless, certain attitudes had to come to an end if the Church is going to be effective in the world. In terms of discontinuity, it brought an end to clericalism that was inherited from the Edict of Milan (313). The liturgy was no longer the exclusive domain of the clergy. What this means is that the Constantinian Era came to an end with Vatican II. It also brought an end to the Church's reactionary attitudes toward the Protestant Reform. With the revival of the 'reform of the reform' the clerical and negative attitudes are embraced once again, often promoted under the banner of 'apologetics.' The impact on religious communities has been tremendous. The religious garb became the distinctive identity among communities; formation withdrew to isolated areas away from the city; liturgical correctness became the issue of the day. It is all about the exterior expressions with little about religious conversion.

Closing of the Mind as Root Cause for Clash

What are the causes of this clash between two paradigms, between the Conciliar and the 'reform of the reform' ecclesiologies? Another way to pose the question is to ask why there is a clash in the first place. Lonergan writes that bias is at the root of the clashes and accumulation of bias causes a spiral of decline. Bias is the closing of the mind for self-centered reasons, for either the individual or for a group. Individual and group bias sees reality only in terms of what benefits itself to the exclusion of others and their needs. Ultimately, it is self-destructive. No serious questions are asked. Understanding falters and there are no insights necessary for the move forward. The heart is closed to conversion and to God's grace.

Such bias is operative on many levels in religious communities. Individual bias moves people toward joining a group because of its customs, nostalgia and an enclosed community safe from the world. Its relationship with outsiders of the community tends to be minimal and clique-like. In male communities, women and young people are viewed as invisible persons. Ideologies are often formed. We must ask what happened to the congregation's original inspiration and how does it contribute to a change in direction?

Religious Congregations & 'Shock Therapy'

Vatican II is a clarion call to transition from one paradigm to another or from one's horizon of understanding to another. What we want to concentrate on is the notion of the 'shift' from the old to the new paradigm and the role for religious communities in this dynamic. A shift is not necessarily a smooth transition, but can be one that is abrupt and a jolt with serious repercussions. Structures are altered through a paradigm-shift; feelings are heightened; insights emerge; consequences lead to other courses of action. We have seen such shifts with the scientific revolutions, regarding the insights from a geocentric to a heliocentric horizon of understanding. In this section we want to analyze what elements contribute to the 'shift.' Lonergan has much to say about this in how he understands history, but first a word must be said about the role of religious congregations in creating conditions for 'shift.'

The religious institution points to something greater, to a light beyond itself, namely "to follow Christ." This is its "supreme rule" and reason for existence (*Perfectae Caritatis*, 2). There are various expressions of what this means for the wider Church. J. B. Metz says religious congregations provide a kind of 'shock therapy' to the institutional Church as a protest movement against Church structures moving away from the radical following of Christ of the Gospels toward more concern with status and self-preservation.[13] Pope Francis encouraged communities during the Year of Consecrated Life to embrace their 'prophetic' dimension.

This 'shock therapy' is also echoed in the Swiss Abbot Martin Werlen's call for a "pro-vocation"[14] in the church filled with ashes and worn out ideas and patterns of behavior. *Embers Under the Ashes* is meant to *provoke* questioning at the deepest levels. The questions are like pebbles

---

[13] Metz, *Followers of Christ*, 11-18.

[14] Werlen, *Embers in the Ashes*, Chapter 5.

dropped in water: one waits and sees the ripple effects. Where do they go? Who is affected? Does anyone care?

Other individuals have lived out their prophetic call to stimulate the Church into thinking about itself and its mission through 'shock therapy.' Franciscan Richard Rohr promotes ecumenical thinking and explorations through various mystical traditions in his conferences like *Conspire*, a program of the Center for Action and Contemplation.[15] A frequent speaker at these events is the Franciscan scientist Ilia Delio who links faith and evolutionary science. Using social media, Benedictine Anthony Ruff raises challenging issues regarding the liturgy at *Pray Tell*. Australian Jesuit Gerald O'Collins has called on all bishops to take a stand on the English translation of the 2011 liturgy and to implement the 1998 Sacramentary.

'Shock treatments' always spring from a connection with the deep inner self and the silent contact with 'You.' Contemplative prayer is a path to the radical following of Christ. An emergence of various forms of prayer and *lectio divina* are found in the programs of the Cistercian Thomas Keating and the Benedictine Laurence Freeman, which spread to lay people in all walks of life. One can remember Karl Rahner's statement that the "Christian of the future will be a mystic or nothing at all."[16]

Commitment to social justice is the fruit of contemplative prayer. Recently, the "Nuns on the Bus"[17] crisscrossed the United States to raise the issue of the economy and the plight of the poor. Others have been radical in calling attention to social justice, like John Deer and Roy

---

[15] See the website for the Center for Action and Contemplation: https://cac.org/

[16] Karl Rahner, "Christian Living Formerly and Today, "in Theological Investigations VII, trans. David Bourke (New York: Herder and Herder, 1971), 15.

[17] As an event of Networklobby.org and conscious of the polarization in politics, "Nuns on the Bus" travel around the United States to listen to people's stories of injustice. These stories will be taken to Congress in an effort to stimulate change. The religious sisters are responding to Pope Francis' call that we must change our politics and not just our policies. One can also take a pledge to be an agent of change and to be bridge builders in politics: (*http://networklobby.org/bus2015/pledge*).

Bourgeois, both suffering consequences from the institutional Church for their actions. All of these individuals touched the source of their spirituality in what it means to 'follow Christ.' They are voices of courage that challenge the established structures within the confusion of the crisis.

Lonergan contributes to these prophetic voices by showing a direction one can choose to facilitate a paradigm-shift and thereby growth into the new paradigm. Growth is built on asking questions and gaining insights; decline is infected by bias, in which shortcomings become cumulative, like a dumping ground. The situation degenerates to a point of no return and needs 'healing.'

Lonergan writes:

> *Growth, progress, is a matter of situations yielding insights, insights yielding policies and projects, policies and projects transforming the initial situation, and the transformed situation giving rise to further insights that correct and complement the deficiencies of previous insights. So the wheel of progress moves forward through the successive transformations of an initial situation in which are gathered coherently and cumulatively all the insights that occurred along the way. But this wheel of progress becomes a wheel of decline when the process is distorted by bias ... the more the objective situation becomes a mere dump, the less is there any possibility of human intelligence gathering from the situation anything more than a lengthy catalogue of the aberrations and the follies of the past.*[18]

Shift Happens

Many factors can contribute to a shift from one paradigm to another. Lonergan offers one approach that involves the accumulation of insights through a continual process of inquiry that leads to intellectual

---

[18] Bernard Lonergan, "Healing and Creating in History" in *A Third Collection*. (Mahwah, NJ: Paulist Press, 1985),105.

conversion. As individuals pursue questions for greater understanding and reflection and move to higher viewpoints, communities are stimulated with insights that may contribute to acts of judgment and action. The insight might contribute to a *prophetic* action and *shock.*

Communities are also free to reject such insights. Thus, the tension within paradigm shifts becomes more felt. Whatever is the case, in order to be authentic to one's self, serious questions -- and the right questions -- must be asked. Lonergan develops this line of thought in the transcendental precepts: "Be attentive. Be intelligent. Be reasonable. Be responsible."[19]

He later adds "Be in love." This is why in the beginning of this essay the reader is asked about the habit of asking questions. Questions open the possibility for intellectual conversion and new values which advance one to higher viewpoints and more questions and more insights.

The 'shift' happens when a person is open to conversion and grace and when there is the accumulation of insights from higher viewpoints toward a new horizon. So, are members of religious communities asking any serious questions?

Final Thoughts for New Directions

This essay on religious life in the post-Vatican II era revolved around the verse from *1 Peter*: *Always be ready to bear witness to any who ask you of the hope that lives in you.* But we began with the question: Is religious life obsolete? For sure, many religious congregations will pass into extinction, and this is not new in the history of the Church. Many more will remain irrelevant and not address the needs in society. The communities that will thrive in their mission will be those comprised of individuals who ask the deep questions about the radical following of Christ and, like 'shock therapy,' prophetically challenge the Church

---

[19] Bernard Lonergan, *Method in Theology* (Toronto: University of Toronto, 1971, reprint 2007), 11-20.

institutions and others at the same time as to their fidelity in following the Gospel.

Where do we go from here as the Vatican II event slips further into the past? Let me make a suggestion for a direction. We begin with what perturbs all people -- world violence and everything it entails. Serious people are becoming more aware that they can be good, compassionate, and loving people who can contribute to the building of a more just society without becoming a Christian. This is obviously true. But they might *ask you of the hope that lives in you*. They might ask what solution you have for world violence.

My reply would be that Christianity makes sense because it does have a response to violence. For me, the symbol of the crucifix is the question mark that embraces all the violence and death that surrounds the human race and planet. The Cross asks: What are you going to do about it? My answer is "the table." The table of fellowship and inclusiveness is where all people sit together as equals and break bread. The table, as an alternative reality, is the place to be "provocative" as Jesus was and continues to be in human hearts and in the Word. This response is summed up in the words of the late Cardinal Joseph Bernardin: "At this table (Eucharist) we put aside every worldly separation based on culture, class, or other differences. This communion is why all prejudice, all racism, all sexism, all deference to wealth and power must be banished from our parishes, our homes, our lives."[20]

The answer to the Cross is the paradigm *shock* of new grace and openness to a new horizon of what it means to be a Eucharistic Church. So, what is the *hope that lives in you?*

You better have a good answer.

---

[20] Cardinal Joseph Bernardin, *Our Communion, Our Peace, Our Promise. Pastoral Letter on the Liturgy*. February 1984, in *Selected Works of Joseph Cardinal Bernardin. Homilies and Teaching Documents*, Vol. 1 (Collegeville: The Liturgical Press, 2000), 11-26, quote at 22.

8

WAKE UP THE WORLD:
RELIGIOUS LIFE AS A PROPHETIC WITNESSING

Emeka Xris Obiezu, OSA

Introduction

'Prophetic witnessing' is a prominent term among the numerous ways that religious life, also called consecrated life, is characterized by the Church and by religious themselves. Even though this term may not be explicitly found in Vatican II language, the concept behind it still was discernible as dominant in the Council's treatment of this way of life. Postconciliar documents do use the concept directly. In his speech inaugurating the year of consecrated life, Pope Francis evokes the same language of prophetic witnessing as he enjoined the men and women in consecrated life to "wake up the world."

Throughout history, many women and men of consecrated life authentically lived out this prophetic character of their vocation. In a very symbolic yet practical way, the movement from hermitage to mendicancy illustrates significant witnessing to the prophetic character of this way of life by making it more socially responsive. Religious maintained the burning desire for the holiness of God and attentively listened to his word in the various circumstances of their history. The particular persuasive power of the consistency between their proclamation and their life bore witness to them as prophets. They proclaimed that word with their lives, with their lips and with their actions, speaking against evil and sin even to Church leaders.

Consecrated for the sake of the kingdom, they never stopped exploring new ways to live the Gospel in their own concrete situation, in their expectation of God's Kingdom coming. Like the prophets of old and like Christ himself, not even the threat of death would deter their commitment to a life marked by self-giving.

As John Paul II recalls in *Vita Consecrata* (VC), "Consecrated men and women have borne witness to Christ the Lord *with the gift of their own lives*. Thousands of them have been forced into the catacombs by the persecution of totalitarian regimes or of violent groups, or have been harassed while engaged in missionary activity in action on behalf of the poor, in assisting the sick and the marginalized; yet they lived and continue to live their consecration in prolonged and heroic suffering, and often with the shedding of their blood, being perfectly configured to the Crucified Lord" (Pope John Paul II, 1996, 86).

However, in the ongoing history of consecrated life, and even more evidently so today, a contrary tendency is also manifest. Consecrated life, like other aspects of Church life, is trapped in the wave of worldliness that challenges us today. According to Pope Benedict XVI, consecrated life has become too settled in this world, adapting itself to worldly standards. Its vocation to prophetic openness has been abandoned in favor of greater weight and attention paid to self-preoccupation, self-centeredness and self-preservation (Benedict XVI, 2011).

To regain its credibility in words and deeds, this great institution needs to change -- and there is a path for that change. It must "constantly re-dedicate itself to its mission, [of] filling the world with God's word and in transforming the world by bringing it into loving unity with God"

(Benedict XVI, 2011). So as consecrated life institutes face contemporary injustices systemic in various societal and ecclesiastical structures, including those of consecrated life itself, a close look reveals challenges of understanding religious life precisely as prophetic. Some people like the Capuchin Franciscan Michael Crosby have even bluntly asked, "Can religious be prophetic?"

In this chapter, we reflect on the meaning and implications of characterizing consecrated life as prophetic witnessing. Following the Council document on religious life renewal, *Perfectae Caritatis* (PC), our reflection here is undertaken on the basis of the Scriptures, of a return to the institutes' founding charism and of the signs of the times wherein religious are called to live. Thus, arise the two questions we tackle in this chapter: In what does prophetic witnessing consist for consecrated life institutes particularly in our time? What examples can we derive from our founding charisms and from the Scriptures to which we must always return?

In response to these questions, we consider the evolution of this way of understanding the meaning and demands of prophetic witnessing in the context of today's challenges in society and the Church. Our response will be enriched by recalling the lived experience of the prophets of old; by grasping the challenges of living in Church and society today; by appreciating why it is necessary for religious to live out their calling; and by being open to suggestions on how to realize this today. All this bears traces of my experience as an Augustinian called to this way of life in the contemporary Nigerian-African situation of Church and society.

Understanding Religious Life as Prophetic Witnessing: Evolution of the Characterization in Church Teachings

The firm conviction that religious life is a prophetic witnessing has colored how we see this way of life within the Church. Prophetic witnessing is at the core of consecrated or religious life. The expression 'consecrated for the sake of the kingdom' used in characterizing this way of life sounds with a prophetic nuance. The radical way of following Christ, the public nature of the vows and the subsequent dedication to mission describing this vocation are all indicative of its prophetic significance.

Vita Consecrata reminds us that, in patristic tradition, prophets such as Elijah were offered as models of monastic religious life. In doing so, this tradition takes on prophetic characteristics --- living in God's presence, contemplating him in silence, interceding for the people, boldly announcing God's will, asserting God's sovereignty and defending the poor against the powerful of the world – and predicates them of religious (Cf. 1 Kings 18-19 and *Vita Consecrata*, n. 84).

Members of religious life institutes have often understood themselves as speaking with a prophetic voice in and out of times and seasons, especially giving voice to the voiceless. Yet it was not until post-Vatican II documents that the explicit language of prophecy gained categorical currency.

It surfaced first in the 1978 document on "religious life and human promotion" where religious life was identified as "prophetic and charismatic" in witnessing to alternative ways of living modeling the Trinity and serving as a challenge to society. The 1994 synod of bishops on religious life once more adopted this language, referring to this way of life both directly and indirectly as prophetic witnessing. In direct terms, the synod states "The consecrated life is a prophetic witness to the primacy of God and to the things that do not pass away" (Walter, 1992).

Sometimes such references are made indirectly by inference from the characteristics either of that life's being or its doing. Examples of such indirect referencing include total self-giving, sign of the kingdom to come, witnessing to eschatological reality, love of Christ, intimacy in following and serving him above any other, open to the spirit, call to total self-giving to God, love for Christ the teacher, Lord and bridegroom of the Church who is intimately followed and served above everything and decision to live according to the Spirit.

Vita Consecrata, the outcome document of the synod issued by Pope John Paul II, crystallized this characterization by devoting a major section to prophetic witnessing in the face of great challenge. John Paul II's conception implied that the prophetic character is necessarily and inseparably linked to this way of life both intrinsically and teleologically. "Intrinsically" refers to its nature as a radical way of following Christ; "teleologically" refers to its very mission.

This twofold characterization is reinforced by the *Instrumentum Laboris* of the Synod, which makes the distinction between being and doing, essence and act, as roots of the prophetic character. The document made a further valuable distinction for appreciating the prophetic nature of religious life: "Indeed, its value lies more in 'being' from God and for God than in 'doing' its mission," though it quickly added that no strict dichotomy between being and doing is ever intended.

Of course, whether intended or not, more often than not, a dichotomy can dominate. Thus it is well worth asking whether this statement is a reflection of living examples or the mandating of their essence by the synod. It does seem that John Paul II's position was an attempt to reconcile the seeming dualism insinuated by the *Instrumentum Laboris*.

The position Vatican II developed that the prophetic is a feature of religious life derives from the sign value the Council appropriates to that way of life as well as its renewed focus upon the influence of the Holy Spirit in the life and mission of the Church. In the pre-Vatican II Church, known for power, conformity and control, attention upon consecrated life institutes was directed more to their conformity with prescriptions permitting their existence, canon law codification and adherence to norms proposed and approved by the Holy See.

This was manifest in some actions toward religious life taken at different times in pre-Vatican II history. The Lateran Council of 1215 decreed against the formation of new religious orders. The Council of Lyons in 1274 refused to accept any other new religious rules beyond the already approved monastic ones. The Council of Trent in 1645 attempted to withdraw all religious from the world and confine them into cloister (Walter, 1992).

In contrast, Vatican II made a significant departure from the practices of the past tradition by putting more emphasis on the Spirit, especially as inspiring the founders and foundresses. This departure turned from uniformity and conformity – indices of control – to following the Holy Spirit's guidance. This is consonant with the entire outlook of the Council marked by a greater awareness of the working of the Spirit and the determination to give the space for the Spirit in charismatic aspects of the Christian life.

In *Lumen Gentium*, Chapter VI, #45, the Council acclaims: "In docile response to the promptings of the Holy Spirit the hierarchy accepts rules of religious life which are presented for its approval by outstanding men and women, improves them further and then officially authorizes them. It uses its supervisory and protective authority to ensure that the religious institutes established all over the world for building up the Body of Christ may develop and flourish in accordance with the spirit of their founders."

The Decree on the Renewal of Religious Life, *Perfectae Caritatis*, speaks of respecting the spirit of founders: "It is for the good of the Church that institutes have their own proper character and functions. Therefore, the spirit and aims of each founder should be faithfully accepted and retained, as indeed each institute's sound traditions, for all of these constitute the patrimony of an institute" (PC, n. 2).

There is, however, a noticeable contrast in the Spirit language of *Lumen Gentium* and that of *Perfectae Caritatis*. While the latter identifies the

Spirit with the founders and foundresses, the former submits the Spirit to the hierarchy by which it receives, approves, supervises, and protects the institutes. Supervisory and protective responsibilities of the hierarchy over the institute are matters of concern, especially when contrasted with acknowledging that religious life is of the Spirit in its proper character and function. It is no wonder that religious congregations encounter challenges from the hierarchy as they fulfill their prophetic function. Even cooptation of the institutes can follow. We shall return to this dilemma later.

Later popes continue to proclaim the prophetic nature of religious life. Pope Benedict XVI, addressing religious and seminarians at vespers in the shrine of Austria 2007 said: "You bear witness to a hope which, against every form of hopelessness, silent or spoken, points to the fidelity and the loving concern of God. Hence, you are on the side of those who are crushed by misfortune and cannot break free of their burdens."

Most recently in the opening letter of the year of consecrated life, Pope Francis writes "I am counting on you 'to wake up the world,' since the distinctive sign of consecrated life is prophecy" (Pope Francis, 2014). This is the priority that is needed right now: "to be prophets who witness to how Jesus lived on this earth... a religious must never abandon prophecy." He had earlier raised the same points with the superiors general of religious institutes (men). He not only recognized the prophetic nature of their life but charged them to see that religious life prophecy becomes open to others. "Radical evangelical living" he said, "is not only for religious: it is demanded of everyone. But religious follow the Lord in a special way, in a prophetic way" (Pope Francis, November 29, 2013).

In most statements, the prophetic categorization of religious life is without limiting qualifications, thus implying that unrestricted prophetic witnessing is taken for granted. However, reality reveals some contention. For instance, there is a sense in various hierarchical teachings that religious prophetic witnessing should be directed towards the world rather than towards the Church. Many people would see that agenda as severely limiting and, in a way, a tactic of the hierarchy to shield itself from the critique of religious prophetism. Returning to the Scriptures as suggested by the Council's call for renewal is a valuable counter here as it helps us put in perspective the meaning, scope and implications of prophetic witnessing as exemplified in the life of the prophets of old.

Returning to the Scripture: Examples from the Life of Prophets

Our understanding of the prophets and the scope of their task has consequences for our appropriation of this metaphor to religious life and how it is lived out. There are numerous ways an overview could be carried out. However, considering the specific focus of this work, we will treat only two themes: the source of the authority and the scope of prophetic witnessing. Prophets believed in the world to come yet are grippingly footed in this world. Thus their primary task was to call the people as a community to accountability and responsibility in their relationship with God as lived in their various social milieus. As mediators of the covenant of God with his people, they needed to identify with what was expected of them in that relationship. In doing so, they often interpreted history, the flow of events, in light of relationship with God. They tried to understand how God was at work in particular historical events and how the people should respond to them. That meant that frequently the prophets were very much concerned about the present, specifically how the people should live in the present as God's people. Even when they spoke about the future, it was for the purpose of calling people to be responsible before God in the present time and space.

Social responsiveness was the measure or the underlying theme for the prophets' witnessing. In that light, we recognize a critique for religious of our time whose life does not conform to the theme of bringing true liberation to the people and society. This fault may have its source in neglect of their duties or from mixed messages of their lifestyle. Though very mindful of their personal relationship with God, prophets of old were not known to be overly self-centered. They lived their lives as though their meaning came only from achieving social transformation. For this they went to where they would rather not want to go. They spoke to people they would rather not want to speak with, as did Samuel and Saul, Elijah and the widow of Zaraphat, Nathan, and David, Elisha and Ahab and the prophets of the eighth century.

In other words, they did not consider personal salvation as very private and individualistically-minded affairs but as bonded to social responsiveness. They are saved only by fulfilling the purpose of their commission. Their call was always precipitated by a particular social need arising from the social conditions of the particular historical time. Speaking to God's chosen people, to kings and priests, they were found in the courts, the temple, the palaces, the synagogue and even the marketplace.

With all this as background, the call of Pope Francis to religious to awaken the world by prophetic witnessing should be heard not challenging a narrowly bounded world 'out there' but the world in its entirety embracing all social and ecclesiastical institutions along with their structures and cultures.

Living out this call entails taking risk. The Scriptures tell the stories of many of these risks embraced by the prophets, not because they wanted them, but because it pleased God and they were aware that he is with them. As we read in Habakkuk 3:15-19, "Decay invades my bones, my legs tremble beneath me ... for though the fig tree blossom not nor fruit be on the vines... God, my Lord, is my strength; he makes my feet swift as those of hinds and enables me to go upon the heights." Religious as prophets must be risk takers, bold enough to take up the challenge of ungodliness everywhere it lurks -- in society or in Church. Religious must speak not only in comfort zones or secure times for that is not the style of the prophets. They must not be afraid of being sometimes labeled as radicals or abnormal because of stepping outside the context of what is normal as allotted by orthodoxy or patriotism. The prophets were willing to disregard rules of orthodoxy and to touch the dead as against the normal practice given in Numbers 19.

We see examples of such in Elijah and Elisha, as well as in the deeds of Jesus and his teachings illustrated in the parable of the Good Samaritan. Amos also very courageously and keenly broke "with the tradition on the negative implications of the day of Yahweh, on the significance of election, and on the uniqueness of the Exodus while at the same time using the same Exodus tradition to indict Israel for its muzzling and misleading" (Ralph W Klein, 1991). As Klein writes, Exodus message was a radical break with the social reality of Egypt. When God told Moses, "Let My people go!" the command was a deliberate subversion of a social order where the Pharaoh was thought of as a god and people could be bought and sold. The Holy One said, "I have seen, surely seen, the fate of my people in Egypt and have heard them cry out because of their taskmasters because I am aware of their pain. I have come down to rescue them."

In the manner of prophets it behooves the religious not to be afraid to break with the traditions and practices that are not liberating as God intended them. An example concerns the practice in communites of priests and brothers that still discriminates against brothers from holding some elected office simply because that is how the Church wants it to be. This practice cannot be God's will and is inimical to a vocation called to be the light of God's justice and love in the world.

Another way of describing the prophets is mystic-advocates of social justice. It illustrates the unbroken bond between the deep spirituality of the prophets and their commitment to the social transformation of their times and context. Carroll Stuhlmuller sees an interplay of ecstasy, international politics and social justice in Amos and thus concludes that ecstasy secured the prophet Amos in his quest for social justice (Klein, 70, 71).

Our concern is not with the argument or the justification of this statement, but rather with the importance of prayer and the need for its interconnectedness with activism in the life of a prophet and for prophetic witnessing. This receives desired attention in this work. Isaiah 63 portrays an example of such communal prayer asking for God's immediate intervention without an agent in the affairs of the community. Indeed, the dynamics and phenomenon of the biblical prophecy are interwoven with power politics of the people of Israel. Though sometimes prophets supported leaders, they more often criticized royal administrations and their policies.

Regarding their source of power, they were commissioned by God, and there was no confusion about that among the people. Even though the leadership might sometimes try to contain them, especially when their prophecy became unbearably uncomfortable to them, prophets were never beholden to the leaders. They were God's mouthpiece through whom his oracles were brought to bear on the people and the various aspects of their lives. God would always watch over them though without necessarily shielding them from attacks from those to whose leadership they brought a contrary and critical voice.

Proclaiming him the greatest among all the prophets, religious imitate Jesus and the way he carried out or fulfilled the prophecies and his prophetic role. His examples become our operative model for assessing prophetic witnessing. As mentioned earlier, he recognized his authority as coming from God his father and thus was not afraid of, nor did he yield to, the plots of the existing institutions and structures attempting to thwart him or otherwise control his activities. He made it clear that his will was to do the will of his father, and this could not be compromised. He understood and fearlessly accepted the risk involved in non-compromised witness to his father's love that must be manifested in speaking out and standing against all forms of structural ills prevalent in the societal and ecclesiastical institutions of his time. Again, we recall that he was comfortable breaking any norms or customs as long as they were oppressive and did not conform to his father's will for his people. Of course, it is no gainsaying that he died for this and that his glorification was embedded in this unique witnessing.

In his apostolic letter instituting the year of consecrated life, Pope Francis referred to this fact that prophets derive their origin from God and by this the empowerment that comes with that realization. According to him, religious like prophets "are free, they are beholden to no one but God, and they have no interest other than God. Prophets tend to be on the side of the poor and the powerless, for they know that God himself is on their side" (Pope Francis, 2014). These two aspects of the prophets' experience, their origin from God as bearers of his words and an alternative way of existing given and lived for the community — secular and ecclesiastical — are evident in the spirit and life of the founders and foundresses of the varied religious communities.

Returning to the Founding Spirits of the Various Institutes of Consecrated Life: The Prophetism of the Founders / Foundresses

Irrespective of their different spirits or charisms, women and men at the founding of consecrated life lived out genuinely this prophetic character of their vocation. Like the prophets of old, their guiding question was "what does God want of us now?" This question was not some other world's reality but an incarnation in the social realities in which these founders lived. In most cases their different charisms are shaped by asking and answering this question. They maintained a burning desire for the holiness of God and attentively listened to his word in the varied circumstances of their history. The particular persuasive power of the consistency between their proclamation and their life bore witness to them as prophets. They proclaimed that word with their lives, with their lips and with their actions, speaking against evil and sin, even to the leaders of the Church. Consecrated for the sake of the kingdom, they never stopped exploring new ways to apply the Gospel in history, in expectation of the coming of God's Kingdom. They never shied away from the implications of the questions either. Like the prophets of old and like Christ, not even the threat of death would deter their commitment, so marked was their life by utter self-giving.

For instance, for St Augustine witnessing to the love of the communitarian God was not an abstract mission but one with strong implication for the social reality of his time. This was the focal point of his charism—community. It must speak to the harsh social relations of the cities of the province of North Africa. There lived the *coloni*, free tenants who cultivated the land with their family and paid rent to the landowner. They worked and depended on very stringent terms of employment that deteriorated significantly on an almost annual basis. By the dawn of the fourth century, the imperial government had enacted laws compelling the *coloni* to remain for life on the land they had been granted to work on. In other words, one was not free to protest or even to leave land when the conditions become unbearable. The landowners increased the burdens, and the state increased the taxes to the extent that these *coloni* were no better than slaves. Augustine reacted to such conditions. In one letter, which is itself an act of preferential option for the poor, he indignantly criticized a rich landowner in Hippo named Romulus for allowing two crooked, dishonest estate managers, *actores*, to reduce the poor peasants to destitution by forcing them to pay a rent twice, even though they could hardly pay it once (Mathiesen, 1999).

On occasion, Augustine had met with resistance when he interceded on behalf of these people since bishops were often accused of obstructing the collection of taxes. St. Augustine's reaction to what we may call today "a materialistic and consumerist society" has become a leitmotif among modern searches for midway between waste of the few and hunger of the many prevalent in today's world. In his words, "God made the world for all, but human pride seeks the accumulation of wealth. Although all have the same skin, all do not have the same dress. All were born naked, but now some swim in abundance while others do not have anything."

Augustine hesitated neither from challenging his fellow Church leaders who did not speak out against these evils nor from reminding the Church of the proclivities of becoming oppressive herself. This is why he restrained from identifying the Church with his image of the City of God. For to him, the city of man is present in every human institution, any structure or situation where lust for selfishness could trump opportunities for love. The duty of any Christian participating in these structures is to strive to increase the space for grace of love by limiting the opportunities for lust, for selfishness, the antithesis of community.

Such ideas are behind Augustine's embrace of community as an evangelical charism that bore witness to the oneness of the Trinity. Those to whom this would become their way of life ought to strive to balance the intolerable waste culture and the agonizing scarcity in the world, the oppressive attitudes of the status quo in the structures of various societal and ecclesiastical institutions. In like manner various founders and foundresses of religious life brought their charisms to bear on aspects of the social life of their time in such a manner that we can call them prophetic.

The movement from hermitage to mendicancy in the thirteenth century was a significant event in the history of religious life that brought to light the socio-political implications of the prophetic witnessing of this way of life. It was indeed symbolical and practical. This movement marked the official beginning of many current religious institutes. The entrance of these holy men and women into society replicates in a way the appointment of the prophets and the inauguration of the prophecy of old. In the manner of the inauguration of the prophecy of old, their inspiration to leave their individual cells was precipitated by the needs of the social conditions of the time. The distinctive meaning and goal of their inauguration were such that their way of life was to shed light on the culture and values of society and the Church drifting away toward the emerging and dominant culture of the time. Their fidelity and consistency to their charism replicated that of their founders and the prophets in realizing their own salvation within the intrinsically bonded relationship with the salvation of social reality of their time.

Thus, religious life by their standard was not a private thing but utterly public and other-focused. It might be significant to know what kind of influence their being commissioned by the Church authorities had on their scope and freedom to discharge their duties. As was earlier mentioned here, adherence to prescriptions and norms set by the Church hierarchy was a serious matter in the pre-Vatican II Church just as were the prophets that served in the courts of kings. Some people may argue that this historic event was crucial to the tendency of the Church hierarchy to subsume the institutes of religious life. Unfortunately, we do not have the time to explore this further as we would have wanted.

The call for religious to return to the basis of their founding is not to satisfy any form of nostalgic feeling for the old or to transport the old to the new. Instead it is to draw inspiration from the experiences of the way these giant leaders responded to the needs of their time, thus empowering the way of religious being present to their time now. This entails seeking always the question of what God is saying to us today. Pope Francis captured this understanding succinctly in his apostolic letter to religious on the occasion of the year of consecrated life.

Recounting our history is essential for preserving our identity, for strengthening our unity as a family and our common sense of belonging. More than an exercise in archaeology or the cultivation of mere nostalgia, it calls for following in the footsteps of past generations in order to grasp the high ideals, and the vision and values which inspired them, beginning with the founders and foundresses and the first communities. In this way we come to see how the charism has been lived over the years, the creativity it has sparked, the difficulties it encountered and the concrete ways those difficulties were surmounted.

We may also encounter cases of inconsistency, the result of human weakness and even at times a neglect of some essential aspects of the charism. Yet everything proves instructive and, taken as a whole, acts as a summons to conversion (Pope Francis, 2014).

Signs of the Time Today & Prophetic Witnessing

Today's religious, irrespective of their geographical, generational and cultural differences, are commonly plagued by the socio-economic culture of consumerism in its individualism and geocentricism—using this earth as the only basis of all values. This culture creates and widens the gulf between the rich and those living in poverty, between the oppressors and the oppressed, the advantaged and the disadvantaged. It thrives on the existence and prevalence of systemic injustices and corruption entrenched in the structures of various institutions of the world to which no one is to be held responsible. As a result, God's people and creation are deprived of opportunities to live the fullness of life promised them by their God. The globalization phenomenon – binding the world together in a way like never before so that experiences at one end of the world are shared by the other end – drives and worsens this dominant socio-political and economic culture.

As in Jesus' time, our generation is entrapped in narratives of anxiety and alienation, of slavery and fear created and enforced by dominant cultures of various institutions. His response to this tendency had implications that are imperial and religious, and it wasn't an inauguration of personal sanctity but of alternative reign — an overthrow by and of God's governance. In this light any attempt at imitating him that limits the scope to a narrow individual personal salvation is antichrist and allows for the domestication of the prophetic voice by the dominant culture.

The Gospel imperative and the tradition of the Church point to a reality forbidding us to regard our choice of religious life as merely personal—setting that meets our human needs or a convenient context from which to minister. The Congregation for Institutes of Consecrated Life and Societies of Apostolic Life in its 1994 document, *Fraternal Life in Community*, cited by the OSA Intermediate Chapter (CGI, 2010), articulates this imperative graphically thus:

> *Religious community in its structure, motivations, and distinguishing values, makes publicly visible and continually perceptible the gift of fraternity given by Christ to the whole Church ... 'it is a sign and instrument,' it is a sacrament.*
>
> *... in the various forms it takes, fraternal life in common has always appeared as a radical expression of the common fraternal spirit which unites all Christians. Religious community is a visible manifestation of the communion which is the foundation of the Church and, at the same time, a prophecy of that unity towards which she tends as her final goal... Above all, by profession of the evangelical counsels, which frees one from what might be an obstacle to the fervor of charity, religious are communally a prophetic sign of intimate union with God, who is loved above all things. Furthermore, through the daily experience of communion of life, prayer and apostolate — the essential and distinctive elements of their forms of consecrated life—they are a sign of fraternal fellowship* (Fraternal Life in Community, 1994 in CGI, 2010).

However, in practice the living of this public dynamics is at the threat of a self-centered attitude that focuses on benefit of the individual more that the public good of all, be it sanctity or development or wellbeing. This in itself is an effect of the current cultural paradigm by which everyone and all institutions, including the Church, have become its slave. The religious are then either entrapped or have withdrawn to self-centered living by spiritualizing the way of life that was originally inaugurated for social transformation.

The reality of religious life today remains what began as a new trend since shortly after the Council: decline in the number of members and diminished interest from new people. According to Archbishop Joseph Augustine Di Noia, OP, Secretary of the Congregation of Doctrine of Faith (CDF), speaking at the provincial chapter of Dominicans in the United States of America in June 2010, this is because many religious institutes are still holding tenaciously to the hermeneutics of continuity and not paying attention to what today's world and ministry are looking for – what God is saying to us here and now – but holding on to old ways of thinking and doing things.

At the root of religious life issues today is the subservience of many institutes and individual religious to the cultural optimism of modernity. This exposes them to an internal secularization leading to disenchantment of the religious life and a lack of clear identity of what it means to be religious, according to Paul Graham OSA. The various unproductive responses religious may have taken as mentioned here are indeed signs of the false prophets. The situation urgently demands making religious life more socially responsive by recovering the prophetic character of its nature. This in turn calls for a critical engagement with contemporary society as in the prophetic ways of witnessing in the old days. This would keep us from succumbing to society or from being simply reactionary against it

This is one of the main expectations of Pope Francis in giving us the gift of the year of the consecrated life. In his words,

> *I am counting on you 'to wake up the world', since the distinctive sign of consecrated life is prophecy. This is the priority that is needed right now: 'to be prophets who witness to how Jesus lived on this earth ... a religious must never abandon prophecy.' Prophets receive from God the ability to scrutinize the times in which they live and to interpret events: they are like sentinels who keep watch in the night and sense the coming of the dawn (Cf. Is 21:11-12). They are able to discern and denounce the evil of sin and injustice ... So I trust that,*

> *rather than living in some utopia, you will find ways to create 'alternate spaces,' where the Gospel approach of self-giving, fraternity, embracing differences, and love of one another can thrive* (Pope Francis, 2014).

We ought to assert our difference from the secularity of modernity not by withdrawing or by being strange. Our life must once again offer hope and alternatives both to those who seek to join us and to many others who recoil from the world's emptiness and non-fulfillment.

Challenges To Living Out the Prophetic Witnessing in the Church & Society: Issues of Cooperation & Domestication

Religious life has to endure a number of challenges in fulfilling its prophetic implications. Michael Crosby has classified these various challenges into internal and external. Internal consists of those arising from within the institution itself, irrespective of pressures from outside. Inversely, the external come from without, including the Church and society (Crosby, 2004).

Two most visible of the internal challenges are the struggle between logic of maintenance and logic of mission, and also the dynamics and implications of institutionalizing a movement. Indeed, they may be seen together, as either one leads to the other. By its very nature, the religious way of life belongs to the category of movements called into existence to challenge the status quo of social living. In most cases, these movements end up within the trapping of what Max Weber refers to as routinization or institutionalization. The consequence of this is the struggle between the logic of maintenance and logic of mission, the struggle to stay alive and the struggle to fulfill the original aim of the institution.

Michael Crosby borrowed Weber's sociological concept of routinization and applied it to the erosion of the prophetic character of religious life.

By routinization, Weber refers to how the charism of movements representing alternative values that challenge the values of the dominant culture become so co-opted and mechanized that they lose their liberative power and influence. This happens when the values and ideals of these movements coincide with viable norms and traditions. In this situation, the values and ideals move further away from the lived reality of the members and the spirit of the founder as institutional norms and traditions become more important. In this case the life pattern becomes mechanical and not charismatic. This occurred at the founding of religious life itself. As the JESUS movement became routinized, turning Christianity into Christendom, living Gospel values and being prophetic became mechanized. The Church followed the norms of the political and cultural system making the Church assume the life of a social institution with all the bureaucracy replacing the communal spirit (Crosby, 2004). As people became more and more alienated and hunger for the original spirit increased, religious life was formed as in the example of Augustine and his early community — as he called his brethren to model their lives on the first Christian community.

Similarly, as most of these religious groups experienced their own phases of routinization, different versions of them emerged from the same feelings of alienation and hunger for the original experience. We have different brands of Augustinians, as the charism gave way to adherence to norms.

Once institutionalized or routinized, movements get caught up in the struggle for existence. This is not unique to the religious life but rather is common to every human institution. It is the story of Christianity itself, as evident in its historical shift from the Jesus movement to the institutionalized faith. This shortcoming is well expressed by Gregory Baum's analysis of the unresolved struggles in human institutions between the *logic of maintenance* and *logic of mission* — between a desperate desire to protect oneself and the burden of doing what it was founded to do — and how the former often takes precedence over the latter.

One of the first side effects of this tendency is the loss of power to effect structural change, for indeed it is movements and not institutions that mobilize structural change. Also associated with this situation is a loss of solidarity among groups for unhealthy competition begins to take place. Each group tries to outwit the other, capitalizing on each other's misfortunes so as to establish cheap popularity and favor with authority -- all in an attempt to survive. Then each group flies the flags of their differences more than of their common ground for the advancement of Gospel values demanded by their common profession of evangelical vows.

Although the two logics should harmoniously work together, for both institutional survival and institutional goal attainment are worthy goals, yet all too often unjustified precedence is granted to maintenance. Good programs are frequently sacrificed to protect the institution, as institutional status is obsessively chosen over the very purpose for which the institution was established in the first place. The institutes of religious life, like any institution, can be overwhelmed by exaggerated attention to maintenance logic. Again, we recall Pope Benedict XVI's remark cited at the introduction to this work that "In the concrete history of the Church, however, a contrary tendency is also manifested ... She gives greater weight to organisation and institutionalisation than to her vocation to openness."

For the sake of their dignity, or better still for fear of losing self-image and recognition in the sight of the Church hierarchy, religious institutes have sometimes passed over an action that would benefit the poor or the marginalized. They conveniently avoided any issue that seemed controversial. So, the primary question was not what God asked of us in that particular situation, but rather how did this make us look in the sight of Church leadership. The same attitude is projected in relationships with secular authorities. For fear of falling out of favor with state authorities, religious communities have, like other parts of the Church, become "too settled in this world, adapting to worldly standards, conforming to worldly values and seeking self-sufficiency." These consequences of choosing institutional maintenance over mission betray the prophetic character of incarnational solidarity, which demands *being-with* even in the face of risk.

The external challenges that religious institutes face regarding authentic witnessing can be classified into domination and cooptation. There are visible attitudes in the Church that seek to clip the wings and seal the voices of prophets, turning them into conformists instead of the revolutionaries intended by their divine origin. In the Church, while on one hand the source of prophetic character of the religious institutes is linked to divine origin, on the other hand the hierarchical part of the Church arrogates to itself the sole determination of authenticity and exercise of such a role by which it seeks to control the religious.

In his work "Max Weber, Charisma and Biblical Prophecy," Ronald E, Clements writes that "The prophet's claim to be able to speak directly on behalf of God placed him outside the more traditional and rational forms of authority of ongoing religious institutions. He felt no compulsion to submit to them, and did not need to appeal to them for his legitimacy" (Ronald E. Clements, 1997). We see this issue manifested in the various individual cases and processes perpetuated by the Congregation for Institutes of Consecrated Life and Societies of Apostolic Life (CICLSAL) that still deny some members of the religious congregations the autonomy that would enhance their prophetic living. This is where the thirteenth century event of commission of religious institutes by the Vatican could be termed problematic, as it may, and many times does, impede their autonomy and freedom to discharge their duties.

Some problematic examples are the refusal for religious brothers to be leaders over priests in groups of brothers and priests. Also, we may cite the now settled case between the Congregation and the Leadership Conference of Women Religious (LCWR). Moreover, many of these religious groups for the fear of losing their face before the Vatican Curia have failed to take active protestation of these acts of the CICLSAL demanded of them as prophetic communities. It is choosing self over others for priests in such communities to keep quiet and play by the rule of CICLSAL and deprive their brothers the opportunity to exercise their God given rights. As we saw in the case of the prophets, they were not afraid to be termed controversial or unpatriotic as long as their decision to stand up against the status quo is for the will of God to prevail. And we know that his will is for the freedom and dignity of all.

Apart from the issues of cooptation, lifestyle poses another challenge for religious life to live out its prophetic witnessing. Imbibing the prevalent dominant consumerism and individualistic cultures opens up some contradictions in the lives of religious and their institutes. Because of these contradictions, religious lack the moral credibility and authority to speak out in the face of social evil. Contemporary religious are plagued by cravings and an insatiable hunger for material things and favor which only the rich and influential people in leadership in either Church or society can satisfy. They may become vulnerable to manipulation by the oppressive authority in society.

Equally the temptation to value human beings only by what they can produce, into which some religious institutes fall, are injurious to those charged with presenting an alternative paradigm of living based on the love of God. Sometimes too institutes of religious life battle with elements of nepotism, tribalism, embezzlement and scandalous displays of affluence. There are also elements of sexism, paternalism, maternalism, class distinction, lack of accountability and transparency, subordination, dominance, accumulation and self-interest. Worse still, their workers may not always receive good remuneration, welfare, medical care, gratuity or provision for their retirement while the leaders may live lavishly in extravagance.

Plagued by all this contradiction, religious cannot afford to challenge any unjust structure without being reminded that it is only too tempting to be blind to the plank in your eye before seeing the speck in your neighbor's eye (Mt 7:3-5; Lk 6:41-42). There is truth in believing that in order to hide their sins, these prophets take up the rational and speculative option in response to the problems of the time. Thus, they fail to emphasize the biblical insistence on the Divine liberation of the oppressed as integral to the evangelical nature of religious life.

This reality warrants that religious take seriously the occasion of the year of consecrated life to engage in a sincere critical reconsideration of the nature and manner of their prophetic witnessing. This would be necessary and possible to the extent that they understand their vocation in terms of, or as incorporating, prophetic imagination and what it implies within and outside the Church. In fact, many religious do not conceive their life as including this aspect of challenging Church structure. Accordingly. they claim they are not in the Church to change it. It is necessary that discussions such as the one undertaken in this chapter begin to flourish among religious groups. Religious can thus be frequently reminded of their prophetic role, constantly urged to question the value of their presence and to ask what is included or not included in their vocation.

These discussions on fruitful prophetic witnessing as part of their task of renewal within the Church called for by Vatican II must include penetrating questions. What opportunities are there to return in fidelity to the revolutionary spirits of our respective founders if the hierarchy protects itself from all forms of critiquing by co-opting and domesticating religious life? How do we embark on dismantling the routinization and institutionalization of the alternative communities formed and/or envisioned by our founders in the way that we may once again fulfill the dual tasks of listening to and questioning the systemic injustices inherent in the institutional structures of Church and society? What does the Church expect from the call for renewal? Is she ready to embrace the result of a genuine return and renewal? Is she willing to allow the impact of religious and their institutes being truly prophetic?

Looking at the Future:
The Case of Alternative Witnessing
– Various Proposals

Responding to the commitment to renewal of religious life by religious institutes in their individual members and organizations and viewing the outcome thus far, Joan Chittister, a Benedictine Sister of Erie, Pennsylvania, concludes that we are still far from the Promised Land. In her opinion,

> *We did well what was required of us then. We have freed religious to be individuals, to be adults. We have changed schedules and living environments to make the leap from an agricultural and parochial period to an industrialized and urban world. We have made cosmetic changes in clothing and governance structures. We have recognized the wisdom of the Spirit in us and among us. But it is not enough. There are new questions to be dealt with now. These questions have come out of the questions before them, true, but they will undoubtedly hold the key to the future. I grapple with them every day. The new questions, I believe, deal with the very existence of religious life, its relationship to the church, its present character, its purpose, its spirituality and its energy* (Chittister, 1994).

Using the exodus experience allegory, she identifies the stages and focus of the renewal in two spheres, namely the internal and external. While I would agree with her that we have done most of what is expected of us in the internal, yet I believe that we need more reeducation of members and institutes on the intrinsic public character of our way of life and also the experiences of subsuming the prophetic voice of the religious way of life.

Faced with the situation of religious not living up to their prophetic responsibilities, people like Michael Crosby suggest the need to refound instead of merely renew religious communities. Their argument is based on the prophetic communities formed by the Old Testament prophets and Walter Brueggemann's concept of alternative imagination that lives the alternative witnessing. Crosby and his group believe that for religious to live up to the demands of their prophetic role there needs to be a select group among the religious institutes that would live this alternative witnessing. They do not see hope in achieving such conversion by the entire system.

I take an alternative approach, one that begins with bringing the individual religious groups and institutes to understand the place where they are called to witness — society and Church and not just with individuals. Thus, we will be well placed to take up the prophetic call. This is why I believe that Pope Francis' call to religious to wake up the world should start with waking up the religious first. For no one deep in slumber can consciously wake up another.

In the light of today's realities, in order to evangelize prophetically the dominant cultures in all ramifications and wherever they exist, religious institutes must formulate a creative re-articulation of the visions of their pasts. But their re-articulation must not simply repeat their age-old truths in updated language, symbols, and practices but rather dynamically engage the hopes, dreams, fears and preoccupations of the present and coming age. Fresh languages, symbols, and practices must be devised. This was at the founding and focus of most of these institutes especially in their thirteenth century existence (Mary Johnson et al, 2014).

In view of the diversity of the challenges of different parts of the world, some serious level of contextuality is necessary. The social location of each individual religious group plays an important and determining factor in the ways of realizing this prophetic witnessing. According to Sandra Schneiders, IHM, "every form of religious life is called to be prophetic in a situation that cannot be generalized to or deduced from some archetypal and abstract context" (Sandra Schneiders, 2014). For instance, viewed from a Nigerian African context, the boldness of prophetic witnessing modeled on Christ is to proclaim the good news with "the great and relentless enemy of silence." That would imply refusing to be subsumed by the lure to patriotism and loyalty to all authorities social or ecclesiastical when they are no longer at the service of the good news. Of course, it means setting ourselves up for the risks that this would bring.

The confusion surrounding the individualizations of the mission of Christ that supports the exclusion of the transformation of social and ecclesiastical structures stems from the tendency to interpret Christ's salvific acts solely in terms of passion-death, resurrection, and Pentecostal events. In this view, the Christian life as imitation of Christ is spiritualized and seen from the narrow individual personal salvific perspective. Such a tendency makes possible the domestication of prophetic voice. The evangelical nature of religious life implies that it is cooperative and beatitudinal, salt to the earth and light to the world. Achieving or living for this is the mark of religious life fulfillment. However, today, the source and kind of happiness many religious identify with are mostly individualistic and therapeutic, the very antithesis of prophetic witnessing. Religious institutes and individuals are so safety- and self-minded that few want to embrace suffering like the prophets and to endure being misunderstood and persecuted in ways inherent in our calling as we read in Mt 5:11-16.

Prophetism is the source of our moral credibility, just as it was for past prophets. The issue however, as people like Crosby would agree, is whether as religious we are ready today to desist from a lifestyle that directly or indirectly provides support to the dominant culture and adopt one that engages actively in compassionate criticism of society and Church. To ask and answer this question would be a proof of the renewal we are called to embark on. The indices for measuring success in this regard include how well we demonstrate freedom from a prevalent culture of privatism, individualism, and personal religion by which we base the assessment of religious life solely on individual development seen in terms of fulfilling personal self-interest of the individual or institute. It also includes thinking less of our individual and institutional security that lures us to territories and temples of power, possession and prestige. No longer will religious boast of how many powerful persons they know and are connected with. Our habits and identity should no longer be exploited for privilege. Rather they would regain their original intention as protest against the values of dominant culture and uncompromising commitment to service and death to self.

Again, citing the example of my religious institute both in general and in particular instances, our challenge in this task of renewal would be genuinely to investigate how the value of community at the core of our heritage and vocation serves as prophetic witnessing today. Included in this investigation is how this way of life speaks to and challenges the dominant culture of today in all territories and temples, empires and cathedrals so that it can be truly called prophetic. How could we show that this way of life remains faithful to the basic idea of Augustine and not co-opted and domesticated by the same culture? We Augustinians often seek the answer to this set of questions in a community versus empire model in which we contrast the relational values of friendship, solidarity, collaboration, and selflessness (characteristics of community) with the impersonal traits of empire such as domination, accumulation, and self-centeredness.

The difference in attitude resulting from a sincere commitment to renewal means that these contrasts between community and empire are no longer posited in terms restricted to 'them and us.' Instead, we apply also to our own system the same critique we subject others to. In this case, we humbly research elements of our living that are incongruous to the community value, name them for what they are and seek processes of redressing them. Such symbolic acts of communal ownership and use of things such as cars, bank accounts, wages etc. have been lost to the comfort and convenience of the individuals. The realism proposed in support of these shifts cannot blind us to the disservice they render to the core values of our way of life as alternative paradigm to the dominant culture of our time. They are feeding the insatiability that feeds the individualism and selfishness of modern consumerism and materialism.

Recovering prophetic witnessing demands also that religious today walk the talk in terms of being advocates for justice. They must be people, as individuals and institutions, known for standing for and standing up for something. We may stand for justice, equality, freedom and common good but may never stand up for their victims when called upon by situations. This has been the story of many religious groups within our institutions, both of Church and of society. The few examples we have explored here result from domestication, from submission to the dominant culture and entrapment by the grip of maintenance logic.

The social context of prophetic witnessing has implications for understanding the meaning and role of religious life and vows. Within this hermeneutic, religious institutes are seen no longer as existing for the service of a few who are eager to make it into heaven but rather as being responsible for all people around the world. This is what we refer to in terms of incarnational solidarity, the realization of oneself in the act of living for the other, in the way that 'I' is not the central focus but 'You,' 'the Other.'

The demand for this service is borderless just as is the Gospel imperative putting all into discipleship to the ends of the earth. Thus, sisterhood and brotherhood transcend beyond the confines of individual religious groups and institutes to assume universal sisterhood and brotherhood. In that way people outside these groups who call them sisters or brothers can relate with them because they see these religious becoming agents of change for their good. This too has begun to impact how these groups understand the scope and meaning of their religious vows. The theology and meaning of the religious vows would become clearer as many would begin to see their evangelical nature removing them from individualistic views and from a focus on individual member sanctity. *Lumen Gentium* prepared for this new understanding with its shift in language of consecrated life from "state of perfection" to "living the Gospel evangelical counsels." By expansion it meant that religious life and vows are no longer seen in terms of ascetical practices but rather of privileged witnessing with concrete signs to critique specific forms of social sin. They are indeed evangelical in as much as they are a "prophetic sign rather than a means of escaping historical reality as pointers to some heavenly future."

Being evangelical, these vows are by nature public witnessing to the love of God for creation made manifest in the lives and service of those who respond to the invitation of becoming religious. Thus, solidarity with the poor and commitment to social justice would be necessary and concrete measures of the realization of this renewal, as is in the case of the prophets of the old and of Jesus. "The disciples of John came to ask Jesus at their master's behest, are you the messiah or shall we look for another. Jesus, pointing to his works said to them go tell John what you have seen and heard, the blind see, the deaf hear, and dumb speak …" This solidarity will necessarily involve being converted by marginalized people, critiquing values and structures, societal or ecclesiastical, calling for systemic change at the roots of poverty, of relationships and of authority issues.

Simplicity of life becomes a prophetic witness that challenges the excesses of greed supporting the social injustices of our time and promotes detachment from undue attention to security and comfort. Our mission cannot be accomplished by and with the power and security which comes from money or social position (Gustavo Gutierrez, 1997). On the contrary, today's Church, including the religious institutes as we remarked in the introduction, is so conscious of precautions and security that it settles in and enjoys the privileges that come from the mission of evangelization. Poverty for instance, as Joan Burke narrates in her chapter of this work, has broadened, or rather shifted, today from having less to "so that all may have enough." This implies that we try both to model an alternative way of living and to restructure our world so that all may indeed have enough.

Opinions may vary as to how to realize this new renewal. People like Michael Crosby would suggest the need for a new brand of community emerging from these groups just as there were various past stages of alienation and hunger for a return to the original. I may differ from this opinion because it suggests that just a few individual religious are needed for the renewal to be achieved; it is a responsibility of the few and not the whole. Nor is there immunity against these few becoming routinized as happened in past experiences.

While I agree that the conscientization would begin from and with a few within all the different groups, my position is that the whole group is needed to realize this renewal. In other words, it is the whole of different institutes that make up this way of life that are called to renewal so that the solution may not lie at all in forming new groups. The first step in this direction might be to make these institutes see value in the admonitions of Pope Francis that we would rather see a bruised Church working to achieve its goals than one suffocating from its self-enclosure by reason of being contaminated.

As with the prophets of old, it would take those leading this return to work within their various groups insistently weathering all the storms of criticism and oppression to see that their various groups take the needed steps to turn around. Multiplication has become a hindrance to progress in this direction. Formation of new groups does not guarantee the reformation of the parent body. Instead it increases the tension arising from the struggle for survival and further departure from the mission. Instead of a narrow application to alternative communities emerging from existing groups, Walter Brueggemann's prophetic community is a charter expected of and defining the entire way of life when a group adheres to the call for renewal. They should not wait for the hierarchy of the Church to lead them on this or for guidelines to achieve it. It is entirely possible that now is the occasion to embark on true self-searching for recovering or reinventing the space for a prophetic witness.

Conclusion

Vatican II was a graced moment then as it is now. The call for renewal of religious life was in no little way one of its gifts to the Church and the world. For in this call individual religious and various institutes of consecrated life find the strength to face current challenges and gain experiences from the story of their histories. Reacting to the 1994 synod of bishops on religious life at the celebration of twenty-five years of Vatican II, Joan Chittister, likening the project of religious renewal to the Israelite exodus journey from bondage to liberation, prophesied that it would take forty years to realize. We are now fifty years since the Council and the project is far from being realized (Chittister, 1994). In a very significant way this occasion of the fiftieth anniversary of the promulgation of the decree on religious renewal is both symbolic and empowering in this search to find its place in the world in which prophetic witnessing remains its only way of being.

Abdicating their prophetic role is disastrous all around, affecting the world and religious institutes in varying degrees. As Isaiah captures it, the world is in disaster as people perish for lack of prophets. So also do these institutes of religious life perish, and the prophets suffer the risk of their own demise for lack of being witnesses. The drastic reduction in numbers of religious today and the disinterestedness of today's generation in religious life are not to be blamed on the influence of modernity without considering the emptiness that this way of life presents today. What religious did before can now be done by others and may be done well. The privileges religious enjoyed before are far gone. People who seek other values in this way of life and cannot see them care little about joining.

One of the inspirations the Council offers us regarding this renewal is the hope that, even though we have not gotten there yet, our commitment to getting there is sufficient. What is asked of us is not success but commitment to faithfulness (*Vita Consecrata*, 63). Thus, the success or fruitfulness is in the process and not in the results; it is in the act of mutual self-gift and not in perfection. The call for perfection is not to individual achieved perfection but in continuous striving for perfection which is conscious of the possibility of falling. For religious are also called to be mirrors to the Church, enabling her to see her shortcomings

But the value of religious life is lost today as long as the institution and its members remain entrapped in the dominant culture. The renowned Canadian theologian and former nun, Mary Jo Leddy, warns, "it would be an illusion for us to think that we can keep treading water forever. Soon we will either go with the flow of the cultural current or we will get tired and start to sink" (Leddy, 1990). We are sinking already as is manifest in all the ways religious are infected by individualism and are fed and sustained in religious communities that compromise their witness as counterculture to society.

These manifestations are visible among religious in profession seeking, work, use of things, exercise of authority and decision making. All that individualism brings about is a dichotomy between theory and practice and between cultural mores and personal morality. We may define ourselves as prophetic and of signs of an alternative life and of the coming kingdom, but our lips are sealed, and our hands tied, so that we do not protest or fight the dominant culture where it oppresses.

Those we are called to serve, those that are marginalized in society by political, economic, and cultural institutions or victimized by the Church's own structures feel bitterly such a loss of value. These marginalized people wander in hunger for authentic prophetic voices to bring them the good news, but their moral leaders witness to nothing but arrogance and abuse of power.

The hope that inspires renewal is recognition of the yearning among individuals and religious groups to move beyond the present realities.

We noted that prophetic witnessing is not a responsibility of a few but rather belongs to the entirety of religious life in all its dynamics. Also, we observed that for it to be effective, it must be responsive to particular situations without any hard and fast rule expected to apply in all situations for that would only make this way of life redundant. Each group, each context, each age is called and expected to respond prophetically as it so fits. However, in the globalization age, without compromise or contextualization, religious life in all circumstances is called to respond to this common phenomenon so as to not slip into a globalization of indifference – according to Pope Francis' characterization of this era.

PART V

LONG RANGE VIEWS & VARIED PERSPECTIVES FROM EXPERIENCE

9

NEW CONSECRATED LIFE: STILL IN THE MAKING

Guillermo Campuzano, CM

Being prophetic does not mean knowing what the future holds,
but rather a willingness to walk into the unknown
knowing that God is walking with us.

Introduction

Each generation is responsible for grasping and being aware of the reality of the world in which they live. Each individual and social group has a moment in life to understand that what they have learned is just a hint for them to begin their journey to freedom. Our founders and foundresses not only grasped the meaning of their time individually, but also helped the people of their generations to face with honesty and creativity the main challenges of their times. They were not afraid to go through their own routes of liberation.

The consecrated life of today cannot continue to live from the stoned dogmatism that gave security to believers of another era – modernism. Today we are on the move, although we have no certainty yet of where we are going, just as Abraham and Sarah when they were called by

God (Heb 11:8). We are walking as nomads following the rhythm of a humanity that continues to look for its destination.

In the past fifty years we have witnessed a profound renovation in consecrated life. This renovation has followed, in many respects, the pace of the transformation of the Church in an always-changing time. From a faithful memory of the way we already walked, we need to continue this process of rereading and deeply renewing our congregations, so we can respond to the new challenges and the cries of reality. We "have not only a glorious history to remember and to recount, but also a great history still to be accomplished! Look to the future, where the Spirit is sending you in order to do even greater things."[1]

Consecrated life exists to show new ways to be a passionate prophetic presence, to offer new means and resources, to respond promptly and boldly to the old and the new eco-human needs as recommended by Pope Francis in many of his communications. In his apostolic letter for the Year of Consecrated Life, Pope Francis told all those who were committed to consecrated life: "So I trust that, rather than living in some utopia, you will find ways to create 'alternate spaces,' where the Gospel approach of self-giving, fraternity, embracing differences, and love of one another can thrive."[2]

Laudato Si',[3] Francis' encyclical on our common home, presents to us the common house of creation as one of those "alternate spaces" where we must review, deepen and testify that the logic of self-giving and fraternity are for us fundamental elements of our way of consecrated life in Century XXI.

---

[1] Pope John Paul II, Post-Synodal Apostolic Exhortation *Vita Consecrata* (Boston: Pauline Books and Media, 1996), 110.

[2] Pope Francis, Apostolic Letter to *All Consecrated People on the Occasion of the Year of Consecrated Life*, II, 2.

[3] Pope Francis, *Laudato Si'* Encyclical "On the Care of Our Common Home" (Boston: Pauline Books and Media, 2015).

It is now commonplace to think that consecrated life is going through times of crisis: declining vocations, aging, departures, overload, economic problems, very small communities, debilitation of spiritual and community life, compulsive activism, double life etc. Facing these challenges, some changes have been initiated: union of provinces, government restructuring, intensification of vocation outreach, priority tasks to find new resources, working hand-in-hand with lay people in our mission etc.

This crisis has led some Church sectors to state that consecrated life has passed and that it is time for the lay ecclesial movements. Others attribute most of these problems to the defective personal and communal testimony of many consecrated people. I recognize how problematic our double standards are, but I do not think we are worse than the generations that preceded us. Blaming Vatican II for the current crisis, as some have, is not fair either.

The problem is more complex and has a socio-historical dimension that cannot be ignored. We live in a moment of epochal change, a real paradigmatic cataclysm that globally affects cultures, politics, economics, science, human relations, the religious sensibility and our ecological environment. Everything has moved from its traditional center. Everything has been questioned, and criticized. This situation affects the Church as a whole and specifically consecrated life. We are facing a crisis of civilization that, like all crises, can mean chaos and death but also the birth of a new life (*kairos*). This is a time in which we can detect with more clarity the authenticity of our life as a whole.

We have to discern this change as a sign of the times, this is also our mission, and a time to ask ourselves what the Spirit is telling us and where it is leading us. Otherwise, we can become prophets of doom, continually longing for a past that probably will never return. This is really not a passing crisis like others before; this is a new situation that probably will remain this way for a long time. As Pope Francis reminds us,

> *At times, like Elijah and Jonah, you may feel the temptation to flee, to abandon the task of being a prophet because it is too demanding, wearisome or apparently fruitless. But prophets know that they are never alone. As he did with Jeremiah, so God encourages us: 'Be not afraid of them, for I am with you to deliver you' (Jeremiah 1:8).*[4]

We have to recognize that there have been and continue to be many profound transformation efforts in consecrated life motivated by different intentions. Some, for example, are motivated by a natural instinct for institutional survival. This type of response to the crisis has led to processes sometimes precipitated, mechanical, and even traumatizing. And in other cases, we have seen transformational processes more missionary, humanizing, programmatic, and systemic.

The new consecrated life cannot simply be a fashionable exercise, nor can it be found in the newness that this world offers. We are not just looking for ways to be attuned with what is useful, functional, productive, and efficient in our world. Our newness comes from the eternal freshness of the Gospel proposals. All throughout the history of consecrated life we can identify eloquent signs of how to live and actualize our consecration at different historic moments. Consecrated life was always a prophetic/meaningful presence in the heart of the Church and humanity. In many ways this form of life incarnates the yearnings of a new humanity in a new world ... These are also the desires and the action of the Spirit, who "makes all things new" (Revelation 21:5).

If we look attentively at the long journey of consecrated life throughout history, we can find the main elements of a "faithful creativity" — newness with roots, sense, and connection -- that *Perfectae Caritatis* (18) proposed to us all. Let us explore some of these elements.

---

[4] Apostolic Letter of Pope Francis, *To all Consecrated People on the Occasion of the Year of Consecrated Life*, II, 2.

Theology of Newness in Consecrated Life

See, I am doing a new thing! Now it springs up; do you not perceive it?
I am making a way in the wilderness and streams in the wasteland.
(Isaiah 43:19).

Theological reflection has always been one of the lungs of breathing for consecrated life. The theology of newness in consecrated life is a "contextual theology." Our theology is a simple reflection of our faith with beginnings in the anguish and the hopes of the poor and those excluded from our society. This was the reflection that all our founders and foundresses went through when they accepted the gifts of the Spirit in their lives. The context that consecrated life's theology finds itself in today is a passing world and a changing reality. This theological reflection has also been a well where that life constantly finds energy and inspiration for its own rebirth.

The newness of consecrated life comes from the Spirit that never ceases to inspire new charisms to fertilize realities that clamor for justice. What we are permanently seeking is our authenticity, that is, to enter into the logic of Jesus of Nazareth and his cause: "the Reign of God, the only thing that is absolute."[5] "From the beginnings of monasticism to the 'new communities' of our own time, every form of consecrated life has been born of the Spirit's call to follow Jesus as the Gospel teaches" (Cf. *Perfectae Caritatis,* 2). "For the various founders and foundresses, the Gospel was the absolute rule ...."[6]

Our newness follows the criteria of the Reign of God, and so it happens in what is hidden, imperceptible, in the silence, from what is as small as the mustard seed (Mt 13:31-32). Consecrated life is willing to withdraw from an "empty-of-God" religious appearance to a real entrance

---

[5] Pope Paul VI, Apostolic Exhortation *Evangelii Nuntiandi,* 8.

[6] Pope Francis, Apostolic Letter *To all Consecrated People on the Occasion of the Year of Consecrated Life,* I, 2.

into an honest search for God to live our love and commitment with the Kin-dom with "creative fidelity."

According to G. Smith, the God of the Bible is the God of the new, of the re-starts and the new beginnings. The weekly structure – seven days of creation – points to this reality. The message of the New Testament is based largely on the concepts of newness and renewal. "Nearly three dozen New Testament passages discuss 'new' things - new wine, new commandment, new creation, new song and the New Jerusalem, to name a few." [7]

Newness images are used by all the authors of the New Testament with just a couple of exceptions. Not only does the biblical concept of newness provide a useful paradigm for the interpretation of the theology of the New Testament, but it can also give us a useful key to discern the journey of consecrated life nowadays.

But the word of God is more than a written document – the Bible. Reality is the place where God wants to meet humanity, the Church and consecrated life! God comes to meet humanity through reality; this is the main way in which God communicates to us. Hence, the creativity in God's experience, as described in Scripture, is based upon God's relationship with reality.

The book of Exodus, the book of liberation, describes the first experience that the people of the Scripture had of God. Even before they understood that God was creator of the universe, they knew a God that was committed to transforming the oppressive reality of God's people:

> *The LORD said, "I have indeed seen the misery of my people in Egypt. I have heard them crying out because of their slave drivers, and I am concerned about their suffering. So I have come down to rescue them from the hand of the Egyptians and to bring them up out of that land*

---

[7] Gregory A. Smith, "Preaching: A Ministry of Newness" (2000). *Faculty Publications and Presentations,* Paper 70. *http://digitalcommons.liberty.edu/lib_fac_pubs/70.*

into a good and spacious land, a land flowing with milk and honey ... And now the cry of the Israelites has reached me, and I have seen the way the Egyptians are oppressing them. So now, go. I am sending you to Pharaoh to bring my people the Israelites out of Egypt" (Exodus 3:7-10).

When consecrated life perceives that its creativity is exhausted, we need to ask this question: what's happening to our relationship with reality?

At all times, that life has the responsibility of reading the signs of history and to interpret them prophetically in the light of the Gospel as an essential dimension of her mission! The reading of the signs of history is even more urgent today due to our anthropological, theological and cosmological uncertainty: we are not certain of how to be human beings in a technological era; we don't know who or what God is in a time of a new global/cosmic spirituality; or even worse, some still naively believe that our planet will survive our continuous aggressions.

If we take seriously reality as the main source of our newness, we will be able to identify new scenarios and emerging subjects of our mission as central themes for a new consecrated life. God is calling us from a possible future—new and germinal—through a new reality. This call from a possible future is what we call Utopia!

Consecrated life has understood this dynamic of theological and pastoral newness that is clearly encompassed in these two concepts: new scenarios and emerging subjects. These two concepts are more than an academic fad. They indeed constitute a theological category for the being and action of that life. If consecrated life engages in an active and permanent discernment of the new scenarios and the emerging subjects of its mission, this can become a source of constant renewal in a world that never stops changing. To understand the cries of life, and to listen without fear to the voice of the Divine *Ruah*[8] through these cries, are both essential dimensions of the identity and mission of consecrated life. This is the way in which we can really understand the meaning of this permanent inventiveness to where the Divine *Ruah* continually pushes us tenderly. The new life of consecration will happen only if we assume, with determination, the challenges of contemporary history and make of this history a vital context of transformation and redefinition.

What if the Church, and in it consecrated life, understood that the huge challenges of today are signs that "we are living one of the most dramatic moments of transformation of human history, a time when we still have a chance to choose our future?" [9] But what are some of those new scenarios and emerging subjects where that life can find principles and ways of newness?

Let us mention some: social exclusion, degradation and natural disasters, forced labor and new forms of human slavery, human trafficking, corruption and impunity, the circle of drug and gun trafficking, injustice and inequality, migration, the crisis of refugees due to war and natural disasters, the new sensitivity for human and sustainable development, social movements and youth, digital culture and social networks, the wisdom of the indigenous peoples, the voice of women and new generations, democratic participation, popular religion in the global South and the growing secularism in the global North, new forms of consecrated life, direct participation of lay people in conse-

---

[8] In the Old Testament, the Hebrew word for "spirit" is *ruah*. It appears 389 times in the Old Testament. Its varied use almost defies analysis, but some emphases are discernible. It is used more often of God (136 times) than of persons or animals (129 times). Its basic meaning is wind (113 times).

[9] Cf. United Nations Charter: The Charter of the United Nations was signed on 26 June 1945 in San Francisco at the conclusion of the United Nations Conference on International Organization and came into force on 24 October 1945. The Statute of the International Court of Justice is an integral part of the Charter.

crated life, presence of consecrated life in public forums like the United Nations etc.

A Consecrated Life That Listens & Responds to the Cries of Humanity & Mother Earth

We are well aware, as the American Poet, Jungian psychoanalyst, and post-trauma recovery specialist, Clarissa Pinkola Estés, has stated,

> *Ours is not the task of fixing the entire world all at once, but of stretching out to mend the part of the world that is within our reach. Any small, calm thing that one soul can do to help another soul, to assist some portion of the poor suffering world, will help immensely ... It is not given to us to know which acts or by whom, will cause the critical mass to tip toward an enduring good. What is needed for dramatic change is an accumulation of acts, adding, adding to, adding more ... We know that it does not take 'everyone on earth' to bring justice and peace, but only a small, determined group who will not give up during the first, second, or hundredth gale.*[10]

Does consecrated life want to be a part of this group? Is that life's newness related to the emergence of a new, just, equal and fair society in which an opportunity for a dignified life is given to all?

God inhabits our world; the world is God's dwelling. Therefore, consecrated life is in the world as a part of it. Today that life is presented as an invitation to follow the Lord in the midst of the world, being embedded in it. The world is our dwelling, our place of life and mission. We are in the world witnessing the values proposed in the Gospel and incarnated in our charisms (Cf. John 17). What we see and experience in this world is that the poor continue to be oppressed, excluded, ig-

---

[10] Clarissa Pinkola Estés, *Desatando a la Mujer Fuerte* (Spanish Edition), (Ediciones B; Poc Tra edition March 1, 2009).

nored and used by socio-political and economic systems. The numbers of people on the peripheries of history continue to grow, while the concentration of the richness of the world scandalously goes to the hands of a small and privileged minority.

Most communities of consecrated people began as a concrete response to people facing the different destructive dimensions of this poverty and exclusion. According to Gustavo Gutierrez, a founder of Theology of Liberation, "material poverty is never good but an evil to be opposed." It is not simply an occasion for charity, as our founders and foundresses understood in their own times, but a humiliating force that denigrates human dignity and ought to be opposed and rejected. Further, as Gutierrez continues, "poverty is not a result of fate or laziness, but is due to structural injustices that privilege some while marginalizing others."[11] Poverty is not inevitable; collectively the poor can organize and facilitate social change. We are called to be at their side in this communal organization, to oppose anything that produces poverty and to provoke systemic-structural change.

Finally, "poverty is a complex reality and is not limited to its economic dimension."[12] To be poor is to be insignificant. Poverty means an early and unjust death. Our option for the poor is an option for a long and dignifying life for all. We radically oppose and denounce the early unjust death of the poor of the earth! This is the greatest injustice. Mahatma Gandhi put it this way: "poverty is the greatest form of violence." In that light Pope Francis concludes,

> *Just as the commandment 'Thou shalt not kill' sets a clear limit in order to safeguard the value of human life, today we also have to say, 'thou shalt not' to an economy of exclusion and inequality. Such an economy kills. How can it be that it is not a news item when an*

---

[11] Gustavo Gutierrez, *Spiritual Writings* (Maryknoll, New York: Orbis Books, 2011).
[12] Ibid.

> *elderly homeless person dies of exposure, but it is news when the stock market loses two points? This is a case of exclusion.*[13]

We are invited to unite, employing all our material, structural and economic resources, with the unrewarded people of good will who serve the poor and join them in this liberating work: this war on injustice. Many of them have religious reasons to do this as we do, and many do this work just for their passion, for humanity and mother earth.

> *From Latin America to Africa, to the Middle East, to our own growing social movements, people are choosing to opt not for the corporations, or the war industry or big money, and dedicate themselves to the struggling masses, our sisters and brothers who suffer needlessly under the weight of global injustice.*[14]

On what side of history are we? On what side of history do we want to be? On what side of history is consecrated life?

Pope Francis is a fresh memory that continually reminds the Church that the Gospel calls each of us to join this campaign of liberation, to do our part in the struggle for justice and peace. He has insisted that, to follow the poor Jesus of Nazareth, consecrated life needs to make an option for the poor as part of our Christological faith. Today, this option for the poor also implies an ecological option because the earth is the poorest of the poor due to our human use, abuse, and destruction of everything on our planet. He has continually invited us to "hear both the cry of the earth and the cry of the poor."[15]

The option for the poor was described in the conference of Aparecida[16] as an essential Christological option for us, if we really want to follow in Jesus' footsteps as we all proclaim in our constitutions. Cardinal Ber-

---

[13] Pope Francis, Apostolic Exhortation *Evangelii Gaudium*, no. 53.

[14] Gutierrez, *Spiritual Writings*.

[15] *Laudato Si'*, 49.

[16] Aparecida (Brazil) is the place and name of the final document of the Fifth Conference of Bishops of Latin America celebrated in May 2007.

goglio – Pope Francis – was the leading Cardinal behind the final redaction of the conclusions of this Conference of Latin American Bishops: "Our faith proclaims that Jesus Christ is 'the human face of God and the divine face of man.'" The preferential option for the poor is implicit in the Christological faith in the God who became poor for us so as to enrich us with his poverty.

This option arises out of our faith in Jesus Christ, God made man, who has become our brother (Cf. Hebrews 2:11-12). Yet it is neither exclusive nor excluding, as this option is implicit in Christological faith. We Christians as disciples and missionaries are called to contemplate, in the suffering faces of our brothers and sisters, the face of Christ who calls us to serve Him in them: "The suffering faces of the poor are suffering faces of Christ." They question the core of the Church's action, its ministry, and our Christian attitudes. Everything that has to do with Christ has to do with the poor, and everything connected to the poor cries out to Jesus Christ: "whatever you did for one of these least brothers of mine, you did for me" (Matthew 25:40).[17]

Consecrated life has to listen to the clamor of people living in this world and to the cries of the planet. The cries of our people and mother earth must become our own cries. We have to hear those cries of pain and suffering arising from a broken world. Violence, war, poverty, hunger, and ecological devastation are among the essential elements that are continually creating the sub-world, the poor global world. More and more victims appear every day, and more and more unjustly condemned innocents continue to provoke us, to call us out of our "consecrated" comfortableness and from our "consecrated" indifference.

The poor, according to the Spanish Jesuit Catholic priest and theologian Jon Sobrino, are "those who are down in history, oppressed, and

---

[17] Document of Aparecida, 392-394.

segregated by society; the poor are not, therefore, all human beings, but the ones who are down, and to be down means to be oppressed."[18]

I have been working with consecrated life for more than 20 years. In reading the constitutions of many congregations, I am always pleased to find that the poor are always in a central place as they are in the Gospels. Theologically – intellectually – we understand the role of the poor in connecting our charisms with the Kin-dom. This relationship is the one that makes these charisms pertinent, valid, universal, and needed in our world today.

Our problem is more existential ... the problem is in the inconsistency of our life style and the inconsistency of our missionary options. For instance, one thing that I cannot understand is why we (religious) continue to educate the rich, making the excuse that we are educating a new kind of leadership for our society. If we review the kind of leadership we have in countries where consecrated life is still responsible for the education of those who are rich, we must ask what went wrong with how we have educated them. Are we willing to change what we do through education so that we can become a real source of social and structural transformation? We clearly need to explore the challenges and possibilities of an education for global citizenship. Global citizenship education has the capacity for structural transformation as it opens up the students to the world's issues.

Although global citizenship education has been a focal point for UNESCO and many other organizations well before 2015, its focus became increasingly prescient after the adoption of the current United Nations global development program: Sustainable Development Goals (SDGs), otherwise known as Agenda 2030. Considering the pivotal role that *Laudato Si'* played in the UN discourse, there is an opportunity for

---

[18] Jon Sobrino, *"Teologia e Realidade"en* Susin, Luiz Carlos (ED). *Terra Prometida: Movimento Social, Engajamento Cristão e Teologia*. *Petrópolis: Vozes*, 2001, 277-309; cit. 287.

members of the Consecrated Life, through their educational institutes, to embrace global citizenship education as a way to highlight, connect and celebrate its unique mission, heritage and history. Our common mission as consecrated people has much to offer the emerging global discourse on integral ecology and integral human development that is now central to the agenda of the common good.

Today we must allow the poor themselves to tell us — with their lives, not only with their words—who they are and how the world is in which they live. We have to open our lives to them. The poor can show us the way for a new consecrated life as they showed the founders and foundresses the way of our charisms in their lifetime. The poor are continually calling us to overcome our inertia and our rigidity. Such respectful and honest attitudes can liberate us from the temptation of continuing to spiritualize or idealize—positively or negatively—the poor and their world. The poor are who they are and not what we imagine or want them to be. Their world is complex and plural. Even though we tend to think of economic poverty when we think of impoverishment and exclusion, there are other forms of impoverishment and exclusion: social, racial, political, religious, sexual, ethnic ... The reality of the poor cannot be reduced to a single dimension, as if the others were not an essential part of the same structural reality.

When we see the systemic relationship among all faces of poverty, we can also see/understand the evident connection among all charisms, as all of them are dedicated to different dimensions of the same reality. Inter-congregational collaboration, a new relational paradigm for consecrated life, is a great possibility in a world in which we are beginning to see the connections between all realities. This kind of collaboration cannot simply be a way to keep alive dying congregations but rather an invigorating energy in an all-connected universe. If we continue to isolate ourselves, we will surely disappear.

This kind of decision implies that we engage in a new relational paradigm, to feel with the poor, to live in solidarity with them, especially the outcast, the excluded, the ones in the historic, existential, and geographical margins of today. "To stand in solidarity with the suffering of those on the underside of history by joining oppressed peoples in their struggle for justice and working for equitable and sustainable global systems"[19] is possible only if we become one with them and stand by them in all circumstances.

In consecrated life this means recovering the prophetic breath and the prophetic vision of our founders and foundresses as men and women who envisioned and were committed to a new reality. They defended those whose lives were threatened, fought for a change in structures, promoted human dignity, prioritized the poor in evangelizing and being evangelized by them. The prophetic breath/vision will necessarily produce changes in our lifestyles, so that we do not continue to be so far away from the ones who are the main reason for our mission. Consecrated life needs to overcome the consumerist tendencies which cause and tend to position us to be closer to the middle and upper sectors of society than to the poor. The necessary transformation of our life can be achieved only with some physical and existential closeness to the world of those living in poverty and misery.

But this return to what is essential to consecrated life demands what Pope Francis is requesting of the entire Church. We need to move from a Davidic (King David) and powerful Church to a smaller, poorer, more insignificant Church and consecrated life. Jesus of Nazareth's lifestyle reveals to us God's way. We do not want to fall into the temptation of yearning and seeking to reconstruct a Davidic, strong, powerful consecrated life; one with the social and ecclesial prestige of the past. Jesus of Nazareth ended his life on the cross. The theology of the cross

---

[19] This is a part of the mission statement of the NGO Partnership for Global Justice. This is an NGO coalition of congregations, groups and individuals grounded in Gospel values who work in partnership by providing workshops and advocacy training to raise consciousness and awareness for the promotion of the UN Charter.
http://www.partnershipforglobaljustice.com

today for consecrated life offers and invites new spaces of comprehension.

We are aware that any personal or institutional action by consecrated life that affects society and is really prophetic must be done in dialogue and collaboration with others, without any "protagonism" syndrome or naïve paternalistic charitable work. Above all are the challenges we face due to our diminishing personnel. We need to ask honestly what justifies maintaining many of our own institutions, if we can join efforts with others who are doing the same kind of work with more vision and resources.

We need to discern the new fields, places where life is calling us to go, inviting us to be a meaningful presence: work with refugees and migrants, people with HIV/AIDS, victims of human trafficking, prostitutes, street children, abandoned women, direct advocacy, social policy making, promoting earth literacy, working for ecological sustainability, promoting systemic change ... etc. What is the meaning then of "periphery" to us today? Where is God calling us to go? Do we have the energy and the willingness to go? How will we respond?

Consecrated life cannot forget that in Christian theology the poor are going to be our eschatological judges at the final judgment, so to be close to them has anthropological and soteriological repercussions for us as Jesus' followers. He was the one who said about himself: "The Spirit of the Lord is on me, because he has anointed me to proclaim good news to the poor. He has sent me to proclaim freedom for the prisoner and recovery of sight for the blind, to set the oppressed free, to proclaim the year of the Lord's favor" (Lk 4:18).

Consecrated Life Has to Return to the "Desert"

The desert (silence and solitude) is the place where big questions can emerge. "Asking the proper question is the central action of transformation – in fairy tales, in analysis and in individuation. The key question causes germination of consciousness. The properly shaped question always emanates from an essential curiosity about what stands behind. Questions are the keys that cause the secret doors of the psyche to swing open."[20] Those essential questions determine the depth of the individual and institutional transformation.

Where will humanity and specifically consecrated life get the incentive and the energy to make urgently needed transformation? To take control of our future we must have a vision of how we would like human society, and in our case, our life, to be. This prophetic vision is possible only if we experience a spiritual rebirth.

This life must regain its mystical dimension, recovering the spiritual experience that was nuclear in primitive monasticism. This dimension is essential for it to return to what is essential, to reclaim its center -- its proverbial place. Mysticism and prophecy are absolutely inseparable. Karl Rahner once said: "All prophets come from the desert!"[21]

According to Sayyed Hossein Nasr, the Iranian Islamic Studies professor at George Washington University, "the ecological/economic/social crisis is only an externalization of an inner malaise. It cannot be solved without a spiritual rebirth of Western humankind."[22] Spirituality is the central concern of the "new cosmology." It seeks to explore our spiritual inheritance over the 70,000 years before religions evolved.[23]

It is necessary to have a spiritual awakening today. This is foundational for everything in the Christian experience: faith, dogma, moral,

---

[20] Clarissa Pinkola Estés, *Women Who Run With the Wolves: Myths and Stories of the Wild Woman Archetype* (Ballantine Books, 1992).

[21] Karl Rahner, "Prophetism,"*Encyclopedia of Theology: The Concise Sacramentum Mundi* (New York: Crossroad, 1986).

[22] Seyyed Hossein Nasr, *Man-and-Nature-the Spiritual Crisis in Modern Man* (London: UNWN, 1968).

[23] M. Hope & J. Young, *Islam and Ecology* on *http://www.crosscurrents.org/islamecology.htm*.

Church, theology, mission, and community. Without this spiritual experience, even our vows are meaningless.

In a deeply secularized and often agnostic world, amidst the crisis and weakening of faith that theologians have detected, it is necessary to have a deep spiritual experience to really have a new beginning. This means that consecrated life must be deeply mystical, if we really want to be meaningfully prophetic. We should rethink this in our spaces and times of silence, prayer, prayerful reading of the Word, celebration of faith and community sharing of our spiritual experience.

Because our culture today is global, our spirituality must be global. "Such a global spirituality presupposes that God not only exists, but that God is present and operative in the whole world, not just in me/us and my/our little universe ..."[24]

The closer we draw to God and the spirit that animates and sustains everything, the closer we draw to all human beings and even to all forms of life. Living in this amazing reality, consecrated life is called to integrative, contemplative spirituality.

If we follow Pope Francis' teachings and actions we can easily identify most of the elements of this global spirituality: spiritual solidarity with all species and earth, deep nonviolence, simplicity of lifestyle, the capacity to live morally (integrity), comprehensive self-knowledge, spiritual practice beyond our chapels, selfless service (overcoming self-reference and worldliness), prophetic action, rediscovering the feminine face of God (consecrated women have a central role in this still unresolved dimension of our Christian theology), sacredness and unity of all life, spiritual wisdom, mercy/compassion, emphasis on relationship, mutuality, new forms of leadership, etc.[25]

---

[24] Caroljean Willie, *Spirituality for a Global Age*, Power Point Presentation.

[25] Caroljean Willie, Ibid.

Consecrated Life Has to Go to the New "Borders" in a Diverse Society

In the beginning the creator created four races, one for each of the four directions: Yellow, Black, Red and White. Each race was given a way of knowing the world and a way of understanding a piece of the truth.
(Lakota & Cherokee Traditions)

Consecrated life is multicultural and plural because the multicultural world is its dwelling. "In the midst of a magnificent diversity of cultures and life forms we are one human family -- one earth community with a common destiny."[26] To comprehend this is very important if that life does not want to be excluded from the table in a society where diversity is an undeniable truth. Many people still think that our world is homogeneous or that they can level and eliminate all differences. These tendencies usually lead to cruel and senseless violence.

Amin Maalouf, a Lebanese-born French author, in his book *Assassin Identities* wrote:

Never has humankind had so many things in common, so many common references, but this is driving everyone to all the more assert their difference. If we assert our differences with such ferocity, that is precisely because we are less and less different: this is lived as an impoverishing standardization, and a threat against which we of necessity must fight in order to protect our own culture, identity, values.[27]

We continue to live in a society where communities coagulate around a confrontation between 'us' and 'them.' The desire for identity can sometimes lead to "murderous slippage."

---

[26] *Preamble – Earth Charter,* UN Documents Cooperation Circles Gathering a Body of Global Agreements. Agenda 21, Chapter 1, Preamble. http://www.un-documents.net/a21-01.htm.

[27] Amin Maalouf, *Les Identités Meurtrières*, translated into English as *In the Name of Identity: Violence and the Need to Belong* and published in 1998.

Intolerance of what is different continues to be a source of violence in our world. Some causes of this kind of behavior may be: the lack of broad vision or awareness, religious, cultural, social, or political perceptions/pretentions, ethnocentrism, our fear and defensiveness (aggressiveness) towards what is different, the power of "the majority" etc.

We are aware that people are still forced today to feel ashamed of their cultural, racial, religious, gender, sexual, social, national, political identities. We still have a long way to go. Our inability to see the dignity in each and every human story causes exclusion, lack of opportunities, culturally constructed privilege, ignorance, fear, entrenchment, irrational violence etc.

According to many studies, "pluralism is a higher-level theoretical response to diversity. Attitudinal and methodological pluralism are two possible responses to diversity. Diversity seems to require such responses which point us to the fact that diversity is often regarded as problematic."[28] Pluralism is the engagement that creates a common society that is recognized as diverse.

The recognition of diversity without any engagement or relationship among the different groups is not enough if we consider the challenges of our world today. "If diversity is a noun, pluralism is its verb."[29] Our challenge is to move our agenda from diversity to pluralism so that we can make our common future sustainable. "There is no room for 'provincialism' (narrow mindedness) in today's global world, and any sign of an exclusively inward-looking search for identity with no relationship to the rest of the world is simply empty and useless ..."[30]

---

[28] "Religious Diversity (Pluralism)", Stanford Encyclopedia of Philosophy. *First published Tue. May 25, 2004; substantive revision Fri. Sept. 4, 2015.*
http://plato.stanford.edu/entries/religious-pluralism.

[29] Ibid.

[30] Caroljean Willie, *Spirituality for a Global Age*. Power Point Presentation.

To be in new, different places in dialogue with sexual, cultural, and religious diversity, and open to new questions that arise in the Areopagus of today is an imperative of a servant, pro-existent, new consecrated life. As we have been insisting, concretely that life needs to engage the new ecological questions as well as the many questions that come from the new emerging subjects such as women, youth, indigenous peoples, and African Americans – knowing that it is the Spirit who guides history and raises new voices from below.

We must engage in dialogue with science, philosophy, biology, politics, mass media, cultures, and religions. We need to engage in a meaningful dialogue beyond ourselves to recreate our agenda and to put the new priorities of a broken world and a wounded humanity at the very top of it. We need to invite lay women and men to embrace fully our charisms and to reinvigorate them with their passion and commitment. We need to learn how to work inter-congregationally, inter-generationally, inter-culturally, inter-religiously etc.

Networking is a possibility that we cannot ignore in an interconnected society. Young people (New Generations) have an important voice in this new frontier that is under the sign of the "inter" and the "network." These new generations of consecrated life need to be educated for global citizenship, a sense of belonging far beyond the borders of our very small houses and communities.

Consecrated life is multicultural and plural because the multicultural world is its dwelling. This diversity forces us constantly to seek multicultural models of coexistence. We need to overcome all forms of theological, moral, pastoral, and liturgical colonialism – always discerning new ways that are more inclusive, respectful of the autochthonous cultures and races. We need an honest evaluation of some models of Church and consecrated life that dehumanize our lives. The humanization of consecrated life is a permanent possibility for people who have founded their lives on the Christ, whose heart is the incarnation process. He became human to validate our humanity and to invite us to humanize our world.

Consecrated life must overcome its political, cultural, scientific, technical anorexia to embrace fully this diverse world as its dwelling. We can mention some possible places where we can go to embrace fully the beauty of this diverse society: new theological places more contextual than theoretical, the economy and the ecology[31] that challenge us to care for our common home, techno-science, media and information in a virtual world, ethics and personal and institutional integrity, written, visual, verbal language, culture and diversity...etc.

In this context, we are continually invited to face our own challenges:

- Re-signification of our vows
- Reconfiguration of our structures
- Implementation of new ways of leadership, in which co-responsibility, circularity, and subsidiarity are part of the norm or become normative
- Special attention to New Generations
- Ecological conversion towards an integral ecology
- New methodologies - inclusive and meaningful ...
- New creative initial and ongoing formation processes

Conclusion

In his words to close the sessions of the Second Vatican Council, Pope Paul VI said:

In this universal assembly, in this privileged point of time and space, there converge together the past, the present and the future – the past: for here, gathered in this spot, we have the Church of Christ with her tradition, her history, her Councils, her doctors, her saints; the

---

[31] *Oikos*, the Greek root of both economy and ecology, means "common home."

> *present: for we are taking leave of one another to go out towards the world of today with its miseries, its sufferings, its sins, but also with its prodigious accomplishment, its values, its virtues; and lastly the future is here in the urgent appeal of the peoples of the world for more justice, in their will for peace, in their conscious or unconscious thirst for a higher life, that life precisely which the Church of Christ can and wishes to give them.*[32]

The challenge today then is to imagine and create something that has not previously existed in consecrated life, a form of communities that are consistently becoming appropriate for religious congregations, that will provide both for relational growth and development of the members (common humanization) and facilitate a ministry that goes beyond restrictive religious scope to embrace the new eco-human paradigm as we argued in previous pages.

All this represents a sharp change in the vision and mission of consecrated life. Today we have another type of vocation that needs to be more mature and experienced. We need a consecrated life that is less interested in seeking safety or in climbing social or ecclesial ladders, a life that is willing to live the adventure of the Gospel, the madness of the cross as our founders and foundresses exemplified. If someone is searching for security and status, they better not enter into that life because this time is not for those kinds of pretentions.

The new world in which we live demands another kind of initial and ongoing formation. Everything in us has to be simpler, more community (humanly) oriented, with a different orientation of our mission, another style of community life, another form of economy and leadership, another lifestyle, with a shared mission with the laity, with other consecrated people, with priests, with any people of good will. We need to learn how to work with others, to collaborate, to create nets, to be

---

[32] Pope Paul VI, Address to the Council Fathers on the Occasion of the Closing of the Second Vatican Council, (Rome: December 8, 1965).

yeast, to give up control and power so we can empower others and follow their lead. Perhaps consecrated life has to live like the primitive community of the Church where ascetics and virgins shared, as equals with other charisms within the community.

We have to get out of ourselves – this is the essential missionary movement – if we really want to go to somewhere beyond us. This means that the first movement of displacement must happen within each one of us and in our congregations. The biggest issue of consecrated life is its self-centeredness. This phenomenon neutralizes all of our possibilities of service, prophecy, collaboration. When we de-center, we are ready to go where life is inviting us to go.

The hermeneutics, the interpretation and redefinition of our charisms in history, are an inexhaustible source of newness and renewal of consecrated life. In the past fifty years many communities changed the words of their constitutions but continued to live a lifestyle more attached to the traditions of the past than to the present incredible challenges before them. Others changed some external forms and customs but settled to live the values of trans-modernity with its overriding worldliness. In either case, fidelity to Jesus' proposal as understood in its historical moment by our founders and foundresses continues to be at risk.

Where are we? Where are our congregations in the process of becoming new? Are we a part of a meaningful group of communities that betrayed the utopia of the poor and the dream of a new humanity as it was sent by the Spirit in the heart of those who gave birth to our charisms? Our identity is to be a prophetic vanguard of the world and the Church more than a simple labor force, as Joan Chittister has said.[33] Are we willing to embrace this mission with all its consequences?

---

[33] Joan Chittister and Rowan Williams, "Uncommon Gratitude Alleluia for All That is, "*New Theology Review,* volume 24, Number 4, November 2011. Reviewed by James A. Wallace, CSSR.

The theological and anthropological key to a new consecrated life that comes from life itself comes to us from the heart of the Gospel as well. The horizon of the Gospel is relational and is based on the human and spiritual meaning of "encounters." This proposal has an amazing significance in a world where we continue to fail in creating a space of peaceful co-existence for all.

This relational horizon is a well of mysticism and prophecy that we are asked to replicate in a relationally wounded and broken world, taking as a model the Trinitarian community. From this perspective, we can understand the incalculable scope of newness and new meaning if we open ourselves to the new scenarios and the emerging priority subjects for consecrated life.

Now is a "time for a theology of encounter," according to Pope Francis.[34] At the United Nations, on September 25, 2015 he spoke of the encounter as the antidote to the "culture of throwaway," in which people are seen as useless and so are discarded: the unborn, the elderly, immigrants, poor. "If we find Christ in those who are typically marginalized, and we know them personally, we won't be able to dispose them."[35]

Consecrated life recognizes today in the "theology of encounter" an extraordinary possibility for re-signification in all dimensions of our identity and our missionary action. Personal and institutional encounters are an essential condition in the experience of Jesus as described in the Gospels.

Newness is a possibility for us. We can embrace it as we encounter reality, the poor, ourselves, our brothers and sisters, consecrated life, our fellow humans, nature and essentially when we meet God in all these encounters as the ultimate source of our newness. Mysticism and prophecy are to characterize and animate the entire life of consecrated

---

[34] The word "encounter" is a favorite of Pope Francis. It appears frequently in his public speeches and 32 times in the Apostolic Exhortation *The Joy of the Gospel*.

[35] Ibid.

communities. A new consecrated life is possible and is still in the making!

10

CONSECRATED LIFE: GLOBAL CONCERNS & THE DEMAND FOR RENEWAL

Ikechukwu Anthony Kanu, OSA

INTRODUCTION

Consecrated life, within the parameters of its historical evolution, is closely bound to Church history and secular history. So much about its high and low periods were based on the sociological and cultural factors that in one way or the other had influence on human history. According to the Cistercian Monk of Mistassini and author Veilleux Armand, OCSO:

> *The religious life is but one of the Church's self-expressions in the course of its historical realization. Consequently, the history of the religious life is inseparable from that of the Church as a whole, and the latter bestows its own significance upon it.*[1]

---

[1] Armand Veilleux, "The Evolution of the Religious Life in its Historical and Spiritual Context, " Abbaye de Scourmont, *http://. Scourmont.be/Armand/writings/evolution-eng.htm.1.*

With this nexus between the history of the Church, secular history, and consecrated life, it is therefore not surprising that the major developments in consecrated life were basically responses or reactions to particular crises in the Church or secular society of the day, or to dramatic social changes in the Church, and in the larger cultural and political arena of Western civilization. Thus, consecrated life can be considered a significant religio-social movement in the history of Western civilization.[2] It is also therefore not surprising that particular historical events such as the legalization of Christianity by Constantine, the French revolution, the emergence of the age of enlightenment, the renaissance period, etc., exerted a great weight of influence on the development of consecrated life.

Prompted by Pope Francis' call for renewal in consecrated life during the Year of Consecrated Life, this chapter seeks a renewal, an adaptation, and a repositioning of consecrated life to maintain her history and patrimony for the purpose of preserving her identity, and reviving the high ideals, vision, and values that define religious institutes. This would involve raising questions regarding what God and the people of our time are asking of consecrated persons.

While recognizing the dialogical relationships in history, this chapter focuses on some worrisome concerns in consecrated life which are most times the consequence of influential historical sociological and cultural indices. These worrisome concerns, among others, include the decline in vocations in the West and the rise in vocations in the Third World countries, which raises questions of the dynamics of quantity versus quality.

There are also the crises of the overthrow of the sacred, mere externalism, disregard for the evangelical counsel of poverty, and the proliferation of new foundations. While these concerns rage, this piece adopts a

---

[2] Lawrence Cada, et al, *Shaping of the Coming Age of the Religious Life* (New York: Seabury Press, 1979), 34.

historical model that envisions the future as the hope of the present: a historical model of growth, decline, and changeover. A cursory glance at the historical evolution of the different epochs of consecrated life reveals that the beginning of each age is always the period of its growth, and this is usually followed by decline and then a changeover to another age.[3] It is therefore within the construct of this historical model that this chapter calls for a renewal that would usher in a new age of consecrated life. The Second Vatican Council document, *Perfectae Caritatis* would be the basis for this renewal.[4]

Consecrated Life:
Meaning & Typologies

Consecrated persons are members of religious institutes and societies of apostolic life[5] who are lay persons or clerics and who assume the evangelical counsels by means of a sacred bond and become members of an institute of consecrated life according to the law of the Church.[6] They totally dedicate themselves to God with the goal of pursuing perfection in charity by faithfully embracing the evangelical counsels of poverty, chastity, and obedience. These counsels are referred to as "evangelical" because the religious vows are centered on the life and message of Jesus, and also because religious consecration is founded on baptismal consecration.[7] Although this way of life has been foreshadowed in the ancient era, its beginning is traceable to the post-apostolic

---

[3] Stephen Toulmin, *Human Understanding* (Princeton: Princeton University Press, 1972), 25.

[4] For Vatican II documents see Austin Flanery, editor, *Second Vatican Council, the Concilliar and Postconciliar Documents* (Ireland: Dominican Publications, 1987).

[5] Ikechukwu Anthony Kanu, *Africae Munus and Consecrated Persons*, in *Catholic Voyage: A Publication of the Conference of Major Superiors of Nigeria*, Vol. 11 (January 2015), 4.

[6] *Code of Canon Law*, 573.2.

[7] Fleming, D.L., "Understanding a Theology of Religious Life, "G.A. Arbuckle & D.L. Fleming, editors, *Religious Life: Rebirth Through Conversion* (New York: Alba House, 1990), 22.

Church that dedicated itself to a Gospel-oriented life-style and to a radical following of Jesus Christ.[8] However, beyond the post-apostolic Church, typologies of consecrated life are observable in the ancient era.

A profound examination of the ancient era reveals a retinue of typologies of consecrated life. At about the fifth century of the Greek world, when mythological and religious interpretations were giving way to the philosophical explanation of reality, Heraclitus left his native Ephesus in disgust at the immorality of his fellow citizens and wandered in the fields outside the city – weeping and eating grass. He rejected the conventional morality of his society and his own conventional role in it and became a self-exiled outcast, a citizen of no state, almost a non-human.[9] Although this might sound extreme, it points to the eremitical era of religious life.

At about the sixth century, Pythagoras, an ancient Greek philosopher, established a band of male and female disciples, which was a religious, philosophical, and political community that shared their possessions with one another.[10] They dedicated themselves to the study of religious doctrines, most likely connected to the worship of Apollo, and to the study of mathematics and science. Their fraternal life with its asceticism and contemplation foreshadowed the religious life of the cenobitic period.

Similarly, two thousand years ago, at a time when the Jewish soul was turned towards the expectation of the Messiah, there also appeared among the Jews a group of holy men and women living together in a community and carrying within themselves all of the seeds of Christianity and of future Western civilization. This brotherhood, more or less

---

[8] Ikechukwu Anthony Kanu, *Africae Munus and Consecrated Persons*.
[9] Bertrand Russell, *History of Western Philosophy* (London: Unwin University Press, 1946), 21.
[10] Ibid., 22.

persecuted and ostracized, would bring forth people who would change the face of the world and the course of human history.[11]

Indeed, almost all of the principal founders of what would later be called Christianity probably were Essenes: St. Ann, Joseph and Mary, John the Baptist, Jesus, John the Evangelist etc. These early models of secluded life are somewhat mirrored in different later and modern forms of religious life.

Worrisome Features: Macro & Micro Concerns

Consecrated life has left so many positive indelible marks on the life of the Church. Thus, John Paul II described consecrated life as a gift and a treasure to the Church. He applauded the religious orders and institutes for their devotion to contemplation and the works of the apostolate, as well as societies of apostolic life, secular institutes, and other groups of consecrated persons. He likewise commended all those individuals who, in their inmost hearts, dedicate themselves to God by a special consecration.[12] Consecrated life, he observes, inspires, and accompanies the spread of evangelization in the several parts of the world.[13]

Being universally present and in no way marginal or isolated, the missionary spirit of consecrated persons represents the *very heart of the Church* as a decisive element for her mission, since it manifests the inner nature of the Christian calling and the striving of the whole Church as bride towards union with her one spouse. Consecrated life has not only proved a help and support for the Church in the past. It is also a

---

[11] John Bright, *A History of Israel* (Philadelphia: Westminster Press, 2000), 39.

[12] John Paul II, *Vita Consecrata*, Post Synodal Apostolic Exhortation, http://w2.vatican.va/content/john-paul-ii/en/apost_exhortations/documents/hf_jp-ii_exh_25031996_vita-consecrata.html No. 1, retrieved 21/12/16.

[13] Ibid., No. 2.

precious and necessary gift for the present and future of the people of God, since it is an intimate part of her life, her holiness, and her mission.[14] These positive dimensions all notwithstanding, there are many worrisome features that have emerged in consecrated life.

Decline in Vocations

Among developed countries of Europe, America, and Oceania, a worrisome feature that has emerged is that of the decline in vocations to consecrated life – gradually tilting towards extinction rather than survival.[15] Commenting on the problem, Benedict XVI avers that this:

> *... is a problem that exists throughout the western world ... the situation in the west ... is a world weary of its own culture ... that has reached a time when there is no longer any evidence of the need for God, let alone Christ, and when it seems, therefore, that humans could build themselves on their own. In this situation of rationalism closing in on itself, and that regards the sciences as the only model of knowledge, everything else is subjective. Christian life too ... becomes a choice that is subjective... arbitrary and no longer the path of life.*[16]

He writes further that:

> *It therefore naturally becomes difficult to believe and ... ever more difficult to offer one's life to the Lord to be his servant. This is certainly a form of suffering which ... fits into our time in history and in which we generally see that the so-called great Churches seem*

---

[14] Ibid., No. 3.

[15] Giancarlo Rocca, *Presnte e Futuro nella Vita Consacrata* (Roma: Edizioni Dehaniane, 1994), 46 – 48.

[16] Jim Sheerin, *Priests for the People – A Reflection on the Nigerian Priesthood: Formation, Renewal & Ministerial Life* (Asokoro-Abuja: Gaudium et Spes Institute, 2008), 105. The Pope spoke in July 2005 to the priests of Aosta Diocese in Northern Italy. See also *Vita Consecrata,*, no 63, par. 1.

to be dying. This is true particularly in Australia, but also in Europe, but not so much in the United States [of America].[17]

Accounting for the loss of vocations, Marcel Onyejekwe of the Tansian Congregation, Nigeria argues that another contributing factor is the sex scandals on the news which have inundated the media at the beginning of this century and millennium: pedophilia, homosexuality, etc. – even in high quarters and by highly-placed Church personnel. Consequently, many became ashamed of identifying themselves with the Church, the clergy, and consecrated life. And so, entrance into these vocations suffers a great set back.[18]

The Overthrow of the Sacred

In the West, developments in science and technology have posed a great challenge to religion, leaving belief in God and the sacred struggling for prominence against secularism.[19] A consequence of this development is that consecrated persons are seen as antiquated, moribund, irrelevant, and strange beings that are in danger of extinction.

Onyejekwe observes that the result of this development is that their big institutions or buildings are being sold off or transformed into secular ends, so by the end of the day there is no longer prospect for religion and consecrated life. The habits are now replaced by secular dresses; charismatic ministries have been left to lay people, with consecrated persons themselves becoming supervisors or directors of the work of others.[20]

---

[17] Jim Sheerin, *Priests for the people – A Reflection on the Nigerian Priesthood*.

[18] Marcel Onyejekwe, "Consecrated Life in the 21st century: The African Experience," in I.A. Kanu. ed., *Consecrated Life: The past, the Present, the Future and the Constant Demand for Renewal* (Ibadan: Paulines Publications, 2015), 30.

[19] Ideas taken from "Pope Calls for Defence of Family,"*The Leader*, LV (43) (Sunday, November 2, 2014), 9.

[20] Marcel Onyejekwe, "Consecrated Life in the 21st Century: The African Experience," 35.

Pope Benedict XVI points out that:

> *Following the Vatican II Council ... religious orders revised their constitutions and their way of life with a 'more evangelical, more ecclesial and more apostolic spirit.' But ... some concrete choices did not offer the world the authentic and life-giving face of Christ. A desire to modernize and ... to speak to contemporary men and women sometimes allowed a 'secularized culture' to penetrate the minds and hearts of some religious. The consequence is that, alongside an undoubtedly generous commitment, capable of witnessing and of total giving, consecrated life today experiences the danger of mediocrity, adopting bourgeois values and a consumerist mentality.*[21]

The Pope told the Major Superiors that the choice to follow Christ always carries with it a renunciation of doing or having other things.

The Rise of Externalism

A cursory glance at the lively examples of the holy fathers and mothers of the Church, in whom shone real perfection and religious life, obviously shows how little -- or almost nothing -- consecrated persons in the twenty-first century do regarding religious discipline.

Saints and friends of Jesus these Church fathers and mothers were! They served our Lord in hunger and in thirst, in cold and in nakedness, in labor and in weariness, in watching, in fasting, in prayers and meditations, in frequent persecutions and reproaches. They waged valiant contests to subdue their imperfections. Purity and straightforwardness of purpose kept them aimed towards God. By day they labored and much of the night they spent in prayer; though while they labored, they were far from leaving mental prayer. They renounced all dignities,

---

[21] Cindy Wooden, "Modern Culture Threatens Religious Order Reforms, Pope says," in *National Catholic Reporter*, 42 (31), 2/6/2006, 6. Benedict XVI met May 22, 2006 with some 1,500 superiors of women's and men's religious orders, representing hundreds of thousands of priests, nuns, brothers and consecrated virgins around the world.

honors and kindred. They hardly took what was necessary for life. They were poor in earthly things but rich in grace and virtue.

However, over the years, there was an increased decline of asceticism, the very virtue that nurtures and sustains consecrated life right from the start. Today consecrated life is far removed from these original features. What is seen now is a direct opposite, much more of externalism than the interior life. There is now so much more emphasis on activity, running businesses, making money for the community, province, or order, than on meditation and contemplation.

Number Verses Quality

While the loss of vocations in the West constitutes a worrisome trend, the vocation-boom in Africa also constitutes a major concern. Benedict XVI, offering a valuable social analysis of the situation, did not delay in making qualifications and identifying another culture as he remarked:

> *Of course, this joy also carries with it certain sadness since at least a part of them comes in the hope of social advancement. By becoming priests, they become like tribal chiefs, they are naturally privileged, they have a different lifestyle, etc. Therefore, weeds and wheat grow together in this ... crop of vocations and the Bishops must be very careful in their discernment; they must not merely be content with having many future priests but must see which really are the true vocations, discerning between the weeds and the good wheat.*[22]

The Roman Pontiff does not completely categorize this trend as a negative one. He also sees faith at work. He writes further.

> *However, there is a certain enthusiasm of faith because they are in a special period of history ... when it is clear that the traditional religion is no longer adequate. People are realizing ... that these*

---

[22] Jim Sheerin, *Priests for the People – A Reflection on the Nigerian Priesthood*, 107. cf. CICLSAL, *Directives on Formation in Religious Institutes*, 1990, n. 14.

> *traditional religions contain a promise within them but are waiting for something ... their culture is reaching out ... and two offerings – Islam and Christianity – are the possible historical response .... In a certain sense there is springtime of faith in these countries.*[23]

The Nigerian Claretian priest, Izum M. Onyeocha, gave statistics of the population of religious persons and an analysis of them:

> *There are 3,627 Nigerian diocesan priests as against 498 missionary or religious priests, 210 Nigerian brothers and 2,936 Nigerian members of indigenous religious congregations. When put together [Nigerian/non-Nigerian, diocesan/consecrated], they total 4,148 priests, 270 brothers and 4,377 sisters. The proportion of priests to sisters is roughly 16:17. The ratio to brothers is 16:1 while sisters to brothers is 17:1. This shows how badly outnumbered the brothers are. These data bring to the fore a number of challenges as follows: number versus quality, modernity versus prudishness, motivation versus individualism, poverty versus personal dignity, chastity versus the survival instinct, obedience versus self-determination.*[24]

While faith is seen at work in the present vocation boom in Africa, there is also the question of the authenticity of such vocations. The commitment of consecrated persons continues to put this to question.

Disregard for Poverty

The vow of poverty, which binds on the consecrated person to empty his or her self after the example of the poor Christ, and to let everything be for everyone in common, is gradually being damaged by a quest for possession and independence. If there is anything in the consecrated person that shocks God's people, it is worldliness and greed, and the ambition to have the best car, the best amenities, the most com-

---

[23] Ibid.

[24] Izum M. Onyeocha, "The future of the Consecrated Life: World African and Nigerian Realities," Izu, M.O. and Amadi, C., eds. *Discipleship and Renewal* (Enugu: SNAAP), 1.

fortable facilities. This incipient greed hurts the consecrated person's spirituality and endangers his or her entire vision of himself or herself as the consecrated of God.[25] This trend is very much common among the consecrated persons who are clergy.

Onyejekwe observes that those concerned often seek to evade the common life, where it is applicable, and its prevailing principles, which they consider hindrances on their way. So, a good number seek to withdraw or live on their own, outside the community, so as to have their way. Various factors are responsible for this: the influence of the external life, popular attitude towards wealth and the rich, greed and selfishness, official neglect and group politicking that undermines the ideals of consecrated life. There is also a growing loss of confidence in authority, as many religious authorities have fallen prey to sectionalism, favoritism, and unjust treatment of fellow consecrated persons. There seems to be a situation where the center can no longer hold.[26]

Focusing on Africa for instance, the underdeveloped nature of many African countries and the strong family ties also affect the disposition of many African consecrated persons towards poverty. Some consecrated men and women who have access to finance may take advantage of it to care for their family members, who are affected by the poor economy in many African countries. Thus, Mary J. Obiora notes:

> *Our society strongly challenges our vocation in many aspects. One of these is the crazy rush to acquire and accumulate possessions. Any obstruction, real or imagined, on the way is forcefully leveled in order to be rich, to be famous and to have titles that perish with human transient life. It is a worm that eats deeply in our society and if the consecrated are not watchful, they can also become unfortunate victims [as indeed some have become]. This will be devastating and*

---

[25] Congregation for Institutes of Consecrated Life and Societies of Apostolic Life, *Directives on Formation in Religious Institutes* (Rome: February 2, 1990), 14.

[26] Marcel Onyejekwe, "Consecrated Life in the 21st Century: The African Experience,"41.

> *contradict our "status" as close friends of Jesus ... When we compete with our counterparts in the World, we suffer derailment from our vocation, which is deeply rooted in the life of Jesus.*[27]

These vices stands in contrast to the vow of poverty and the principle of community life.

Proliferation of New Foundations

Alongside the vocation boom is the proliferation of religious institutes in developing countries. Both are connected, in the sense that the vocation boom provides the market for the proliferation of religious institutes. Unfortunately, most of these institutes come with dubious purposes, with similar, confused, or undefined charisms, or with utter disregard for the laid-down canonical and hierarchical rules. Many do not have a clearly written Episcopal approval, a reliable and rightly-earned sustenance, or a solid foundation by way of formation, orientation, and openness to consecrated life tenets etc.

In Nigeria, there are cases of seminarians founding religious groups which operate underground. Some have also been founded by ex-seminarians and ex-members of female religious institutes. Some of the seminarians or female religious, who have been sent away on account of questionable character, go on to form new religious institutes.[28]

Onyejekwe observes that the purpose of such foundations is seemingly for mere ostentation, on the part both of the founders and the members. The founders consciously or otherwise may simply be creating a domain for themselves, a people to parade in public with the concomitant homage and reverence by the boys/girls, with little or no show of interest in their spirituality, and no visible interest to be on the side of

---

[27] Mary Jerome Obiora, "Discipleship: Its Meaning and Implications in the Scripture and in Our Cultural Set-up,"Onyeocha et.al. *Discipleship and Renewal*, 35.

[28] Marcel Onyejekwe, "Consecrated Life in the 21st Century: The African Experience, "49.

the Church or defend her positions, all of which raise questions and doubts concerning the part of the Spirit in the project.

On the part of the members, it may all be the quest for ordination or profession, so as to validly parade oneself as a priest or consecrated person – definitely for some ulterior motives other than spirituality or salvation. In some cases, it is to evade the hammer of the perceived enemy superior and his/her cohorts, or a solution to an endemic crises, dissension, and division stemming from the political, social, and economic inconveniences of the affected.[29]

Consecrated Life & the Need for Renewal

The Church has always made several sincere efforts towards the renewal of consecrated life. Popes Leo XIII, Pius X, and Pius XII had dealt with several issues with the aim of renewing the commitment of consecrated persons. In 1950, Pius XII proposed a reform with an Apostolic Constitution *Sponsa Christi*. In it, he wrote:

> *We find also in the Institute of Nuns some things that are neither necessary, nor complementary in themselves, but simply historical and external, that were born of circumstances of past times, that today have also changed much. When these other characters are no longer advantageous to or can impede another greater good, there is no special reason to be seen to conserve them.*[30]

With several other issues and concerns coming up, the Decree, *Perfectae Caritatis* became inevitable. The Decree on the Up-to-Date Renewal of Religious Life, *Perfectae Caritatis*, is one of the sixteen documents of Vatican II that dwells squarely on consecrated persons. *Perfectae Caritatis* is a Decree, ranking lower than the Constitutions and higher than the

---

[29] Ibid., 50.

[30] Cf. AAS 43 (1951), 37-44, as cited by Castellano J. Daniel in "Commentary on *Perfectae Caritatis,*"*www.arcaneknowledge.org/catholic/councils/comment21-07.htm*.

Declarations. The term "*Perfectae Caritatis*" is Latin for "perfect charity." Accordingly, the document sees consecrated life as a call to pursue perfect charity.[31]

Perfectae Caritatis understands the renewal of consecrated life as a return to the beginnings, a going back to the Gospel and original charism of the founders. Thus, all accretions of time in the observances and apostolates that do not correspond with the Gospel and modern conditions must be cut off.[32] The call for return to traditional norms is not a recommendation to retain the *status quo* at all cost.

> *The up-to-date renewal of the religious life comprises both a constant return to the sources of the whole of the Christian life and to the primitive inspiration of the institutes, and their adaptation to the changed conditions of our time.*[33]

The two important considerations in the renewal of religious life, in the view of *Perfectae Caritatis*, are the Gospel and modern times. Talking about the document *Perfectae Caritatis*, the Chicago-born Carmelite Ernest Larkin said: "One could characterize the decree as basically conservative, balanced, almost dialectical in its effort to assert both sides of each question. But it is positive and practical."[34] The Nigerian Augustinian Jude Ossai points out five general principles or foundation stones for the renewal of consecrated life in *Perfectae Caritatis*:

1. *Since religious life is sequela Christi, the Gospel which tells us about Him should be the supreme rule of all religious institutes.*

2. *The spirit and aims of the founders of the religious institute and all their patrimony should be accepted, respected and retained.*

---

[31] Jude A. Ossai, "*Perfectae Caritatis* and the Constant Demand for Renewal," Kanu, I. K, ed., *Consecrated Life: The Past, the Present and the Constant Demand for Renewal*, 61.

[32] Ernest E. Larkin, "Religious Life in Light of Vatican II", www.carmelnet.org/larkin/larkin068, 305.

[33] Second Vatican Council, *Perfectae Caritatis*, 2.

[34] Ernest E. Larkin, "Religious Life in Light of Vatican II,"303.

> *This is because it is for the benefit of the Church that institutes have their proper character and peculiarity.*

3. *All institutes should share in the life of the Church. Religious are part of the Church and as such should, to the best of their ability and in consonance with their own natures, align with the Church in her undertakings in biblical, liturgical, dogmatic, pastoral, ecumenical, missionary and social matters.*

4. *Institutes should ensure that their members have a proper understanding of the people, of the conditions of the times and of the needs of the Church. This is aimed at arming the religious better as they serve humanity and participate in the evangelizing and missionary mandate of the Church.*

5. *A spiritual renewal of the religious. This last point is believed to be the most important of the five. The reason is that "even the best-contrived adaptations to the needs of our time will be of no avail unless they are animated by a spiritual renewal ..."*[35]

These five principles touch on the consecrated person's commitment to the evangelical counsels in various ways.

Regarding chastity, the renewal of *Perfectae Caritatis* would maintain that candidates should not be allowed to take the vow of chastity if they are not adjudged to be "psychologically and affectively" mature. This is very important as chastity and its demand of continence touches "intimately the deeper inclinations of human nature". To lead them to this maturity, they should be warned of the dangers to chastity, and also taught that chastity that is dedicated to God is beneficial to the whole personality.[36] In other words, formation should be integral, positive, and truthful. Beyond formation, there must be healthy communities for the preservation of chastity.

---

[35] Jude Ossai, *Perfectae Caritatis* and the Constant Demand for Renewal, 66-68.
[36] Cf. Second Vatican Council, *Perfectae Caritatis*, 12.

Regarding poverty, *Perfectae Caritatis* calls on consecrated persons to choose poverty *voluntarily*, in fact and in spirit, as a way of imitating Christ who, though was rich, chose to be poor so that we could become rich through his poverty. In the practice of poverty, Consecrated persons should put their trust in the providence of God. In other words, there should be no unhealthy preoccupation about tomorrow. Beyond the individual, institutes as a community, should endeavor to bear "a quasi-collective" witness to poverty, taking the local conditions into account. This they have to do by giving up part of their resources for the other needs of the Church and the poor.

Regarding obedience, *Perfectae Caritatis* stresses that by the vow of obedience a religious offers his will as a sacrifice of himself to God. He does this in imitation of Jesus Christ who came to do his Father's will (Cf. John 4:34; 5:30; Hebrews 10:7: Psalm 39:9) and actually did his Father's will. The religious, moved by the Holy Spirit, subject themselves in faith to their superiors who hold God's place.

Conclusion

The practice of renewal, adaptation, re-evaluation, and *aggiornamento* is necessary for every institution, social and otherwise, that wants to survive and stand the test of time. This even becomes more important when the focus is on the spiritual life. Consecrated life, being an intimate relationship with God, requires a constant renewal that is based on charism, apostolate, and social setting. Thus, *Vita Consecrata* teaches that,

> *the first missionary duty of consecrated persons is to themselves, and they fulfill it by opening their hearts to the promptings of the Spirit of Christ ... to whom they must therefore direct and offer everything*

that they are and have, freeing themselves from the obstacles which could hinder the totality of their response.[37]

This is the basis for a call to renewal.

This would involve a total rethinking of the basic dimensions of consecrated life, especially a rethinking of the evangelical counsels as a source of freedom for their vocation rather than perhaps a burden or source of enslavement.[38] The counsels become a source of joy that God found them, unworthy though they are, worthy to receive such great gifts. From this perspective, the evangelical counsels become an empowerment to consecrated persons to excel in their vocation to holiness, which the Christian tradition speaks of as the fundamental reason for the consecrated life.[39]

This chapter, having pointed out the different faces of worrisome features that threaten the value of consecrated life, strongly believes that a renewal of this kind would bring about a new age for consecrated life.

---

[37] John Paul II, *Vita Consecrata*, No. 25.

[38] John Paul II, *Vita Consecrata*, No. 22.

[39] John Paul II, *Vita Consecrata*, No. 18.

REFERENCES & SOURCES

Introduction

Francis, Pope. Apostolic Letter *To All Consecrated People on the Occasion of the Year of Consecrated Life.* November 21, 2014.

John Paul II, Pope. Post-Synodal Apostolic Exhortation *Vita Consecrata.* March 25, 1996.

Second Vatican Council. *Lumen Gentium,* Dogmatic Constitution on the Church. November 21, 1964.

_____ . *Perfectae Caritatis,* Decree on the Adaptation and Renewal of Religious Life. October 28, 1965.

USCCB [United States Conference of Catholic Bishops] Committee on Clergy, Consecrated Life and Vocations. *Days with Religious.* 2014.

Chapter One

John XXIII, Pope. *Appeal of the Pontifical Commission to North American Superiors.* August 17, 1961. The pope delivered this appeal through Monsignor Agostino Casoroli.

_____. *Opening Speech to the Council* at the Basilica of St Peter. October 11, 1962.

Pius XII, Pope. Encyclical *Mediator Dei.* November 20, 1947.

Second Vatican Council. *Ad Gentes,* Decree on the Missionary Activity of the Church. December 7, 1965.

_____ . *Dei Verbum,* Dogmatic Constitution on Divine Revelation. November 18, 1965.

_____. *Gaudium et Spes,* Pastoral Constitution on the Church in the Modern World. December 7, 1965.

_____. *Perfectae Caritatis,* Decree on the Adaptation and Renewal of Religious Life. October 28, 1965.

_____. *Presbyterorum Ordinis,* Decree of the Ministry and Life of Priests. December 7, 1965.

_____. *Sacrosanctum Concilium,* Constitution on the Sacred Liturgy. December 4, 1963.

_____. *Unitatis Redintegratio,* Decree on Ecumenism. November 21, 1964.

Chapter Two

Bergant, Dianne. "The Rebirth of an Apostolic Woman." *Ministerial Spirituality and Religious Life.* Edited by John M. Lozano, CMF et al. Chicago: Claret Center for Religious Resources in Spirituality, 1986. 73-90.

Flannery, Austin, OP editor. *Vatican Council II, Vol. 1&2, The Conciliar and Postconciliar Documents.* New Revised Edition. Northport, New York: Costello Publishing Company, 1996.

Francis, Pope. Apostolic Exhortation *Evangelii Gaudium.* November 24, 2013. h*ttp://w2.vatican.va/content/francesco/en/apost_exhortations/ documents/papa-francesco_esortazione-ap_20131124_evangelii-gaudium.html.*

Schneiders, Sandra M., IHM. *Buying the Field: Catholic Religious Life in Mission to the World.* Paulist Press, 2013.

Chapter Three

Anameje, Humphrey. "Mission of the Laity as Mission of the Church— Emergent Contemporary Theological Discussion." *Bulletin of Ecumenical Theology,* Vol. 19 (2007) 103-142.

Boff, Leonardo. *Francis of Rome & Francis of Assisi: A New Springtime for the Church.* New York: Maryknoll, Orbis Books, 2014.

The Code of Canon Law. Vatican City: Libreria Editrice Vaticana, 1983.

Flannery, Austin, OP, editor. *Vatican Council II, Vol. 1&2, The Conciliar and Postconciliar Documents.* New Revised Edition. Northport, New York: Costello Publishing Company, 1996.

Francis, Pope. Apostolic Exhortation *Evangelii Gaudium,* On Proclamation of Gospel in Today's World. Vaticana: Libreria Editrice, 2013.

Garvin, Mary. "Religious Life." In *The Modern Catholic Encyclopedia Revised and Expanded Edition* edited by Michael Glazier and Monica K. Hellwig, 705-706. Collegeville-Minnesota: Liturgical Press, 2004.

Higgins, W. Michael and Douglas R. Letson. *Power & Peril: The Catholic Church at the Crossroads.* Toronto: HarperCollins Publishers Ltd, 2002.

John Paul II, Pope. Apostolic Exhortation *Pastores Dabo Vobis,* On the Formation of Priests in the Circumstances of the Present Day. Vaticana: Libreria Editrice, 1992.

_____ . Apostolic Exhortation *Vita Consecrata,* On the Consecrated Life and Its Mission in the Church and World. Vaticana: Libreria Editrice, 1996.

Lakeland, Paul. *Catholicism at the Crossroads: How the Laity Can Save the Church.* New York: The Continuum International Publishing Group Inc., 2007.

Lowney, Chris. *Pope Francis: Why He Leads the Way He Leads — Lessons From the First Jesuit Pope.* Chicago: Loyola Press, 2013.

Nolan, Albert. *Jesus Today: A Spirituality of Radical Freedom.* New York: Orbis Books, 2006.

Ploch, Lauren. "Nigeria: Current Issues and U.S. Policy." *Congressional Research Service, www.crs.gov* (Accessed: May 13, 2013) 1-13.

Sarah, Cardinal Robert. *God or Nothing: A Conversation on Faith with Nicolas Diat.* San Francisco: Ignatius Press, 2015.

Sobrino, Jon. *No Salvation outside the Poor: Prophetic-Utopian Essays.* Maryknoll, New York: Orbis Books, 2008.

Sullivan, Maureen, OP. *The Road to Vatican II: Key Changes in Theology.* New York: Paulist Press, 2007.

Walsh, J.P.M. "Evangelical Counsels." In *The Modern Catholic Encyclopedia Revised and Expanded Edition* edited by Michael Glazier and Monika K. Hellwig, 280-281. Collegeville-Minnesota: Liturgical Press, 2004.

Chapter Four

Dorr, D. (1983). *Option for the Poor: A Hundred Years of Vatican Social Teaching.* New York: Orbis Books.

Freire, Paulo. (1970). *Pedagogy of the Oppressed.* New York: Seabury.

Massaro, T. (2008). *Living Justice: Catholic Social Teaching in Action (Classroom Edition).* New York: Rowman and Littlefield Publishers.

Merkle, J.A. (2004). *From the Heart of the Church: The Catholic Social Tradition.* Collegeville, MN: Liturgical Press.

Neal, Marie Augusta. (1990). *From Nuns to Sisters: An Expanding Vocation.* Mystic, CT: Twenty-Third Publications.

_____. (1981). *The Gospel Agenda in Global Perspective: A Pedagogy Project.*

_____. (1987). *The Just Demands of the Poor: Essays in Socio-Theology.* Mahwah, NY: Paulist Press.

O'Brien, D.J. & Shannon, T.A. (1992). *Catholic Social Thought: The Documentary Heritage.* New York: Orbis Press.

Paul VI, Pope (1967). Encyclical *Populorum Progressio,* On the Development of Peoples.

Schneiders, Sandra M. (2011). *Prophets in their own country: Women bearing witness to the Gospel in a Troubled Church*. New York: Orbis Books.

Internal documents of the Sisters of Notre Dame de Namur [Listed in chronological order]:

Constitutions of 1964.

Chapter Acts of 1975.

Chapter Acts of 1978.

Constitutions of 1989.

Triennial Report of the General Government Group, 1999.

Mission Statement drafted by the General Government Group in 1999.

Report of the General Government Group to the Chapter of 2002.

Chapter Acts of 2002.

Chapter Calls of 2008.

Proposals for the Chapter of 2014.

Chapter Five

Arbuckle, G.A. *Out of Chaos: Refounding Religious Congregations.* London: Geoffrey Chapman, 1988.

The Bible – New Jerusalem Version. New York: Doubleday, 1985.

The Craighead Institute in Scotland. *www.craighead.org.uk* (accessed September 17th 2014).

Ferder, Fran. *Words Made Flesh: Scripture, Psychology and Human Communication.* New York: Ave Maria Press, 1988.

Flannery, Austin editor. "Perfectae Caritatis." *Vatican Council II, Conciliar and Postconciliar Documents.* New York: Costello Publishing, 1975.

Hoffman, Dominic and Basil Cole. *Consecrated Life, Contribution of Vatican II.* Bombay, India: St. Paul's Publications, 2005.

McVerry, P. "Blessed, Broken and Shared." In *Religious Life Review*, vol. 51, #277, Nov./Dec., Dublin: Dominican Publications, 2012.

O'Murchu, Diarmuid. *The Prophetic Horizon of Religious Life.* London: Excalibur Press, 1989.

Rulla, L.M. *Anthropology of the Christian Vocation II.* Rome: Gregorian University Press, 1986.

Schneiders, Sandra M. *Selling All: Commitment, Consecrated Celibacy and Community in Catholic Religious Life.* New York: Paulist Press, 2001.

Chapter Six

Church Documents

Francis, Pope. (2013). Apostolic Exhortation *Evangelii Gaudium,* On Proclamation of Gospel in Today's World.

_____ . (2015). Apostolic Letter *To All Consecrated People on the Occasion of the Year of Consecrated Life.*

John Paul II, Pope. (2000). *Novo Millennio Ineunte.*

_____ . (1996). *Vita Consecrata.*

Vatican Council II. (1965).*Gaudium et Spes* (GS), Pastoral Constitution on the Church in the Modern World.

_____ . (1965). *Perfectae Caritatis,* Decree on the Adaptation and Renewal of Religious Life.

Congregation for Institutes of Consecrated Life and Societies of Apostolic Life. (2008).

Faciem tuam, Domine, requiram, The Service of Authority and Obedience.

_____. (1994). *Fraternal Life in Community.*

Pontifical Council for Social Communication. (1971). *Communio et Progressio,* Pastoral Instruction on the Means of Communication.

Sacred Congregation for Religious and Secular Institutes. (1978). *Religious and Human Promotion.*

(All above documents are online at Vatican Archive, http://www.vatican.va/archive/index.htm).

Other Sources

Buber, Martin. (2000). *I and Thou.* New York: Simon and Schuster Pub.

_____. (1992). *On Intersubjectivity and Cultural Creativity.* Chicago: University of Chicago Press.

Foucault, Michel. (1980). *Power/Knowledge.* Brighton: Harvester.

Gaventa, John. (2003). "Power after Lukes: An Overview of Theories of Power since Lukes and their Application to Development." Unpublished Paper, Participation Group, IDS, Sussex, August.

Gilbert, Margaret. (2006). *A Theory of Political Obligation.* Oxford: Oxford University Press.

Hegel, G. W. F. (1977). *Phenomenology of Spirit,* trans. A. V. Miller, Oxford: Clarendon Press.

Honneth, Axel. (2014). *Freedom's Right: The Social Foundations of Democratic Life.* New York: Columbia University Press.

_____. (2012). *The I in We: Studies in the Theory of Recognition.* Translated by Joseph Ganahl. Cambridge: Polity Press.

_____. (1996). *The Struggle for Recognition: The Moral Grammar of Social Conflicts.* Cambridge: Polity Press.

Moore, Donald. (1996). *Martin Buber, Prophet of Religious Secularism.* New York: Fordham University Press.

O'Malley, John W. (2010). *What Happened at Vatican II.* New York: Harvard Univ. Press.

Ricoeur, Paul. (1990). *Oneself as Another*. Translated by Kathleen Blamey. Chicago: University of Chicago Press.

Rigby, Ken. (2007). "Bullying in Schools and What to do about It." Revised and Updated.

Australian Council Educational Research. Victoria: Acer Press, Hibutani, Tamotsu. (1961). Society and Personality: An Interactionist Approach to Social Psychology. New Jersey: Prentice-Hall, Inc.

Tillich, Paul. (1954). Love, Power and Justice. Oxford: Oxford University Press.

Chapter Seven

Bernardin, Cardinal Joseph. "Our Communion, Our Peace, Our Promise. Pastoral Letter on the Liturgy." February 1984, in *Selected Works of Joseph Cardinal Bernardin. Homilies and Teaching Documents*, Vol. 1. Collegeville, MN: The Liturgical Press, 2000.

Center for Action and Contemplation: *https://cac.org/*.

Hart, Patrick editor. *A Monastic Vision for the 21st Century: Where do We Go from Here?* Cistercian Publications, 2006.

Hughes, Kathleen. *Becoming the Sign. Sacramental Living in a Post-Conciliar Church.* Mahwah, New Jersey: Paulist Press, 2013.

Lombardi, Federico, speaking for Pope Francis. *Comunicato della Sala Stampa della Santa Sede: Alcuni chiarimenti sulla celebrazione della Messa.* July 11, 2016.

Lonergan, Bernard. "Healing and Creating in History." in *A Third Collection*. Mahwah, New Jerssey: Paulist Press, 1985.

_____. *Insight. A Study of Human Understanding,* Collected Works of Bernard Lonergan 3. Edited by Frederick E. Crowe and Robert M. Doran. Toronto: University of Toronto, 1992 [1957].

_____. *Method in Theology*. Toronto: University of Toronto, 1971, Reprint 2007.

Metz, Johann B. *Followers of Christ. Perspectives on the Religious Life*. Mahwah, New Jersey: Paulist Press. Translated 1978.

Rahner, Karl. "Christian Living Formerly and Today." *Theological Investigations* VII. Translated by David Bourke. New York: Herder and Herder, 1971.

Van Bavel, Tarcisius. *The Basic Inspiration of Religious Life*. Villanova, PA: Augustinian Press, 1996. *https://goo.gl/1YdJG7*. (Accessed on April 8, 2016)

Werlen, Martin. *Embers in the Ashes: New Life in the Church*. Mahwah, New Jersey: Paulist Press, ebook edition, 2013. Edited by Patrick Hart. *A Monastic Vision for the 21st Century: Where do we Go from Here?* Cistercian Publications, 2006.

Chapter Eight

Augustine, St. (2007). *Sermons*, 39.4; 247.1; 61.2; 177.6-7. *Essential Sermons: (Classroom Resource Edition) (The Works of Saint Augustine: A Translation for the 21st Century) (Works of Saint Augustine. Part III, Homilies)*. Edited by Daniel Doyle. Translated by Edmund Hill. New York: New City Press.

Baum, Gregory. (1987). *Theology and Society*. New York: Paulist Press.

Benedict XVI, Pope. "It is Time for the Church to Set Aside Her Worldliness," A Speech to Representatives of Catholic Society Active in the Life of the Church and Society, Freiburg, September 25, 2011. PV-GERMANY/ VIS 20110926 (750) Pope Benedict XVI message in Germany.

Brown, Peter. (2002). *Poverty and Leadership in the Later Roman Empire*. Hanover, New Hampshire: University Press of New England.

Chittister, Joan. (1994). "Religious Life is Still Alive, but far from the Promised Land: Ten Questions Get to the Heart of What Future Might Hold," *National Catholic Register*.

Clements, Ronald E. (1997). "Max Weber, Charisma and Biblical Prophecy," In *Prophecy and Prophets*. Edited by Yehoshua Gitay. Atlanta: Scholars Press.

Congregation for Institutes of Consecrated Life and Societies of Apostolic Life. (1994). *Fraternal Life in Community*. Rome.

Crosby, Michael. (2004). *Can Religious Life be Prophetic?* New York: Crossroad Publishing.

Francis, Pope. (November 29, 2013). "Address to the General Assembly of the Union of Superior Generals at the Conclusion of their 82nd Annual General Meeting in Rome."

_____. (2014). "Apostolic Letter To All Consecrated People on the Occasion of Year of Consecrated Life."

Gutierrez, Gustavo. (1997). *Sharing the Word through the Liturgical Year*. Maryknoll, New York: Orbis Books.

Intermediate General Chapter (CGI). Order of St. Augustine. (2010). "The Unity of the Order in Service to the Gospel."

John Paul II, Pope. (1996). *Vita Consecrata:* "Post-Synodal Apostolic Exhortation on Consecrated Life and its Mission in the Church and in the World."

Johnson, Mary et al. (2014). *New Generations of Catholic Sisters: The Challenge of Diversity*. New York: Oxford University Press.

Klein, Ralph W. (1991). "Prophet-Mystic and Social Justice: a Response," *Biblical Research*, XXXVI: 69-73.

Leddy, Mary Jo. (1990). *Reweaving Religious Life: Beyond the Liberal Model*. New York: Twenty-Third Publications.

Mathiesen, Ralph W. (1999). "Society, Social Thought." Edited by Allan D. Fitzgerald. *Augustine Through the Ages: An Encyclopedia.* Grand Rapids, Michigan: William B. Eerdmans Publishing Co.

Sacred Congregation for Religious and Secular Institutes. (1978). *Religious and Human Promotion.*

Schneiders, Sandra M. (2014). *Finding the Treasure: Locating Catholic Religious Life in a New Ecclesial and Cultural Context.* New York: Paulist Press.

Walter, Patricia. (1992). "Religious Life in Church Documents." *Review of Religious Life* 51.

Chapter Nine

Conference of Bishops of Latin America (CELAM). *Final Document of Aparecida V.* Bogota: 2007.

Estes, Clarissa Pinkola. "*Desatando a la Mujer Fuerte* (Spanish Edition)." Ediciones B; Poc Tra edition, March 1, 2009.

_____. *Women Who Run with the Wolves: Myths and Stories of the Wild Woman Archetype.* Ballantine Books, 1992.

Francis, Pope. Apostolic Exhortation *Evangelii Gaudium.* New York: Pauline Books and Media, 2015.

_____. Encyclical *Laudato Si',* On the Care of Our Common Home. Boston: Pauline Books and Media, 2015.

_____. Apostolic Letter *To All Consecrated People on the Occasion of the Year of Consecrated Life.* 2014. *https://w2.vatican.va/content/francesco/en/apost_letters/documents/papa-francesco_lettera-ap_20141121_lettera-consacrati.html*

Gutierrez, Gustavo. *Spiritual Writings.* Maryknoll, New York: Orbis Books, 2011.

Hope, M. and Young, J. "Islam and Ecology." *http://www.crosscurrents.org/islamecology.htm.*

John Paul II, Pope. Post-Synodal Apostolic Exhortation *Vita Consecrata*. Boston: Books and Media, 1996.

Maalouf, Amin. *Les Identities Meutrieres (Murderous Identities).* Paris: Grasset & Fasquelle, 1998.

Nasr, Seyyed Hossein. *Man-and-Nature-the Spiritual Crisis in Modern Man.* Wandala. UNWIN Paperback. London: 1968.

Paul, VI, Pope. Address to the Council Fathers on the Occasion of the Closing of the Second Vatican Council, Rome: December 8, 1965.

_____. Apostolic Exhortation *Evangelii Nuntiandi.* 1975. *http://w2.vatican.va/content/paulvi/en/apost_exhortations/documents/hf_p-vi_exh_19751208_evangelii-nuntiandi.html.*

Rahner, Karl. "Prophetism." *Encyclopedia of Theology: The Concise Sacramentum Mundi.* New York: Crossroad, 1986.

Smith, Gregory A. "Preaching: A Ministry of Newness." *Faculty Publications and Presentations.* 2000. *http://digitalcommons.liberty.edu/lib_fac_pubs/70.*

Sobrino, Jon. "Teologia e Realidade." en Susin. Kuiz Carlos Editor. *Terra Prometida: Movimento Social, Engajamento Cristao e Teologia.* Petropolis: Vozes, 2001. 277-309.

Stanford Encyclopedia of Philosophy. "Religious Diversity (Pluralism)." 2004. *http://plato.stanford.edu/entries/religious-pluralism/.*

United Nations. "Documents Cooperation Circles Gathering a Body of Global Agreements."*Agenda 21,* Chapter 1,,m Preamble. *http://www.un-documents.net/a21-01.htm.*

Wallace, James A. "Uncommon Gratitude for All that Is" by Joan Chittister and Rowan Williams. *New Theology Review. Vol. 24* (2011).

Willie, Caroljean. "Spirituality for a Global Age." PowerPoint Presentation. 2013.

Chapter Ten

Bright, John. *A History of Israel*. Philadelphia: Westminster Press, 1987.

Cada, Lawrence et al. *Shaping of the Coming Age of Religious Life*. New York: Cross Road Books, 1987.

Castellano J. Daniel in "Commentary on *Perfectae Caritatis*". Published online at *www.arcaneknowledge.org/catholic/councils/comment21-07.htm*. Retrieved 21/12/16.

The Code of Canon Law. Bangalore: Theological Publications in India, 1983.

Congregation for Institutes of Consecrated Life and Societies of Apostolic Life. *Directives on Formation in Religious Institutes* (Rome: February 2, 1990),

Flanery, Austin. Editor. *Second Vatican Council, the Conciliar and Postconciliar Documents*. Ireland: Dominican Publications, 1987.

Fleming, D.L., "Understanding a Theology of Religious Life." In *Religious Life: Rebirth through Conversion*. Edited by G.A. Arbuckle and D.L. Fleming. New York: Alba House, 1990.

John Paul II, Pope. Post Synodal Apostolic Exhortation *Vita Consecrata*. http://w2.vatican.va/content/john-paul-ii/en/apost_exhortations/documents-ii_exh_25031996_vita-consecrata.html No. 1. (Retrieved 21/12/16.)

Kanu, Ikechukwu Anthony. "Africae Munus and Consecrated Persons." *The Catholic Voyage*. Vol. 11. (January, 2015).

_____ . "The Concept of Family as the Contribution of Africa to the Consecrated Life." *The Catholic Voyage*. Vol. 12 (January, 2016), 31-40.

_____. "Consecrated Persons as Agents of Pastoral Care of the Family." *JORAS: Nigerian Journal of Religion and Society. Volume 5* (2015), 74-84.

_____. "Obedience and Discernment in the Life of Consecrated Persons." *Vincentian Pastoral Journal 27. 2.* (2016), 49-53.

_____. "*Quitte Ton Pays*: On Consecrated Persons and the Challenges of Family Obligations in Contemporary Africa." *Jos Studies Volume 23* (2015), 45-57.

Larkin, Ernest E. "Religious Life in Light of Vatican II." In *carmelnet.org/larkin/larkin068*. Retrieved 21/12/16.

Obiora, Mary Jerome. "Discipleship: Its Meaning and Implications in the Scripture and in Our Cultural Set-up." In Izu, M.O. and Amadi, C. eds. *Discipleship and Renewal*. Enugu: SNAAP.

Onyejekwe, Marcel. "Consecrated Life in the 21st Century: The African Experience." In Kanu, I. A., editor. *Consecrated Life: The Past, the Present, the Future and the Constant Demand for Renewal*. Ibadan: Paulines, 2015.

Onyeocha Izu M. "The Future of the Consecrated Life : World African and Nigerian Realities." In Izu, M.O. and Amadi, C., editors. *Discipleship and Renewal,* Enugu: SNAAP.

Ossai, Jude A. "*Perfectae Caritatis* and the Constant Demand for Renewal." In Kanu, I.K. editor. *Consecrated Life: The Past, the Present and the Constant Demand for Renewal*. Ibadan: St. Paul's Publications., 2015.

"Pope Calls for Defence of Famil" (Report). In *The Leader* LV (43) (Sunday, November 2, 2014).

Rocca, Giancarlo. *Presnte e Futuro Nella Vita Consacrata*. Roma: Edizioni Dehaniane, 1994.

Russell, Bertrand. *History of Western Philosophy*. London: Unwin University Press, 1946.

Sheerin, Jim. *Priests for the people – A Reflection on the Nigerian Priesthood: Formation, Renewal & Ministerial Life*. Asokoro-Abuja: Gaudium et Spes Institute, 2008.

Toulmin, Stephen. *Human Undertsanding*. Princeton: Princeton University Press, 1972.

Veilleux, Armand. "The Evolution of the Religious Life in its Historical and Spiritual   Context, " Abbaye de Scourmont, *http:///. Scourmont.be/Armand/writings/evolution-   eng.htm.1.*

Wooden, Cindy. "Modern Culture Threatens Religious Order Reforms, Pope Says." In *National Catholic Reporter* 42 (31) (2/6/2006).

CONTRIBUTORS

DIANNE BERGANT, CSA, PHD is Carroll Stuhlmueller, C.P. Distinguished Professor Emerita of Biblical Studies at Catholic Theological Union in Chicago and a former President of the Catholic Biblical Association of America. She has served on the editorial boards of *The Bible Today*, *Biblical Theological Bulletin* and *Chicago Studies*. Her current interests are in biblical interpretation and biblical theology, particularly on issues of peace, ecology, and feminism.

JOAN F. BURKE, SND DE NAMUR, a holder of a doctorate (D.Phil., Oxon.) in social anthropology from Oxford University, is Senior Lecturer in the post-*graduate Maryknoll Institute of African Studies and the Centre for Leadership and Management* at Tangaza University College, Kenya. She has served her congregation in leadership roles on both the general and provincial levels, as well as was the first SND de Namur NGO Representative to the United Nations. Sister Joan brings with her a wealth of missionary experience and academic work with Catholic women religious in both East and West Africa.

GUILLERMO CAMPUZANO, CM is a Vincentian priest from Colombia holding two Master Degrees: Master of Psychology from San Buenaventura University, Medellin, Colombia and Master of Clinical Counseling from DePaul University, Chicago. He currently represents the Congregation of the Mission at the United Nations. Guillermo advises the National Board of Directors of Latino Young Adult Ministry. He is also part of the Theological Team of the Latin American Conference of Religious Life (CLAR). He has studied and lectured at various institutions of higher education in Latin America and the United States.

ROBERT F. DUEWEKE, OSA received his PhD in Theology / Spirituality from St. Paul University, Ottawa, Canada. He has worked in a wide variety of ministries, including fifteen years as a missionary in the Chulucanas Diocese in northern Peru, concentrating on forming basic Christian communities and implementing the vision of Vatican II. He is former director of the Tepeyac Institute, a school for ministry, theology and lay leadership training for the Diocese of El Paso, Texas. He was also a fellow at the Lonergan Institute at Boston College, Chestnut Hill, Massachusetts, USA and currently serves as the representative of the Augustinians International Non-Governmental Organization at the United Nations.

THERESA EKE, DC, of the Daughters of Charity of St. Vincent de Paul, holds an MSc and a Licentiate in Clinical Psychology from the Gregorian University, Rome. Sister Theresa has worked in initial formation in her congregation for ten years and has also served in congregation leadership in several capacities. She engages in psychological assessment and counseling for various congregations, dioceses and individuals in Nigeria and other parts of Africa. She is particularly adept at integrating spirituality with psychology as well as issues of religious community with group dynamics.

FRANCIS CHIDI EZENEZI, PHD is a theologian, a canonist and a researcher on the interconnectivity of theological studies and canonical disciplines, as well as on the thought of the Second Vatican Council in relation to ecclesial administrative procedures and practices. He obtained his Doctorate in Systematic Theology from the University of St. Michael's College in the University of Toronto. He holds a Master's degree and a Licentiate in Canon Law from Saint Paul University, Ottawa, Canada. He belongs to the Catholic Diocese of Awka, Nigeria and is currently the pastor of St. Gerard Majella Parish in the Sault Ste. Marie Diocese, Ontario, Canada.

CHRISTIANA N. IDIKA, DMMM is a member of the Congregation of Daughters of Mary Mother of Mercy. She holds a PhD in political philosophy from Universität Würzburg, Germany. She is currently a junior researcher in the University of Kassel, Germany and Research Assistant at Institute for World Mission, St. Georgen Philosophical and Theological University, Frankfurt am Main, Germany.

IKECHUKWU ANTHONY KANU, OSA, PHD, is a friar of the Order of Saint Augustine of the Province of Saint Augustine of Nigeria. He is the Executive Secretary of the Conference of Major Superiors of Nigeria (Men). He has served as a lecturer and administrator at various academic institutions in Nigeria: Veritas University of Nigeria, Abuja; the Augustinian Institute, Makurdi; Saint Albert the Great Institute, Abeokuta; and Saint Augustine Major Seminary, Jos. He is the founder and editor-in-chief of IGWEBUIKEPEDIA: Internet Encyclopedia of African Philosophy and *IGWEBUIKE: An African Journal of Arts and Humanities.*

EMEKA XRIS OBIEZU, OSA, holding a PhD from the University of Toronto, is a systematic theologian with specialization in political theology and Christian social responsibility. He was the Augustinian NGO representative at the United Nations, working in UN ministry for more than ten years.

JOHN PAUL SZURA, OSA, holding a PhD in Systematic Theology from Fordham University, New York and a PhD in General Psychology from Illinois Institute of Technology, Chicago, has taught in seminaries in the United States, the Philippines, and Peru. His focus is on the integration of theology and psychology. John is a member of the Karl Rahner Society and of the Peace Psychology Division of the American Psychological Association.

OTHER BOOKS
FROM PACEM IN TERRIS PRESS

POSTMODERN ECOLOGICAL SPIRITUALITY
Catholic-Christian Hope for the Dawn of a Postmodern Ecological Civilization Rising from within the Spiritual Dark Night of Modern Industrial Civilization
Joe Holland, 2017

LIGHT, TRUTH, & NATURE
Practical Reflections on Vedic Wisdom & Heart-Centered Meditation In Seeking a Spiritual Basis for Nature, Science, Evolution, & Ourselves
Thomas Pliske, 2017

THOMAS BERRY IN ITALY
Reflections on Spirituality & Sustainability
Elisabeth M. Ferrero, Editor, 2016

PETER MAURIN'S
ECOLOGICAL LAY NEW MONASTICISM
A Catholic Green Revolution Developing Rural Ecovillages, Urban Houses of Hospitality, & Eco-Universities for a New Civilization
Joe Holland, 2015

PROTECTION OF RELIGIOUS MINORITIES
A Symposium Organized by Pax Romana at the United Nations and the United Nations Alliance of Civilizations
Dean Elizabeth F. Defeis & Peter F. O'Connor, Editors, 2015

BOTTOM ELEPHANTS
Catholic Sexual Ethics & Pastoral Practice in Africa: The Challenge of Women Living within Patriarchy & Threatened by HIV-Positive Husbands
Daniel Ude Asue, 2014

CATHOLIC LABOR PRIESTS
Five Giants in the United States Catholic Bishops Social Action Department Volume I of US Labor Priests During the 20th Century
Patrick Sullivan, 2014

CATHOLIC SOCIAL TEACHING & UNIONS
IN CATHOLIC PRIMARY & SECONDARY SCHOOLS
The Clash between Theory & Practice within the United States
Walter "Bob" Baker, 2014

SPIRITUAL PATHS TO
A GLOBAL & ECOLOGICAL CIVILIZATION
Reading the Signs of the Times with Buddhists, Christians, & Muslims
John Raymaker & Gerald Grudzen, with Joe Holland, 2013

PACEM IN TERRIS
Its Continuing Relevance for the Twenty-First Century
(Papers from the 50th Anniversary Conference at the United Nations)
Josef Klee & Francis Dubois, Editors, 2013

PACEM IN TERRIS
Summary & Commentary for the Famous Encyclical Letter
of Pope John XXIII on World Peace
Joe Holland, 2012

100 YEARS OF CATHOLIC SOCIAL TEACHING
DEFENDING WORKERS & THEIR UNIONS
Summaries & Commentaries for Five Landmark Papal Encyclicals
Joe Holland, 2012

HUMANITY'S AFRICAN ROOTS
Remembering the Ancestors' Wisdom
Joe Holland, 2012

THE "POISONED SPRING" OF ECONOMIC LIBERTARIANISM
Menger, Mises, Hayek, Rothbard: A Critique from
Catholic Social Teaching of the Austrian School of Economics
Pax Romana / Cmica-usa
Angus Sibley, 2011

BEYOND THE DEATH PENALTY
The Development in Catholic Social Teaching
Florida Council of Catholic Scholarship
D. Michael McCarron & Joe Holland, Editors, 2007

THE NEW DIALOGUE OF CIVILIZATIONS
A Contribution from Pax Romana
International Catholic Movement for Intellectual & Cultural Affairs
Pax Romana / Cmica-usa
Roza Pati & Joe Holland, Editors, 2002

*This book and other books from Pacem in Terris Press,
or by Joe Holland from other publishers,
are available at:*

www.amazon.com/books

www.ingramcontent.com/pod-product-compliance
Lightning Source LLC
Chambersburg PA
CBHW060113170426
43198CB00010B/881